# War, Suffering and the Struggle
# for Human Rights

## ABOUT THE AUTHOR

Peadar King is director of KMF Productions and the presenter/
producer of the RTÉ documentary series *What in the World?*
As a commentator on international politics, he makes regular
contributions to Irish broadcast and print media. He is also
author of *What in the World? Political Travels in Africa, Asia
and the Americas* and *The Politics of Drugs: From Production to
Consumption* both published by The Liffey Press.

# War, Suffering
# and the Struggle
# for Human Rights

Peadar King

The Liffey Press

Published by
The Liffey Press Ltd
'Clareville', 307 Clontarf Road,
Dublin D03 PO46 Ireland
www.theliffeypress.com

A catalogue record of this book is
available from the British Library.

ISBN 978-1-9160998-2-1

Front cover photo by Antoine Makdis
Back cover photo by Bob O'Brien

Printed in Spain by GraphyCems

# CONTENTS

# ACKNOWLEDGEMENTS

Almost a half century ago at the age of twelve years I was sent to a boarding school. It was a tough place for a child to be. It also had its compensations. Among them was Liam Ashe, one of the best teachers I have ever known. Having worked as a teacher for fifteen years I have known many fine ones. Liam Ashe has the qualities of a fine teacher - well read, well prepared, an ability to tell stories, a deep respect for learning and for students. All of which he employed in his reading of this book and for which I am hugely grateful.

Liam's contribution to this book is immeasurable. Each word has been carefully read and re-read. Each sentence parsed and analyzed. Each chapter commented on in detail. And then on the round, how that chapter sits, the content, the representation and the politics. His presence as a reader was at times a call to think again, and at times a reassurance. And above all, an encouragement to keep writing. For all of that the final call was mine and if there are mistakes in this, they are mine alone. To have such a presence in writing a book is invaluable. To do so is generosity personified.

Mary Byrne too. I have known Mary Byrne for fifteen years. Another friendship. Mary has meticulously proofread every word, sentence and paragraph. Knowledgeable about the minutiae of grammar, nothing goes unnoticed. That said

# Acknowledgements

(again), the final changes were mine and if there are mis-beats or mangled words and sentences, they are mine.

This book is based on the RTÉ television Global Affairs series *What in the World?* Colm O'Callaghan has nursed and nurtured this series for almost a decade. In all likelihood it would have fallen by the wayside without him. It is an indication of his longstanding commitment to public service broadcasting.

Documentary making is a collective undertaking. Central to that undertaking is my partner in KMF Productions, Mick Molloy. For two decades now, Mick and I have worked together. Twenty years thinking how best to fund and make the *What in the World?* series that does justice to all the people with whom we work. Mick's patience and attention to detail is phenomenal. And equally important, his is a calm reassuring voice when most needed.

In making the television series, I have worked with some of the best, most creative and dedicated people in the independent television sector. And beyond the sector. I wish to acknowledge and thank each of them for their contribution to the work over a two-decade period: Abdirisak Heibe, Bernie O'Connell, Colm O'Meara, Dearbhla Glynn, Enda O'Connor, Gerry Nelson, Jack O'Flynn, Jayro Gonzalez, Jerry O'Callaghan, Joe Farrell, John MacMahon, Kevin O'Sullivan, Kim Bartley, Liam Mac Namara, Liz Gill, Maeve Taylor, Mairéad Ní Nuadháin, Mark McCauley, Mary Fitzgerald, Maurice Sweeney, Molly O'Duffy, Nuala Finnegan, Paul Mullan, Philip Graham, the late Sr. Phyllis Heaney, Rodney Rice, Ronan Fox, Rory Byrne, Seamus Martin, Sebastián Hacher, Stephen McCloskey, Willie Van Velden and Zaid Ahmed.

Mick Cassidy has travelled with me more than any other person, and in addition to his superb work on sound he is a talented photographer. A selection of his work is featured here. Mick O'Rourke, likewise, has filmed many of the documentaries, and in addition to his resolute skill as a cameraman he is the perfect cycling companion. Ken O'Mahony, also a perfect travelling companion, is a consummate cameraman, some of his still photographs are also included here. We too have travelled far together. Skilled craftspeople directors Bob O'Brien, Stephen O'Connell and Ruth Meehan are also gifted still photographers and terrific companions on the road. Some of their work is also included here. We four, too, have travelled far together. Three editors in particular I wish to acknowledge and thank for their longstanding commitment to the series and the hours and hours and hours of slow painstaking work, Andrew Stewart, Seamus Callagy and Rónán Ó'Mhuirgheasa. It has been a pleasure working with all three.

To Antoine Makdis, thanks for the cover photograph, and to Julián Cardona for the photograph of the wall on the Mexican/ USA border.

Some of this work first appeared on RTÉ Radio 1's *World Report*. I wish to acknowledge John Burke and Colm Ó Mongáin for facilitating these broadcasts.

I wish to thank Clare Daly for writing the Foreword to the book. Clare's contribution to Irish politics has been immense on national issues, and more particularly international issues. Work that now continues in the European Parliament.

I wish to thank my immediate family, Margaret King, Órla O'Donovan, Sadhbh Ní Dhonnabháin and Ríon O'Donovan. Thanks. And to my extended family too. Thanks.

I also wish to thank David Givens of The Liffey Press. This is our third book together and for very good reasons I keep coming back to him. Thanks David.

And finally, I wish to thank all those people who shared their stories. People in Afghanistan, Brazil, Iraq, Libya, Mexico, Palestine/Israel, Russia, Somalia, South Korea, South Sudan, Syria, Uruguay and Western Sahara. Thanks for trusting me with your stories. I hope in the recounting of them in this book that trust has been honoured.

# FOREWORD

Along with Mick Wallace TD and some peace campaigners, I first went to Aleppo in Syria in late 2017. Our journey began in Damascus where the mortar bombs pounded the city. Two hours north, to a school in Homs. A place where young people of all faiths and none were educated together. A school where fifty children had been killed by two suicide bombers. Now rebuilt. The recycled rubble and war materials now used for artwork. Children learning and experiencing that love conquers violence. We were struck not just by the scale of the destruction, but the resilience of those who carried on. Despite it all, people carrying on.

In June 2018, along with a number of other Independents4Change Dáil colleagues, I had the privilege of returning to Syria. In the industrial zone of Aleppo, once home to 65,000 factories and workshops, a textile manufacturer had re-opened his factory on the first floor of a bombed building. Five hundred meters from where the jihadists continued to fire, a small number of workers went to work there every day... "Life goes on" as Peadar concludes in the eerie chapter describing the devastation of Afghanistan after decades of foreign interference.

We were the first tourists to visit Aleppo's Citadel since the war, in a country where fourteen per cent of GDP came from tourism in 2010. Such was the rarity, we got a mention

on the TV news. Everywhere we went people were both surprised and delighted to see us. Why did we come? Were we
not afraid, with everything that was being said about Syria
in the West? This is what is at the heart of Peadar King's out-
standing narrative.

Against the backdrop of the enormous human cost of war
and foreign interference in countries which, although household names, we know little about – Iraq, Afghanistan, Libya,
Syria, South Sudan, countries synonymous with death and
destruction, unrelenting carnage and casualties – we find real
people, just like us. People whose lives have been stood on
their head by conflicts that have little to do with them, and
bear precious little resemblance to the way they are reported
on our screens.

This book is the human face of war and poses the questions, "Is there ever justification for war?" and "What can be
done?" In answering, Peadar says the first thing is "to know
the reality of war". That's what we were doing in Syria and
that's what this book does. Not just in relation to war but also
foreign interference.

*War, Suffering and the Struggle for Human Rights* humanises
the statistics and confronts us with war's horror. "People don't
realise what it's like to live in a war zone. You have to live it to
understand it," Reem Aslo tells Peadar in Aleppo.

Story after story. Brazil, Mexico, South Korea, Uruguay...
Peadar narrates for the people.

Amaro – "the authorities don't respect us, we who are poor
and black" – lost his son Matais in Brazil. Here more people
died from homicide in 2015 than lost their lives in the war in
Syria.

Carmen Castillo's chilling account of the death of her daughter: "They dumped my daughter like you would dump an animal." The pink crosses in the desert mark the disappearance of
the women whose only crime was to try to earn a living in the

maquiladoras, Mexico's sweatshops feeding the global market, while many more die trying to escape poverty or drug gangs.

Tangerine farmer Jung Young Hee: "It hurts me very much. I've been living here in Gangjeong village for twenty-four years." Jeju, South Korea, a UNESCO heritage site, is now home to the wholly owned South Korean Jeju Civilian-Military Complex Port to which US warships have unlimited access. The US now has military bases in eighty countries or territories.

This is a world where women suffer most, from being almost banished from public life in Afghanistan, to the sex work that follows the military bases, most tragically articulated by the elderly "comfort women" of Korea, forced into "service", repeatedly raped over years.

Stories from history too. Eighty-five-year-old Russian Serafimove Kazakova remembers. Stories of quiet courage. "The woman they were looking for, the landlady was able to hide her on top of the stove and later when the Germans searched the house she escaped and hid in a haystack."

Young people too. Harrowing accounts of the gratuitous violence meted out on them. They can be killed because they are "seen as less than human". It's nothing more than "racial and class genocide". Young people introduced to Peadar by the incredible Kiltegan missionary Jim Crowe from County Clare, along with Lula, former president, one of the founders of the Brazilian Workers' Party almost forty years ago.

Africa. How can we explain the lack of any news coverage for the deadliest bomb attack ever on its continent, incinerating over 600 people and injuring many more in Somalia in 2017? Ahmedweli Hussain, a young Somali journalist, reported: "The scene I visited was unspeakable. I can't say any word about that day. Everyone was calling for help. There is no tragedy worse than what I have seen". Peadar's account of his visit to that devastated country will remain with you for a long time.

Colonialism, brutal economic policies, corruption. This book gives you the real stories of the consequence of foreign interference as the world moves into yet another phase of militarism. The legacy of Europe's colonization of Africa. The ongoing United States' destabilization of Latin and South America. The more recent wars for oil and regime change in the Middle East. Wars that profit the military industrial complex.

There is open talk of an EU army, the establishment of a European Defence Fund. One that will, for the first time, directly access EU funds. Tens of billions of European citizens' monies to be spent on security and defence. For the same companies to profit on the double. For the bombs that make people refugees and the barriers to keep *them* away from *us*...

But this book, more than anything else, shows that they *are* us! The interview with former revolutionary and present farmer, Jose 'Pepe' Mujica, president of Uruguay at age 75, graphically shows the way forward. Identifying hyperconsumption and the pursuit of wealth over happiness as the problem, he points us to Seneca, the Roman stoic, who wrote *On the Shortness of Life* to help get our priorities right. Don't waste precious time. "Being alive is a miracle, and sometimes people, in the middle of the noise around us, do not realize that. But being alive is miraculous. So, we have to be happy in this life. Because we have only one life, and it is always going away."

I encourage you to read this book, to read it slowly, to listen to the testimonies: Amaro's testimony. Ahmedweli's testimony. Serafimove's testimony. Reem's testimony. Read them ... read them all ... chapter by chapter. Take your time ... let them sink in.

Within these pages, people from across the globe and across the ages have shared with us harrowing, deeply personal stories ... stories of our time ... very often stories of our making.

And in the process they have posed deeply troubling questions for us … for you and for me. Questions we need to think about … and act on.

From all those questions one thing stands out. There is never justification for war. To know that means to do something about it.

Stand up for Justice!

**Clare Daly MEP**
September 2019

*Independent socialist Clare Daly was elected a member of the European Parliament for the Dublin constituency in 2019. A well-known Dáil Deputy for Dublin North (2011-2019), she was previously a member of Fingal County Council (1999-2011). For over ten years, Clare Daly was an Aer Lingus shop-steward in Dublin Airport and prior to her involvement in trade unionism was Students' Union President in Dublin City University.*

# Dedication

*For Michael*

# INTRODUCTION

# *We Need to Talk About War*

It has always seemed to me that what I write about is humanity in extremis, pushed to the unendurable, and that it is really important to tell people what really happens in war. War is not so terrible for governments because they are not wounded or killed like ordinary people. – *Marie Colvin*

One hundred years after the ending of World War I, black limousine after black limousine pulled up in front of the Élysée Palace in Paris. Waiting for those who had the doors open for them were a soberly dressed French President Emmanuel Macron and his wife, the equally soberly dressed Brigitte Macron. It took forty-five minutes and fifty-one seconds for the procession to complete. Occasionally, sobriety gave way to smiles, even jocose interactions. Photo opportunities too. Not quite selfies but the opportunity to be photographed on a red carpet in front of the Élysée Palace, once the home of Napoleon Bonaparte, was not to be passed up. It was the start of a ceremony that lasted three hours and forty-seven minutes. German Chancellor Angela Merkel was the last to arrive.

Another city, another Armistice commemoration. This time London. Another three hours. Three hours and thirty minutes. The BBC's David Dimbleby the commentator. "It is one hundred years to the day the guns fell silent..." Dimbleby intoned. "A day set apart to honour those who gave their lives and those whose lives were destroyed by war." The music is solemn. A soberly clad Theresa May carries a poppy wreath to the Cenotaph, Britain's foremost World War I memorial. Military figures follow. On a balcony stands England's Queen Elizabeth with Camilla Parker Bowles to her right, dressed in black with poppy flowers on their lapels. The severity is briefly broken as Camilla is caught on camera whispering a jocose remark to her mother-in-law. A shot that tells its own story. Her husband Charles Windsor is dressed in military uniform. His brothers and sister too. All dressed in military uniform. Big Ben rings out two minutes of silence. A silence broken by the sound of gunfire.

Charles was the first to lay a wreath, "on behalf of the nation", Dimbleby tells us. And later, one on his own behalf "with its distinctive Prince of Wales feathers". Prime Minister Theresa May too. Followed by the anti-war Labour Party leader Jeremy Corbyn who has consistently voted against the use of UK military forces in combat operations overseas. Last of the politicians was Secretary of State for Foreign and Commonwealth Affairs Jeremy Hunt, with a wreath "made up of exotic flowers representing the overseas territories". Better than having the territories represent themselves.

Another city, this time Dublin, with newly inaugurated President Michael D. Higgins, his second term in office, at Glasnevin cemetery. "One hundred years ago the guns finally fell silent on the Western Front..." President Higgins declared. Echoes of a colonial narrative.

Another country. Yemen. November 2018. One hundred years after the end of the war to end all wars. November was one of the bloodiest months in the war in Yemen with at least 3,058 documented deaths according to the Armed Conflict

Location and Event Data (ACLED). At least 28,182 fatalities were recorded in the first eleven months of 2018, marking a sixty-eight per cent increase compared to 2017. ACLED estimate that 60,223 people were killed in Yemen between January 2016 and November 2018, six times higher than the frequently cited UN figure of 10,000. Save the Children reported that an additional 85,000 children may have died from hunger and starvation in the same period.

Some of the very people who stood at the Cenotaph are responsible for all those deaths, Jeremy Corbyn exempted. Every day Yemen is hit by British bombs, dropped by British planes, flown by British-trained pilots, maintained and prepared inside Saudi Arabia by thousands of British contractors. An army leadership well represented at the Cenotaph. A *Guardian* newspaper article put the value of British arms sales (2014-2018) to Saudi Arabia and the United Arab Emirates, key participants in the war in Yemen, at £6.2 billion. In June 2019, a British court ruled that British arms sale to Saudi Arabia were unlawful. Three judges accused Tory Ministers Boris Johnson, Jeremy Hunt and Liam Fox of illegally signing off on arms exports without assessing the risk to the civilian population. The newspaper also reported that in December 2018, one month after the commemoration ceremonies were done and dusted, France signed a new military contract with Saudi Arabia.

The First World War was not a war to end all wars. Nor was it a war to protect the rights of small nations. It was a catalyst for the Second World War. Itself a catalyst for the Cold War. In turn a platform for the Korean War. The war in Vietnam. The war in Cambodia. The war in Afghanistan. The war in Iraq. The war in Syria. Seamless wars. To suggest that this was a war to end all wars is a lie, a misrepresentation of the history of the last century.

All wars are based on lies.

The guns did not fall silent on the eleventh hour of the eleventh day of the eleventh month in 1918.

Some of the people who attended the ceremony in London, most notably the children of England's Queen Elizabeth, have never known war. Not intimately. They may wear the uniforms, but they are protected from its insidious impact.

Their ancestors caused World War I. King George V of England, the current monarch's grandfather, was first cousin to both Russia's Czar Nicholas and his wife, Alexandra. He was also first cousin of Kaiser Wilhelm II. Wilhelm II and Czar Nicholas were third cousins. Not that people are responsible for the actions of their forebears.

But some acknowledgement of their family's complicity would have been appropriate. Some apology too. An apology to the working class who were mere fodder in their wars. Charles Windsor had the opportunity to apologise during an insert interview in the BBC coverage of the commemoration ceremony. From the comfort of his palace in London, he opted not to do so. Cloaking himself in a comforting narrative instead, he extolled "the extraordinary courage, gallantry and endless devoted service" of those who fought in the war. A narrative underscored by a self-serving smugness that refuses to acknowledge the horror that unfolded.

On that centenary day, none was forthcoming. Rather, this was a day of triumphalism. One that ignored war's reality. The shattered limbs. The broken bodies. The mass slaughter. The agonising cries of the dying. The suffocating poison gas attacks. The heaps of putrefying bodies in the trenches. The shellshock that lived on long after the shells stopped falling.

Of which one French soldier wrote:

> Men were squashed. Cut in two or divided from top to bottom. Blown into showers; bellies turned inside out; skulls forced into the chest as if by a blow from a club.

On 1 July 1916, first day of the Battle of the Somme, 60,000 British soldiers were killed or gravely injured – 30,000 in the first half hour. At the end of four-and-a-half months of battle, 1,300,000 casualties had been sustained by both sides, and the British and French front line had advanced five miles.

None of this featured in the commemoration ceremony. The commemorations in London and Paris were nothing more than an exercise in obscene hypocrisy. An opportunity for grandstanding by the French president, the British monarchy and the British military class.

Following the war, the world did not change for the better. The old militaristic impulse reasserted itself. Those who survived the war did not return to a better Britain. In the same way, years later, those US soldiers who fought in Vietnam did not come back to a better or welcoming United States. Reduced to silence, many could never bring themselves to talk about it.

We have lost track of war's insidious presence. As we have become inured to all its horrors. And there are countless victims of war. All over the world. Countless victims of cluster bombs that continue to maim and kill. Countless shattered limbs that ache at every move. Countless hours of sweated nightmares. People living and re-living the trauma. In the morning and in the evening. In their waking and in their sleeping.

We need to talk about war. Actual war.

About the insufferable pain it causes. The dead and the slowly dying. The injuries that never go away. The destruction it brings. The mayhem it causes. The fear it induces. The grief that clings on. And the pain, the physical and emotional pain.

There is no glory in war. There is no heroism in killing other human beings, whatever the cause. There is nothing heroic in invoking war, even as a metaphor, whatever the cause.

And yet the war mindset runs deep. We invoke war as if it is something gallant, something to be celebrated, and we do it all the time. Even when we are seeking to do the right thing. War on Want. War on Poverty. War on Drugs. War on Terror. War on Waste. War on Everybody. Want and poverty can never be alleviated by war: war exacerbates poverty and want. The War on Terror has just done that: terrorised millions of people. An estimated 1.3 million lives have been lost. The figures vary. It's a matter of "take your pick". But nobody disputes the carnage that has taken place. Killing on a scale that is beyond imagining. And then there are the injured: those who envy the dead.

Today's wars are not just the product of contesting ideologies, faith systems or geography. Class wars, race wars and gender wars are also a feature of contemporary conflict. As are the wars on drugs, the poor, people of colour, other ethnicities and others.

This book encompasses all of these wars.

War is not inevitable. War is always a conscious choice. Not by those who fight, but a choice nonetheless.

War is a failure.

A failure of diplomacy.

A failure of empathy.

A failure of intellect.

A failure of statecraft.

A failure of imagination.

I hope this book will be a small reminder that we have the vision and the capacity to not just imagine but to create a world beyond war.

And forever end war's suffering.

# 1

# Enduring Freedom

# *Afghanistan*

The departure lounge in Dubai airport was like any other international departure lounge. We joined the queue for our 09.55 flight number EK640. Airports are liminal spaces, spaces that allow for quick glances knowing that you will never again be in the same place with the same people. Quick eye contact can be easily averted and carries no threat, no risk. And so, a quick surveillance revealed a group of people lost in various electronic devices – phones, tablets, laptops. Whatever happened to books? Except this journey was somewhat different. The destination was Kabul, the capital city of Afghanistan, the site of the first war of the twenty-first century. This was not the eclectic travelling party one usually finds in such places. There was an absence of women. Children too. Neither seen nor heard. Lots of middle-aged men. Some clearly of Middle East origin. Afghans too.

But what was noticeable was the number of western middle-aged men, Ken O'Mahony and me included. Some travelling alone, some in pairs but no noticeable large groups. One man had an American flag emblasoned on his t-shirt – brave, if not foolhardy, I thought. Once boarded, two guys sitting in front of me watched Rambo-type films all the way on the three-hour flight. As if they haven't had enough of it in the real world, I thought. Passport control was a formality. Just as my passport was handed back to me the official said: "Welcome to Afghanistan". As I walked through the concourse, I noticed the tourist office was closed. And it seemed to have been closed for quite some time.

In truth, Afghanistan has always had a difficult relationship with foreigners, particularly those who come uninvited. But we were invited, or so we had presumed. As we entered the concourse, however, the people who invited us were nowhere to be seen. There was no-one about. Not the usual line of people with names on cards. Not the scrum of taxis touting for business. No hotel representatives jockeying for our attention. There was an eerie emptiness about the place. And it wasn't just the tourist office that was closed. Every place was. Suddenly it seemed to me that even the passengers on board had disappeared.

For years I had been negotiating with those who I had always presumed to be the close associates of Malalai Joya, the human rights activist once described by the BBC as the bravest woman in Afghanistan. At no stage did they give me their names, their location, or any corroborating evidence as to who they were. I had no idea if they were operating within Afghanistan or not. She was the reason we were here. This was to be a documentary about her life. And now what? As the concourse emptied and as the telephone numbers I had been given rang out, I had a sinking feeling deep in the pit of my stomach that I had been duped. That whoever had represented themselves to me as associates of Malalai were not. And that for whatever reason Ken and I were now in Kabul airport with nowhere to go. It was a sobering thought that lasted more than a moment. I had managed to track two journalists, one in Denmark and one in The Netherlands, who vouched for them, but at that moment I had even begun to doubt their veracity.

Perhaps sensing my growing anxiety, a late-leaving passenger stopped to tell us that because of security restrictions the whole airport was cordoned off. Nobody was allowed in except travelling passengers and security-cleared staff and that we had to walk about a kilometre outside the cordon to a rendezvous point. It was a tense walk in the blistering sun. With a huge sense of relief what we had expected inside the concourse was in full voice outside. Among the signs was one for Ken and myself.

Two cars and four armed guards were assigned to bring us on the three kilometre airport road to the city, once regarded as the deadliest in the world. It was the first time we had ever travelled under armed guard but on this we had no choice. For years this route had been a Taliban target. Suicide bombers, mortar attacks, kidnappings, this road had seen it all. But as we looked out on the four-lane highway clogged with cars, trucks, lorries, overloaded motorbikes and cyclists, it looked no different to many other capital cities around the world. On arrival at a safe house located within a warren of back streets, we were given a security briefing that emphasised that when we were told to move we did, and on this trip there was to be no free-wheeling.

The following morning Ken and I travelled in separate cars for what was our first meeting with Malalai Joya. The meeting was shrouded in secrecy. Even the driver did not know the precise location of our meeting when we set out, travelling hither and thither, reversing and going forward, interspersed with lots of phone calls. Final directions arrived when we got to the district in which Malalai had spent the night. The cars drove up to the door. We were told to exit quickly kerbside and ushered up a narrow concrete stairway into what initially looked like a comfortable middle-class apartment. Our rushed entry was protection for those who hosted her as much as for our protection. The hallway, now filled with men with guns and up to a half a dozen people there, was such a melee that I didn't at first recognise Malalai when she entered.

Polite, gracious and smiling with an outstretched hand, she greeted and welcomed us. Wherever and whenever she can she subverts the norms that hold women in an inferior place. It is a policy of hers to shake hands with men. We met as equals. But it was a hurried welcome. She had just received notification that the apartment was no longer safe; perhaps the sightings of two western men had something to do with it and she had to leave immediately. Apologising, she packed as she talked. Somewhat breathlessly she explained: "This is my difficult life. Most people live with fear," she told me. "When they go out of their house and say goodbye to their families, they are not sure if they will return safe back home or not".

Everything she had – her clothes, books, laptop and a photograph of her "lovely" four-year-old son when he was one year old – was squeezed into one suitcase. Her son was born, she says with a smile, on the day that marks International Day for the Elimination of Violence against Women. She dare not carry a photograph of him as a four-year-old as it would endanger his life. It's a further indication, if one were needed, of her commitment to Afghanistan (a commitment her husband, whom she married in 2005 at the relatively older age of twenty-six, shares with her) and its transformation into a secular rights-based democracy. Above all, she wants an end to the oppression by the criminal warlords, the terrorists and fundamentalists whom she accuses of working in tandem with foreign governments against the people of Afghanistan.

Malalai has long black thick hair of which she is immensely proud. Dressed in a deep blue head-to-heel dress with beautifully embroidered inlay cuffs and collar, she quickly dons her disguise. The hijab, "a shroud for dead bodies", according to Malalai, provides the perfect cover. Over her dress, she wraps around her head a long black headscarf which covers her mouth and her nose with only a slit for her eyes to see. She then puts on a long black coat, takes a quick check in a hand mirror, puts on sunglasses, grabs her suitcase and, with her armed guard preceding her, disappears down the stairway where we had entered the building.

Hated it may be, but her hijab is her ultimate disguise. It is clear that it ill-fits her and not just the physical inconvenience of it. "I'm a social feminist, secular independent person who believes in women's rights, social justice and democracy. I believe faith is a personal issue and Islam should never feature in the name of any country," she tells me in one of three long conversations we had over the ten days we were in Afghanistan. A social feminist forced to take cover under the hated burqa, the prescribed dress code of those who wish to silence and kill her. The irony of it all. The prescribed dress code of her oppressors is the main plank in her protection from the very same oppressors. On the open street below she is well hidden, safer than in her safe house in this war-saturated and most unsafe of countries.

And Afghanistan has known war. The British (1839-1842, 1878-1879 and the month-long war in 1919) then the Soviets, and still the Americans. Not to mention their own interminable internal conflicts. An instability fed by neighbouring Pakistan from which a crude distortion of Islam was co-opted for political gain. Hassan Abbas argues in *The Taliban Revival: Violence and Extremism on the Pakistan-Afghanistan Frontier* that "mainstream Islam with its soft and egalitarian essence ... was squeezed marking the end of Pakistan's founding father Mohammad Ali Jinnah's dream of a tolerant secular and pluralist polity ... and the rise of sectarianism and misguided religious fervour". The "zealots" had taken over.

But first the Soviets had to be dealt with and towards that end the West would sup with anyone who would help undermine what US President Ronald Reagan characterised as "this evil empire". That undermining preceded Reagan. In a 1998 interview, US President Jimmy Carter's National Security Advisor, Zbigniew Brzezinski, admitted that the US provided covert support to the Mujahideen, the opponents of the pro-Moscow government in Kabul six months before the Soviet intervention. "That secret operation was an excellent idea," Brzezinski later claimed.

> It had the effect of drawing the Russians into the Afghan trap. The day that the Soviets officially crossed the border, I wrote to President Carter: We now have the opportunity of giving to the USSR its Vietnam war. Indeed, for almost 10 years, Moscow had to carry on a war unsupportable by the government, a conflict that brought about the demoralisation and finally the break-up of the Soviet empire.

Once the US-reviled Soviet empire was defeated, the West disengaged and any prospect of nation-building was lost. Chaos ensued, leaving the hard-pressed, poverty-stricken, disenchanted Afghans vacuous and rudderless. Years later, when Brzezinski was asked if the Carter administration support for the Mujahideen was worth it, he replied:

> What is most important to the history of the world? The Taliban or the collapse of the Soviet empire? Some stirred-up Muslims or the liberation of Central Europe and the end of the Cold war?

Further evidence, Malalai Joya claims, that the US government is willing to sacrifice millions of Afghans to meet its own strategic interests.

From the age of four Malalai Joya has been on the move. One year after her birth in 1978, the year of the Soviet invasion in which an estimated one million Afghans and 100,000 Soviet soldiers died, she left Afghanistan. Her first stop was Iran, where she and the family lived in Khunuk Buzghala refugee camp in which 85,000 Afghans were squeezed into "filthy, overcrowded camps" in the desert frontier of the Birjand district in eastern Iran about 500 kilometres from Malalai's home province of Farah. The successful Mujahideen-led opposition in which her father participated – losing his leg to a landmine in the process – was followed by a bitter internecine civil war as warlords, drug lords and what Malalai Joya calls "rival thugs" fought each other with US weapons that had been supplied to the Mujahideen in their fight against the Soviets. Tens of thousands Afghans were killed, an estimated 62,000 people in the city of Kabul alone, a figure Malalai claims may be closer to 80,000 although there are no official numbers for this staggering death toll. And it is staggering. It is as if the population of Galway city was wiped out. Ironically, given this death toll, Kabul is now home to 4.5 million people spread across 100 square miles as people fleeing violence across the country are drawn to the capital in search of security. At the time of the US invasion in 2001, the city was home to just 1.5 million people.

Jaded and war-weary, the Afghan people thought some reprieve from the violence might come with the rise of the Taliban. The Taliban, described by Joya as "these ignorant misogynist dark-minded stone-age terrorists," did not emerge out of nowhere. Their genesis is rooted in Cold War imperialism and the cack-handedness of the Soviet empire that sought to bolster what nobody realised at the time, not least the Soviet apparatchiks themselves. This was the beginning of the end of its (and their) existence.

Originating in Pashtun, an area that straddles the Afghan-Pakistan border, a group of fanatical young men – "Talibs" (literally "seekers of knowledge") – with a rudimentary understanding of Islam, schooled in local madrasas or seminaries, set up checkpoints near the city of Kandahar in an effort to stem the violence and extortion. As their influence spread, the war-weary public embraced the Taliban in the hope of a fresh start, but they never signed up for what was to come.

13

It had all the hallmarks of the 1970s Khmer Rouge revolution in neighbouring Cambodia.[1] The Khmer Rouge was intent on transforming Cambodia into a revolutionary utopian society modelled on eleventh-century Cambodia. Theirs was to be a nationalist, communist idyll uncorrupted by urbanisation, learning, science or religion. The Taliban too wanted to turn back the clock to the time the Qur'an was written, even though many of them could not read.

The Taliban was led by the reclusive and elusive one-eyed Mullah Muhammed Omar (his injury occurred in 1993 while fighting the Soviets alongside the Mujahideen), the self-styled Commander of the Faithful who envisaged a spiritual idyll modelled on the Prophet Mohammed's seventh-century world. He assumed full control of Afghanistan, entered Kandahar's grand mosque, wrapped himself in the rarely seen holy cloth once worn by the Prophet Mohammed and waved to his followers from a roof-top building. His legitimacy among his followers was beyond questioning.

Like Cambodia's Pol Pot, he foreswore having his photograph taken, partly out of religious zeal and partly for security reasons. Even when, as leader of the Taliban, he became emir of Afghanistan between 1996 and 2001, he so seldom left his house in Kandahar that most of his followers had no idea what he looked like. He met with few journalists, and according to his obituary in *The Economist* hardly talked when he did.

Marie Colvin was among those who sought to interview him, and his response is detailed in Lindsey Hilsum's book *In Extremis: The Life of War Correspondent Marie Colvin*. Declining the invitation, Mullah Omar sent Colvin a handwritten message on pink paper. "I am extremely busy and I only receive visits from those who are important and highly responsible. As women in our society do not have very important responsibilities, up to now the necessity of receiving any woman is not felt".

---

[1] See *What in the World? Political Travels in Africa, Asia and the Americas.*

After the 2001 US invasion Mullah Omar was in hiding, flitting between Afghanistan and Pakistan. "Nobody recognises him," said Hamid Karzai, Afghan President 2001-2014. "This is a man nobody has seen." He died on 23 April 2013 aged about sixty years

Apart from the Khmer Rouge regime, this was a government like no other. The Minister for Finance had no budget and no qualified economists. Mullah Omar collected and dispersed cash on a whim. Only twice did he visit the capital Kabul while in power. There were no policy statements, no political parties, no elections. Ministries included the Ministry for the Propagation of Virtue and the Prevention of Vice. There were no salaries for state officials or soldiers. "Sharia law does not allow such things," claimed Mullah Wakil, Mullah Omar's aide and spokesman. "That is why we give no salaries to officials or soldiers, just food, clothes, shoes, and weapons. We want to live a life like the Prophet lived 1400 years ago, and jihad is our right."

At seven years of age Malalai Joya moved to Peshawar in Pakistan, about 150 kilometres from Kabul through the famous Khyber Pass, where along with thousands of other refugees they lived in "an assortment of shacks and earthen huts". In 1998 her family – there were ten children in all, Malalai the eldest of seven girls – moved back to Afghanistan while the Taliban were in power. Her activism stems from this period. Clandestinely, she started teaching girls, an activity branded by the Taliban as un-Islamic and if discovered punished by public flogging, lashings, beheadings, hangings. In these small groups, Qur'ans were always to hand in the event of being stumbled upon by the upholders of Taliban rule. Even the dead, Malalai told me, were not safe from lashings. The family of a just-deceased fourteen-year-old boy had his coffin checked. When they opened the coffin they discovered the boy had no beard. He was "an infidel", the Taliban said, so according to their rules he must be lashed. "They actually took the corpse out of the coffin and whipped it in front of the family."

"We are a war generation", she tells me. "We were born in war and we were reared in war. We have lived through bloodshed and barbarism. We have seen nothing in our lives but war."

Women bore a heavy burden under Taliban rule. Forced to wear the cobalt blue burqa that covered the whole body from head-to-toe, a grill over the eyes providing the only view on the world, women were not allowed to work outside the home, leave home without the permission of their menfolk, receive education after the age of eight, and then only to study the Qur'an, and were not allowed to be treated by a male doctor unless accompanied by a male chaperone. Householders were ordered to blacken their windows so women would not be visible from the outside. Without male support, war widows could not feed themselves and their children. And there was worse. Rape of women was routinely used as a weapon to dominate and terrorise. Children too, "often as young as four", Malalai told me. A regular punishment for a woman who was perceived to have digressed was to have her breasts cut off.

Men were compelled to grow beards, beards as long as a clenched fist according to the rules governing male grooming. Men were also forced to pray at the mosque five times a day. All of which was strictly monitored. Music, television, the taking of photographs – daily newspapers could not carry any photographs – dancing, clapping during sports events and even kite-flying were banned. Images of frayed cassette and VHS tapes hanging from trees were commonplace. More sinister were the beheadings, often public Hand chopping, too, in what might be the world's most misogynistic regime, although there is much competition, not least the Wahhabism of Saudi Arabia from where Osama bin Laden learned his particular theology, if theology it be. "After the Taliban fled," Malalai told me, "one of the first things people did was to blast loud music on the streets. Afghan music, Iranian music, Indian music could be heard everywhere." The Taliban silence was broken.

Presaging US President Donald Trump, who in 2019 urged his elected critics to leave if they don't like it – "if they're not happy here they can leave" – Commander Mullah Niazi from the Central Mosque declared "you either accept to be Muslims or leave Afghanistan". But Niazi went further. "Wherever you go, we will catch you. If you go up, we will pull you down by your feet: if you hide below, we will pull you up by your hair."

From 1996 to 2001, the Taliban imposed a grotesque distortion of Islamic law from which women like Malalai yearned to be free. Yet when the United States invading force deposed the Taliban in 2001, there was no relief for the people of the country. "Under the banner of liberating our people," Joya has publicly stated, "the Americans attacked Afghanistan. They pushed us from the frying pan into the fire."

On foreign intervention, Malalai is quite clear.

> Democracy, human rights, women's rights can never come by military intervention. Never come by the barrel of a gun. Never come by massacres. Never come by foreigners. They occupied our country with nice banners of war on terror but in reality it is a war on innocent civilians. Fear is now part of the lives of millions of Afghans. Fear inspired by fundamentalist warlords, ISIS and the Taliban. When I receive death threats I don't fear death. I fear remaining silent in the face of injustices.

Again and again Malalai emphasised her desire to be rid of all foreign troops.

A parliament of sorts merged from the invasion and in 2003, at the age of twenty-five, Malalai Joya declared as a candidate and was elected, the youngest woman ever to be elected to the Afghan parliament. From the outside, Joya challenged what she perceived as a sham parliament, accusing her fellow-parliamentarians of misogyny, criminality, of being drug lords and war lords. Threatened with death and rape, and amidst accusations of prostitution following her outspoken comments, she was expelled from parliament in 2007. "A stable or a zoo is better than this parliament," she declared, "at least there you have a donkey that carries a load and a cow that provides milk." Malalai was branded as "impertinent", an "infidel" and "out of the frame of humanity" and was suspended from parliament for her views. She describes the country as a "narco state". Quoting an old Afghan saying, she says that the post-Taliban regime "is the same donkey with a new saddle".

Her expulsion did not go unnoticed and generated strong international protests. Noam Chomsky condemned her expulsion. So too did Naomi Klein, Nobel Peace Prize laureates Kenyan social and environmental activist Wangari Maathai, Guatemalan feminist and indigenous rights activist Rigoberta Menchú Tum, US campaign against landmines activist Jody Williams, Iranian children and women's rights activist Shirin Ebadi, Irish peace activists Betty Williams and Mairead Corrigan, along with a host of Canadian, German, English, Italian and Spanish parliamentarians.

An advocate for women's rights, secularism and non-violence, Malalai Joya accuses the United States and NATO of using the catastrophic situation of women under the Taliban to justify its invasion of the country and what she regards as their criminal war on Afghanistan.

Malalai has survived seven assassination attempts. Travelling with a few armed bodyguards in Afghanistan's underground of hideaway locations, she moves from safe house to safe house every few days so that she can continue her cause. "It's not easy as a human being. It really is a big problem just to be alive."

Half of all Afghans suffer some form of mental health problems according to a 2019 Ministry of Health report. Stress and anxiety induced from suicide attacks, bombings and poverty are cited as the main causes of the country's mental health problems. War's legacy. The dead cannot speak for themselves, but some of the injured, people wounded physically and otherwise, can. And Malalai was anxious for us to meet with those who survived.

We were driven, along with Malalai Joya, to an area in the city to meet with survivors of the Shah Shaheed massacre that took place at midnight on 7 August 2015, and to what was once the home of thirty-one-year-old Basira Sultani, her husband Masoud, their son Abdullah, her husband's brother Mohammed Zaher, her father-in-law and her mother-in-law. It was once a prosperous, middle-class home. Masoud was a master craftsman and his father had a shoe-making business elsewhere in the city, employing about half a dozen men and selling directly to other middle-class men. Abdullah was a Maths teacher and the two women kept the home and looked after the children. Then one night it all fell apart.

When we arrived at the house, the front walls were blown out. Inside there was nothing. Everything had been destroyed. What was once a home was now a shell. "Every time I enter the house, the pain and sorrow grow stronger," Basira's father-in-law told me.

Pain and postponed pain. Hanging somewhat precariously on the outside are four large photographs of his two sons. Masoud is on the left in a light blue suit and matching tie with a flower in his buttonhole, his beard neatly trimmed. It might well have been his wedding photograph. To his right is a much more relaxed, casual and younger Abdullah, barely bearded, perhaps in his late teens or early twenties, carrying what could have been his gym bag. In between were the macabre images of their mutilated corpses, Masood's blood-splattered face, Abdullah's barely recognisable. Along the street other gruesome images look down on us. The wounded dead live on. The dead and the living dead.

There is still tea to be had. Basira serves. The night her husband was killed was the night of their two-year-old son's birthday. They had cake to celebrate. As she holds her eleven-month-old baby she lifts her dress to her knee in what is perhaps a breach of custom to show us her injuries. Her leg darkened with bruises, the muscles seem to have collapsed inwards, stitches run along each side of her leg. "My whole body is like this," she says. "My head, my neck, also my ear, all over my body." At the time she was twenty-two years of age. In all she has had eight operations and even now glass remains lodged in her body.

Her body is broken. She has difficulty walking, difficulty sitting, difficulty sleeping. Pain wracks her body.

> When the bomb exploded there, I was asleep in the bedroom with my husband and baby. I was pregnant at the time. When the bomb exploded I didn't hear its voice or sound. I was deaf and blinded by its impact. The power had gone. I couldn't hear anything. I couldn't find anything. The room was dark. I was trying to find my phone to turn on its light, to find where my husband is. Then I heard the voice of my father-in-law. He was shouting – where are all my sons, Masoud and Abdullah? When I woke up, I saw everywhere was destroyed. There was smoke everywhere. My leg was hurt. Everywhere was blood on my body. I didn't know where my husband was. I didn't know where my son was either. There was blood from my head to my feet. I was seriously injured.
>
> My room was on the second floor. When I came down to the first floor, I saw all the walls had collapsed. I noticed my mother-in-law had my son in her arms. She was also bloody.
>
> That night I went to the hospital. When I woke up, I noticed all my body was injured. I didn't know my husband had died with his brother. I was brought home

after twenty-four days and I was told that my husband died.

Days later we set out early for Jalalabad, Afghanistan's fifth biggest city located close to the Pakistan border and about a three-hour drive from Kabul on a road built by the Soviet invaders. I had wanted to go to Pashtun, home of the Taliban. It was out of the question. The scenery on the road to Jalalabad is breathtaking. Huge craggy clumps of rock and crevice towering above us to our left. Between us a deep ravine and a dry river bed, our only protection a foot-high, occasionally breached wall. And driving like we have seldom seen. Breakneck speed as cars and trucks weave in and out and between each other with inches at most to spare.

This is Taliban-controlled territory, we are told. Distracted by the speed of our driver, that news doesn't disturb us. We have enough to be getting on with. By journey's end we are not so sure on which side of the road Afghans drive. Overtaking on the left and right. Where there is a space, claim it before someone else does. The only consolation is that we saw only one car accident en route. Luck seems to be with us. But then again, I thought, we only have to be unlucky once.

Only once, Ken and I reminisced, had we experienced such driving. That was back in 2011 in Ethiopia as we raced against the darkness to get to our hotel in Addis Ababa. Here in Taliban country, even Ken, who is normally unflappable in such situations, was unnerved. On this road we weren't allowed to stop. It was as hot in the car as outside. Drinking water had to be kept to a minimum. Even a quick pee break was considered risky. Perhaps on the return journey. As it transpired we were allowed a rushed brief stop, the armed guards standing by nervously. The landscapes cried out to be photographed and Ken was aching to get out of the car but it was strictly disallowed. Perhaps they were right. We arrived safely.

Abdul Miamat, a key supporter of Malalai Joya, is our host for the next few days. Security here was even stricter and Ken and I had to wear the traditional long shirt known as the Paraahan, the Pakool hat and the baggy pants known as the Tonbaan in an effort at minimising our presence. Given that the temperatures are close to forty degrees, the clothes are remarkably comfortable. Malalai arrived separately in full burqa. As she disrobed, she said: "It's really oppressive. It affects your peripheral vision. And it's hot and suffocating in there. Getting used to it is more difficult than you think and it takes a while to get the hang of it." Apparently her father used to joke that he could pick her out of a crowd of burqa-wearing women in that she looked like a penguin when she walked.

Abdul lost seven of his brothers in Afghanistan's many wars. Photographs of each are kept behind a glass case. Carefully he lifts each out, recounting the location and timing of each death. A bearded Qubat looks directly at the photographer. He was twenty-eight when he was killed, martyred as Abdul says, fighting the Soviets. A clean-shaven, smiling Abdul Shoker with sunglasses was also twenty-eight. The photograph looks like it could have been taken on a holiday. Abdul Karin was twenty-two when he was killed, unsmiling in a grainy black and white photograph that may very well have been taken shortly before his death with his younger brothers Morwais and Mahmood. Morwais was twenty. Then Abdul corrected himself. No, he said, he was nineteen. In the photograph he's about twelve years old. Mahmood, a hint of a smile creeping across his face, was seventeen when he was killed by a warlord. In the photograph he's about ten years old. Mohammed Sawood, wearing a military-style jacket, was thirty when he was killed. A preppy-looking Sultan Ahmad in check jacket, white shirt and dark tie was thirty-four when he was killed.

Seven more people killed in Afghanistan's killing fields. All of this Abdul tells us without emotion.

Dubbed Operation Enduring Freedom, the British and US-led war has resulted in an estimated 147,000 people killed and 100,000 people injured since 2001, plus the more precise figure of 3,458 coalition forces killed. The Soviet invasion, initiated by the sclerotic Leonid Brezhnev who died three years into the war – the last of the Soviet Union's imperial adventures and a precursor to its demise – cost an estimated one million Afghan lives and prompted the civil war in the intervening years. This is a country drenched in bloodshed. Then there are the countless injured. In this country the injured envy the dead. But it reaches a point where numbers are redundant, beyond comprehension, beyond imagining. It sounds trite to say but occasionally we need to be reminded, as we were in Juba, the capital of South Sudan, by Anglican Archbishop Daniel Deng Bul in his equally splintered country, that one death is one too many. For Abdul Miamat, seven were too many.

Back in Kabul, we re-visited Basira, now living away from her parents-in-law. Socially too her situation has drastically changed. Now a widow, she is expected to return to her own family but her family wants her new one to take responsibility for her. So she has rented a room. A one-roomed home with a one-year-old child, caring for whom is a challenge with which she can barely cope. She is in despondent mood.

> Now that I don't have a husband, I lost my house. I'm homeless. I have nothing. I have no future. My father and mother are very old. Now I don't have a husband. I have no one, except Allah. I want my husband to be alive.

As we leave, I have this image of her sitting outside her one-roomed home, her eleven-month-old baby crawling around her. We gave her some money but it seems wholly inadequate, a mere stopgap. She accepted without comment. As we drove away, I look back. There is a stillness about her. She is sitting cross-legged on the floor, her upper body almost imperceptibly rocking to and fro, looking into the mid-distance. The living dead. And the dead living. Lost and alone, apart from her child. It is a forlorn image that has stayed with me. War.

One last conversation with Malalai Joya before we leave. Inevitably the future and her aspirations feature. On a potential run for President of Afghanistan in 2019, she was non-committal. "Even I am not sure tomorrow if I'm alive or not." Malalai Joya decided against it. All candidates are male, as are all deputy president candidates bar three. But politics is more than presidential politics. "It is the strong support of the Afghan people – and of freedom-loving people around the world – that gives me courage. The silence of good people is worse than the actions of bad people."

Then she said: "And now we have to say goodbye." And she was gone.

On the day we left Afghanistan, we rose early to catch the sun rising over Kabul, as it has done since the city was first founded in the fifth century. And despite the carnage, despite the killings, despite the injuries, the shutters go up in the shops, the markets open and the early morning cars escape the inevitable snarling of later traffic. And despite the incessant war, women and men continue to make love (women and women and men and men probably do as well, but that is well hidden, deeply disguised and highly proscribed). Children are born, grow up, and as we make our way down from a mountaintop overlooking the city, they make their way to school. Life. Whatever it is about the human spirit. Its resilience. Its determination to go on. Regardless.

It's as if the words of Samuel Beckett's *The Unnamable* come to life on the streets of Kabul.

> You must go on, that's all I know.
> You must go on.
> I can't go on.
> You must go on.
> I'll go on.

# 2

# BLACK DEATH

## *Brazil*

With tears rolling down his cheeks, fifty-one-year-old single father of three boys Amaro Jose de Silva recalled the death of his son Matais, killed by police. Struggling to get the words out, Amaro recounted in detail the day his son was killed.

> It was a Saturday. February the 11th, one week after his seventeenth birthday. I was coming home from work. And I heard that my son was shot. Another boy was with him at the time and this boy died too. There were two police officers. One drew his gun and killed Matais's friend. He was shot five times in the face. My son was shot in the leg, staggered and fell. The police officer came closer and shot my son three times in the head.

Amaro is not alone in his grief.

Brazil is a bitterly divided country. But then, Brazil has always been divided. A scandalously rich, white European elite owns and controls the enormous wealth of the country to the exclusion of their black and mixed-race co-citizens who make up an estimated half of its 211.5 million population (2019 estimate), the fifth most populous country in the world.

Homicide, the ultimate crime. Globally, nine out of ten homicides (defined by the UN as the intentional killing of another person) occur outside armed conflict, 464,000 according to a United Nations Office on Drugs and Crime (UNODC) 2019 report based on 2017 data. A disproportionate number of these deaths occur in Central and South America. The statistics are depressingly bleak. Beyond them is the bewildering, heart-wrenching grief, the trauma, the utter incomprehension personified in the lost and broken lives of the bereaved. The onomatopoeic Irish phrase *croí bhriste* is more resonant for hundreds of thousands of grief-stricken people across all continents than its English counterpart.

Sixty-one-year-old Zilda Maria de Paula's grief-stricken face holds my gaze as she drags on yet another cigarette. Long pauses punctuate her description of her son's killing, her eyes glassy with pain. Her mouth tightens as she recalls what she regards as his execution, her voice verging on cracking. But does not. Zilda refuses to cry. In public at least. Like Amaro, her telling is etched with deep emotion. But try as she might, her grief seeps from her. Breath by breath. Sigh by sigh. Pore by pore.

> For me this is really traumatic. People tell me I'm strong. I can't cry in front of people. I cry in my house. My house is empty. I can't listen to the radio any more, just watch the TV sometimes. There are some days that I cry a lot. And I go to the cemetery and I have this impulse to open the grave.

And then consider the sheer terror encountered by the about-to-be-killed. No one to comfort them as, convulsed with fear, their bodies writhe in pain, the air sucked from their lungs. No one to hold them as their bodies shudder for breath. No one to ease their pain as the first bullet enters their body, the first thrust of the knife, the first kick in the head, the chest, the stomach, the groin.

> This mass attack happened between 8.00 pm and 10.00 pm on August 18th 2015. What upsets me most is that

I can feel his fear when he saw the gun pointing at his
head.

Home to just eight per cent of the world's population, but
thirty-three per cent of its homicides, Latin America is an out-
lier. Not North America. Not the United States with its succession of mass shootings, its permissive gun laws and its highly
militarised civilian force. Not the ravaged South Africa still
reeling from the legacy of apartheid.

More than 2.5 million Latin Americans have been murdered
since the turn of this century. No other continent comes near.
Just four countries in the region — Brazil, Colombia, Mexico
and Venezuela — account for a quarter of all the murders on
Earth. Of the 20 countries in the world with the highest murder rates, 17 are Latin American, as are 43 of the top 50 cities.
In 2017, Los Cabos, Mexico had the unenviable distinction of
being the most dangerous city in the world with a murder rate
of 111.33 per 100,000 people. Caracas, Venezuela, previously
number one, is second with 111.19 murders. In third place is
Acapulco, Mexico, with 106.63 murders per 100,000 and Natal
in Brazil is fourth with 102.26. Young men are especially at
risk, with a homicide rate for those aged 18 to 19 estimated at
46 per 100,000 – far higher than the risk faced by their peers in
other regions.

But not just the cities, Latin American countries as well.

With 23,047 homicides (81 per 100,000 people), Venezuela tops the deadly 2018 list followed by El Salvador's 3,340
homicides (51 per 100,000), Jamaica's 1,287 homicides (47 per
100,000) and Trinidad and Tobago's 516 homicides (37.5 per
100,000), the second deadliest in the country's history. Notwithstanding the much-publicised litany of mass shootings,
the United States had five homicides per 100,000 people in
2015. Ireland 0.9 per 100,000.

Towering above all these statistics in absolute terms is Brazil.

Data from the Brazilian Forum of Public Security highlights Brazil's chilling record for homicides. Between 1980 and 2010, there were one million homicides in Brazil. Slightly less than the population of Cyprus, more than the population of Fiji. It's as if one-fifth of the Irish population were wiped out in a 30-year period.

In 2015, more people died violent deaths (58,383) in Brazil than in war-torn Syria.

The 2019 *Violence Atlas*, published by the Institute of Applied Economic Research, in association with the National Public Security Forum in Brazil, recorded 65,602 intentional violent deaths in 2017.

That's 180 deaths per day.

The Brazilian Igarapé Institute, an independent "think and do tank devoted to integrating security, justice and development agendas", reported that 218,580 children and adolescents were murdered between 2005 and 2015. Three black children/ adolescents for each white victim. The incidence of homicidal violence varies over the life cycle of young people.

A 2016 UNICEF report, *Situation of Children and Adolescents in Brazil*, stated that 11,403 boys and girls aged 10 to 19 were victims of homicides the previous year. Of these, 10,480 were boys.

That's an average of 31 children (10-19) murdered per day.

A 2017 United Nations report concluded from its analysis of Brazil's death toll that a young black man dies every twenty-three minutes in Brazil. A black youth is twelve times more likely to be murdered than a white youth.

Police are as likely to kill many of these young people as protect them. In 2017, the police killed 5,144 people, a twenty per cent increase over the previous year.

That's fourteen killings by police per day.

They too have not escaped unscathed: 367 members of the police force were killed in 2017.

That's one policeperson killed per day.

While men suffer disproportionately from this spiralling violence, women do not escape. In 2015, Brazil passed a law giving legal definition to femicide. Black women are more than twice as likely to be victims of homicide as white women. Also at risk are lesbian women and politically active women. So too are women in their own homes, many shot by current or former boyfriends. The murder of 39-year-old black feminist politician Marielle Franco on 14 March 2018 in Rio de Janeiro sparked a national and international outcry. Her killing remains unsolved. Following her death Amnesty International wrote:

> Marielle Franco was born and raised in a favela in Rio, Brazil. An elected councillor, she worked tirelessly to promote the rights of black women, LGBTI and young people.

> She refused to stay silent about police killings and continued to speak out against injustice right up until hours before her brutal killing. A car pulled up beside hers, and Marielle was shot four times in the head.

A total of 1,133 women were killed in 2017. That's three women killed every day.

The following year (2018) brought some respite from the slaughter. That downward trend continues into the first three months of 2019.

Except.

Except the number of police killings has risen significantly. Police killings rose a colossal eighteen per cent in early 2019, promising to become the deadliest year in decades. Six months after the inauguration of right-wing President Jair Bolsonaro in January 2019, 414 people had been killed by military police in São Paulo, the highest number since 2003, and 881 people were killed by the police in Rio de Janeiro.

Hidden within these cold, stark statistics are the lives that could have been. Lives that no longer hold the promise of sun, wind and sea. Rain too. No longer hold the promise of joy. The promise of love and companionship. No longer hold the promise of a present or a future. Lost, too, to their disorientated, anguished relatives.

Solange de Olivera Antonia carries her grief not just in her face but in her whole body. As she tells her story it's as if each word, each breath, rattles her body. Lips clasped tightly. Reluctant words unwilling to leave her body. Forced out. Hard-birthed words. Words Solange wants heard, not just in her community, not just to be heard in Brazil, but worldwide. This was her son's life. Her boy. Her flesh. Her blood.

> When he was 20 years old, unfortunately Victor was arrested while he was robbing a bank and he surrendered. And a police officer was doing an occasional job as a security guy. He surrendered and threw himself on the ground. Protecting his head like this. And despite all of these, the police officer came closer and shot my son three times. Before he shot the first time Victor raised his hand and the police officer shot him in the face, on the shoulder, and in his back.

The malevolent violence, the punitive policing, the soaring death rate, all of these have soaked the continent in blood. Blood-letting that, despite statistical peaks and troughs, shows no signs of abating. Violence that is hidden away in the cities' dark streets and poorly lit areas. Violence that targets the young, obliterating any remnants of childhood innocence that might have remained in a life framed by state-backed and societal-backed poverty, racism and class divisions. Physical violence, verbal violence, psychological violence, sexual violence. Violence that leaves everyone struggling for answers. How has it come to this? How did it all happen?

On Friday, 18 August 2017, I arrived in São Paulo, Brazil. Over the next eight days I met with thirteen young people and three adults, all victims of Brazil's relentless violence and police brutality.

Coming to Brazil I had hoped to get some answers to these questions. There were clues in the statistics and in the telling of stories.

Black seventeen-year-old Yasmin Cristina da Silva Efigenio...

> Everything started when I was fifteen years old. I was arrested. I was a drug dealer. A police officer pointed the gun to my face. One of them hit me in the face. Then they cuffed me, took me to the police station. When we arrived, two female police officers made me squat three times, strip off. She started to beat me, hit my stomach, slapped my face, verbal violence too. I didn't say names. They beat me even harder and took me to another police station and all this way I was beaten until I opened my mouth. When I said the names they wanted, they stopped beating me.

Black seventeen-year-old Mikael dos Santos...

> The first time I was beaten by the police I was sixteen years old. It was in the beginning of 2016. I was in front of my house. I was with two friends. The police were passing, stopped us, searched us, and found some cigarettes on my friends. And then they started beating us. It was 11.00 pm. They started to beat us. They got my cell phone from my pocket and took it.

Black seventeen-year-old Cicero Hugo Nunes de Lima...

> When I was sixteen years old, unfortunately I went to jail. They waited for my parents to go away and then they came back to the jail to beat me. They hit me a lot. They beat me on the kidneys. In the stomach, in the chest and in my face. They put my hands back and started to beat my face. To hit my chest. I hated everything, I felt really humiliated. I never felt so humiliated in my life.

Here if it's dark, the police beat you. They put your face in the ground. Step in your face. Step on your back. Punch your face, your stomach. Your chest. They mock about you. After they beat me a lot and offended me, they threw me in jail like a dog, not even like a dog 'cos no dog deserves that. Nobody deserves that. They left me there with my hands back until next day.

Black twenty-one-year-old Guilherme de Oliveira Mascarenhas…

When the police officers beat us, they use the pepper spray on our eyes. They hit our neck, legs, and in the chest, stomach, and kick us in the same places. Every time they hit us, they hide us behind the police car so nobody sees their aggression. They say they are going to kill me; they are going to throw drugs at us and say it's ours. They call us names. They say they are going to kill my family.

Black twenty-one-year-old Tomas Alves…

I was fourteen years old when I was coming out of a club. Police officers approached. I put my hands on my head and they told me to spread my legs. I didn't do it properly so they hit my legs. Called me a lazy nigger. And tried to punch my head. One of the police officers got my hand and the other one and they started to balance my feet. And they broke my fingers. Another time four or five months afterwards the police officers approached again and I was near a place where drug dealers hang out. They tried to hit me again. To hit my face again. They kicked me. That's when they broke my jaw. Broke some teeth. Another time when I got arrested, I went to the casa. One day before I went to the casa, the police officers hit my head here and here. And another time they hit me with the police stick. That's when they broke my ankle.

Black twenty-two-year-old Hebert Douglas Ribeiro da Silva...

> One night in October I was fourteen years old, about to be fifteen, I was with two friends. It was about 8.00 pm. I has this haircut and I had about 300 dais in my pocket. These police officers once caught me with weed and they suspected I was drug dealing. The police told me to get inside the police car and then they cuffed me. I said I didn't have any drugs. They stopped the car in a deserted place, an empty place. And told me to strip. I was alone with the boss of the police officers. He punched me and he tortured me, told me to be naked and touched my penis. I have scars on my body.

Black twenty-nine-year-old Edmilson Silva Filomeno...

> It was around 11.00 pm, midnight when the police approached. They left the car with a gun pointed to my head asking me not to move. And all the time they offended me, called me son of a bitch, thief. After the search they found my college ID in my pocket. The police officers called me names, said that a thief doesn't go to college. He threw everything from my backpack on the ground and left it there and kept saying that I shouldn't look in his eyes and saying that if I told anyone about the violent approach, he would remember my face.

Underpinning all the violence is racism. All the young people recognised this.

Yasmin Cristina da Silva Efigenio...

> There are some people that don't like our colour. They judge us just by the colour without knowing us.

Mikael dos Santos...

> When the police stopped me, they called me nigger, black son of a bitch.

Cicero Hugo Nunes de Lima...

I am just black. What's the difference? If you're white and if you're black, what's the difference? There is no difference. Everybody is a human being. They don't look at that. If you're black, they are going to beat you. That's what matters. If you're black, you're going to get hit. If you're white you can go. That's how Brazilian society looks like.

Guilherme de Oliveira Mascarenhas...

When the police approach us they tend to call us black, monkey. When they arrive, they call us son of a bitch, addicted drug dealer.

Tomas Alves...

I have lots of white friends. And when we hang out together, they don't approach my friends. But they approach me. So that's how I see the prejudice of the police officers.

Hebert Douglas Ribeiro da Silva...

When the police approached, they ask if you have tattoos because of your colour...

Edmilson Silva Filomeno...

We black people are considered a dangerous class in the society because we are viewed as thieves, as criminals. When you leave home for work, you don't know if you are going to come back.

Racism is deeply embedded in Brazilian society, a racism that stems from Brazil's history of slavery.

Brazil was late abolishing slavery. By the time it did so in 1888, an estimated four million slaves had been transported from Africa – forty per cent of the total number of slaves brought to the Americas. Old bitternesses have metamorphosed into overt hatred and fear. The gulf between the black and white people who came in waves to Brazil after it was "discovered" in 1500 has never been bridged.

A United States government-backed 1964 military coup copper-fastened white supremacy. Forty years later, another revolution, this time a bloodless one, resulted in the election of the charismatic democratic socialist Lula da Silva as president in January 2003. He and the Workers' Party transformed the country. A relentless campaign by the all-dominant, white, elite-controlled right-wing media, allied to sections of the military and the judiciary, resulted in the prosecution and imprisonment of Lula in 2018 on what many within Brazil believe were trumped-up corruption charges. Charged with manipulating the budget, Lula's successor, Dilma Rousseff (president 2011-2016) was ousted from office, clearing the way for the election of the right-wing Michel Temer, followed by the election of far-right former army captain Jair Bolsonaro. As in 1964, the not-so-subtle spectre of Brazil's North American neighbour loomed large. The far right had taken over.

> In congratulating Bolsonaro, US President Donald Trump talked of closer economic and military cooperation. There is no pretence here. Two white supremacists aligning with each other. Denying accusations of racism, Bolsonaro once stated: "If I was racist, what would I have done on seeing a black fall into the water? I'd have folded my arms."

Brazil is a vast, expansive country (8.51 million square kilometres), the fifth largest in the world with the sixth largest population (211,049,527) and the ninth highest ranking economy. According to the 2010 census, about six per cent of Brazil's population live in favelas or shanty-towns, around 11.25 million people. Given the informality of favela life and the population growth in the intervening years, these are conservative estimates.

It is in these favelas that police violence is most keenly experienced. "The problem here in Brazil," human rights lawyer Valdenia Paulino told me, "is that the state is the main violator of human rights that we have in the country."

> Black people living in poverty and on the periphery of large cities are seen as less human than others, that's why they can be killed at any moment. That's how Brazilian whites perceive the poor, indigenous and black population.

She claims that São Paulo, where we met, is at the heart of this genocide. The demarcation lines in this heaving metropolis of twenty million people are the Tietê and Pinheiros rivers. Those who live outside the rivers, known in São Paulo as the three Ps – *pobres, preto, puriferia* (the poor, the black and those on the periphery) – are the most likely victims of what Paulino characterises as Brazil's genocide.

It was in Jardim Ângela, a peripheral neighbourhood on the outskirts of São Paulo, that I met with the young black people and the bereaved parents. My host was Jim Crowe, a County Clare-born Catholic priest. Three features stood out when I first met Jim Crowe.

First, his name. Those at his naming ceremony in 1945 would not have been aware of the significance of his naming. For years the name Jim Crow, particularly in America's Deep South, has been synonymous with what Michele Alexander, in her powerful and uncompromising book *The New Jim Crow: Mass Incarceration in the Age of Colorblindness*, calls the white terror of the all-pervasive racism that permeates large swathes of society in the United States to this day. Brazil too. This Jim Crowe is the antithesis of that Jim Crow. The difference is more than the letter e.

Second, his accent. Unchanged, despite living for forty years in Brazil.

Third, his hands. Jim Crowe has remarkable hands. Farmer's hands. Just like his father and grandfather, he tells me. But these hands have been marked by social and political struggle rather than tilling the rich and fertile soil of his homestead. To paraphrase Seamus Heaney's oft-quoted poem "Digging", Jim Crowe has been digging with an altogether different tool. Those whom he admires are first to greet you as you enter his home whose door is open all day to whoever strays in or deliberately stops by. Greeting those who enter are poster images of India's Mahatma Gandhi, Dom Hélder Câmara, the now deceased Catholic Archbishop of Receife known as the Red Cardinal, and the Argentinean/Cuban Marxist revolutionary Che Guevara.

Poster boys are just that. Poster boys. Digging in and getting your hands dirty are the difficult parts. And that's what Jim Crowe did. Distancing himself from the petite bourgeosie of his class of origin, along with Lula, he co-founded the Workers' Party. "There were just fifteen of us at the first meeting," he told me. Since then the pipe-smoking farmer's son from Clare has been at Lula's side throughout all his triumphs and tribulations. In taking a courageous stance against corrupt, military dictatorship from 1964-1985 and the forces that sought to undermine Lula's pro-poor policies, he was not alone.

Central to those policies was Lula's Programma Bolsa Familia (PBF). Introduced by President Lula in 2003, and described by the World Bank as "Brazil's quiet revolution", low-income families received cash transfers on condition they sent their children to school and had them vaccinated. Panned by Lula's right-wing critics as indulgent and wasteful, the equivalent of throwing money from a helicopter, it had an altogether different impact. Fourteen million households, fifty million people, around a quarter of the population, benefited from the programme. Inequality was reduced. Extreme poverty was halved from 9.7 per cent of the population to 4.3 per cent. It was, according to Deborah Wetzel and Valor Econômi-cot in a November 2013 World Bank report, "a global success story and a reference point for social policy around the world".

A brave and bold policy.

Brave too was the Mothers of May Movement, a network of mothers, family and friends of victims of state violence, located in São Paulo. The group's mission is to fight for truth, memory and justice for all victims of discriminatory, institutional and police violence against the poor, the African descendant and Brazilian social movements. My introduction to these women and to the young people of Jardim Ângela, I owe to Jim Crowe.

And this is the life they described for me.

Yasmin Cristina da Silva Efigenio…

> I live with my mother and my brothers. The neighbour-hood where I live is humble, is simple. And that's it. We come from a humble family. When we were young, my father left my Mom. Abandoned us. My mother, she never abandoned us. And my mother has taken care of us since we were kids. She never leaves us. We love her a lot. Where I live is really dangerous. There are lots of places to sell and buy drugs. We don't have peace. I wish I didn't live there actually. I want to live in a peaceful place. That's it.

Mikael dos Santos…

> When my life started it was when I experienced the major pain in my life. My father died. I went to a child shelter when I was five. And they became my family. It was hard sometimes. There were times when I could wish I was near my family and I couldn't. In the begin-ning I had eight brothers. It was hard for my Mom to stay with me. And I had to go to the child shelter. It was really hard for me. I was adopted. And it was good for me to be with them but I wanted my Mom and my Dad to be beside me. And I couldn't have that. It was really terrible. I couldn't handle it.

Cicero Hugo Nunes de Lima...

When I was sixteen years old, unfortunately I had to buy a gun because one guy near my house stabbed my father and because of that I felt threatened and I felt that he was threatening my family. I bought a gun on-line and I paid 800 dais. The next day I ran to a soccer game. I noticed the boy was following me. The guy that stabbed my father. I went back home and got the gun. When I was coming back from the game, police officers approached. And then I went to jail.

Guilherme de Oliveira Mascarenhas...

When I was twelve, I met the world of crime. I started to go to parties, started to drink. To have fun. When I was seventeen and a half, I started to steal. That's where I started to steal to help my Mom inside my house. On my second attempt to steal I went to jail.

Tomas Alves...

My childhood was really painful. Since I was a kid, I was never the type to play with other kids. Since I was a kid, I had to bring money inside the house because we didn't have my father. I used to beg for money on the street to ask for food and money. I had to give money to my family. I had to take a chance. To be part of the traffic, to be part of drug dealing, because we didn't have conditions to eat. To wash our clothes. We didn't have it so that's when I started as a drug dealer.

Hebert Douglas Ribeiro da Silva...

My parents divorced when I was seven years old. When I was ten years old, I lost my grandmother who raised me. She was a really special person for me. When she died my world fell. I got into depression. When I was depressed, I started to use drugs with weed. I was ten years old. When I was fifteen years old I went to jail. I was a drug dealer for five years and lived on the streets. And I ate from the trash. I spent two weeks there eating from the garbage. Taking a shower in the rain. I don't even like to remember that.

Bearded with long Rastafarian-styled hair, Rafel Mantovani was twenty-eight when we met. He too grew up in Jardim Ângela. His Italian father abandoned the family when he was young. His Brazilian mother worked as a maid, raising five sons. While his family background may have been different, his experience of the police was all too familiar. It's an experience he still carries with him.

> Once when I was riding a motor cycle (without a licence), the police officer approached. I was sixteen years old. They threw me against the wall. They beat me in front of the school. It was something that marked me because I was in front of some of the people I admired. I was a teenager. And they beat me. Hit me a lot. The police officer told me I was stealing and then they cuffed me and put me inside the car. It was humiliating. It was a bad experience for me not just because of the physical violence but because of the verbal violence, moral violence in front of the school you study. They put you inside the car just because you are riding a bike. They are here to humiliate us.

Both Jim Crowe and human rights lawyer Valdenia Paulino argue that the targeting of young black men in the favelas is grounded in racism and is of genocidal proportions. "That's how the rich people in Brazil see the Indians, and the poor people in Brazil," Paulino told me. From north to south, for black and poor people, there is no escaping the genocide.

A racial genocide. A class genocide. Perpetrated by the white wealthy elite and those prepared to do their bidding. It is an audacious claim, one that challenges many people when first heard. Based on the stories I heard, and influenced by both Crowe and Paulino, I named the documentary *Black Genocide in Brazil*. It, too, was intended to provoke. The extent of the killing of young black men is of such scale that it comes within the definition of genocide. It's one of the standard questions I get asked when screening the film. Why "genocide" in the title?

In 1944 Polish Jewish lawyer, refugee and linguist Raphael Lemkin, fluent in nine languages, coined the term *genocide*. No single word, he felt, could capture what was happening at that time and until a word was found, he believed that people would not come to realise the absolute horror of mass killing. For Lemkin, the word had to pass the George Eastman test. Eastman coined the word "Kodak" for his new camera because (a) it was short, (b) it was not capable of being mispronounced and (c) it cannot be confused with anything else.

The then twenty-one-year-old Lemkin was studying linguistics at the University of Lvov in Ukraine, about seventy kilometres from Poland, when he first heard of the Armenian massacre. One of the Armenian survivors, Soghomon Tehlirian, assassinated former Turkish interior minister Mehmed Talaat who had presided over what Pulitzer prize winning author Samantha Power describes as "the killing by firing squad, bayoneting, bludgeoning and starvation of nearly one million Armenians". For what Talaat did there was no punishment, but for what Tehlirian did there was. Murder. "It is a crime for Tehlirian to kill a man but it is not a crime for his oppressor to kill more than a million men," Lemkin remarked.

Defining this word and gaining international recognition for the crime of mass murder became a lifelong obsession for Lemkin. That obsession was further fuelled by the mass murder of Jews, gypsies, gay people, priests, people with mental or physical disabilities, communists, trade unionists, Jehovah's Witnesses, anarchists, Polish and other Slavic peoples, resistance fighters and others in Germany's extermination camps during the Second World War.

Winston Churchill's fury at the crimes of Nazi Germany provided a further impetus for Lemkin in his all-consuming search for the elusive name for the crime of mass murder. "The whole of Europe has been wrecked and trampled down by the mechanical weapons and barbaric fury of the Nazis," Churchill thundered. "As his armies advance, whole districts are exterminated. We are in the presence of a crime without a name." Finding that elusive name became a lasting preoccupation for Lemkin. Having toyed with the words barbarity and vandalism, he eventually decided on genocide: the ultimate crime.

*Geno,* meaning race or tribe or people or nation, owes its origins to Greek; *cide,* meaning killing, owes its origins to Latin. The word eventually became associated with the sheer barbarity – a word Lemkin felt did not encapsulate the absolute horror of what happened during World War II – of mass killing, and would, he hoped, send shivers down people's spines every time it was invoked.

All of which is detailed in Irish-American Samantha Power's masterful 2003 book, *A Problem from Hell: America and the Age of Genocide.*

Genocide involves the attempted destruction of the political and social institutions, the culture, the language, national feelings, religion and economic existence of national groups. It also marks the end of people's personal security, liberty, health, dignity and the lives of individual members of targeted groups.

The legal definition of genocide, as stated by the Office of the UN Special Advisor on the Prevention of Genocide (OSAPG), is defined in Article 2 of the Convention on the Prevention and Punishment of the Crime of Genocide (1948) as:

> … any of the following acts committed with intent to destroy, in whole or in part, a national, ethnical, racial or religious group, as such: killing members of the group; causing serious bodily or mental harm to members of the group; deliberately inflicting on the group conditions of life calculated to bring about its physical destruction in whole or in part; imposing measures intended to prevent births within the group; [and] forcibly transferring children of the group to another group.

The crime of genocide has no statute of limitation.

The Genocide Convention came into force on 12 January 1951, six years after the ending of World War II. Raphael Lemkin died eight years later having fulfilled his lifetime ambition. Singlehandedly, he gave the world a solitary word. Genocide. A crime against humanity.

As of May 2019, the Genocide Convention has been ratified or acceded to by 150 states, Brazil included. Forty-three other United Nations member states have yet to do so. Of those, twenty are from Africa, seventeen from Asia and six from the Americas.

The scale of the killing in Brazil, the sanctioning of the killing by the state, is of such an order that many Brazilian activists believe it comes within the definition of genocide.

The war (genocide) against young black people in Brazil has intensified following the election of Jair Bolsonaro in January 2019. And that war has become more explicit. On 7 April 2019, musician and part-time security guard Evaldo dos Santos Rosa and his family were travelling to a baby-naming ceremony when the car he was driving was mistaken for another. Ten soldiers fired eighty bullets at his car, killing him, but miraculously his wife, their seven-year-old son, her step-father and a thirteen-year-old girl survived.

Eighty bullets. Fired at a family car. No questions asked. No attempt to stop and search.

State-sanctioned killing with impunity. Following the shooting dead of eleven bank robbers by police in São Paulo in April 2019, Governor Joao Doria congratulated the police for sending "more than ten gangsters to the cemetery. Bandits from now on are not going to the police station, not to the jail, they go direct to the cemetery."

Time and time again Bolsonaro has spoken approvingly of extra-judicial killings. In August 2019 he declared that "criminals will die in the streets like cockroaches and that's how it should be" following his proposed changes to the criminal code. Among his trademark utterances are: "a good criminal is a dead criminal; the dictatorship's mistake was to torture but not kill."

Speaking in 2017 about a black settlement founded by the descendants of slaves, he said: "They do nothing. They are not even good for procreation." To the former head of the Secretariat of the Presidency of the Republic for Human Rights, Congresswoman Maria do Rosario, a campaigner against homophobia and for the establishment of a truth and reconciliation commission to investigate the crimes perpetrated by public office holders during the dictatorship, Bolsonaro declared in 2014: "I wouldn't rape you because you don't deserve it."

The extra-judicial killings, the class hatred, the racism and the misogyny that underpin the utterances of Bolsonaro and his supporters are most keenly felt by the poor of the favelas.

By Amaro, Zilda and Solange. By Yasmin, Mikael, Cicero, Guilherme, Tomas, Hebert, Edmilson and Rafel. And by hundreds of thousands of beaten, broken and bereaved people across Brazil. And the monumental scale of the killing that holds the country in its vice-like grip and leaves its people reeling and grieving.

Known by his nickname Boosie, Zilda's son was killed in a bar by the police along with seven others, a fourteen-year-old girl included. Eight people killed. In a bar. By the police. Without provocation. As if that would be a justification. And no recourse to justice. Zilda's thirty-four-year-old and only son was among those killed, shot once through the head.

Zilda Maria de Paula…

> My son had a hole in his forehead. He was executed, all of them were executed. The only survivor was asleep in a chair. They shot him in the mouth, his mouth was completely destroyed. He is like a zombie now. That was terrible what they did there. Everybody in their way they shot, they executed, including a fourteen-year-old

girl. Aiming at another guy, they shot the girl. They shot ten and eight died. It was an atrocity.

When they took him to the cemetery, they told me they would have to lock the coffin. I agreed. His friends put a picture on his coffin. I have this picture in my head of seeing that horrible coffin, coffins are ugly. When I close my eyes, I see the face of my son, my dead son.

They buried lots of futures. Buried lots of dreams. Not just my boy. But other boys too. And it doesn't stop.

The killing continues.

And then she added…

He was thirty-four at the time. My only son.

Solange de Oliveira Antonio has sought justice for her dead son Victor. He was killed on 3 March 2015.

After a year I got a record of the shooting that shows what I told you, that my son surrendered. That the police officer shot my son after he had surrendered. That he was on the floor. I've been with the DA with this case. He said that he can't help me to take this police officer to court because it's clear that it was an execution but the judges, the police officers are protected by the state and we can only try and punish this police officer through the state. How is the state going to punish this police officer that was trained to kill?

And then she added…

My family was complete. My daughters Lena, Caroline, and there's Gustavo. He's fourteen years old. And then there's Victor. He would have been twenty-two years today. He would have been twenty-two.

As the tears flowed down Amaro Jose de Silva's cheeks he wistfully remarked, "the authorities don't respect us, we who are poor and black".

Matais was killed on 11 February 2017.

I couldn't recognise my son's body. In the cemetery, I spent the whole night with his body. The funeral was simple, was humble. The coffin was locked. My son died on a Saturday morning. And we just got his body on Sunday night. We had to pay money to release my son's body to bury him. His body arrived in the cemetery on Sunday night. It was about 10.00 pm. We went to pray with his body. And on Monday around 10.00 am he was buried. That's what I have to say but it was really hard. It was painful to see my son in a coffin.

And then he added…

I asked God, please God take me and bring my son back to life…

Please.

# 3

# A Bitter Anger

# *Iraq*

Honking of horns amidst throngs of traffic. Thursday night in downtown Baghdad. Thursday night is wedding night. And if weddings are a symbol of hope and trust there is no shortage of them here. Woody Allen was right. The heart is a resilient little muscle. Wedding party after wedding party. Young men, hair highly coiffed, hanging out of car windows. Music at full volume competing between the various wedding parties. Less visible are the women at the party. What glimpses we get of the brides and grooms suggest that people marry very young here. The social and religious mores prohibit any pre-marriage intimacies – a bit like Ireland when it was another country.

For those not attending wedding parties, Thursday night is ice-cream night. Prohibition of alcohol consumption is strictly enforced here – at least in public. While many people do not consume alcohol they make up for it in tea – served in what we might regard as a sherry glass with lots of sugar – and of course ice cream. The Al Fakma ice-cream café, the most popular in all of Baghdad. Families gather here, the young and the old and all those in between. Loud music blares from a nearby tannoy system. It's hard to hear and be heard.

It's hard, too, to imagine that this same city was pummelled from the sky in the Bush-Blair invasion of Iraq in 2003, an invasion that despite the carnival atmosphere around us has left a deep imprint. All of which seems like a long time ago now. Another country to us. But not to those who lived through the carnage.

For the people of Iraq, the legacy lives on. And not just of that war but of the preceding Gulf War. The 1991 invasion known as Operation Desert Storm. Estimates put the combined death toll at ... well ... it's almost "pick a figure", half a million, a million, more than a million.

And if we are ever to begin to comprehend what has befallen this country, our only hope is to take time to hear individual stories of loss and grief. And as we travelled from Basra in the South, stopping off in Babylon (the epicentre of the great Mesopotamian civilisation), Baghdad, Erbil and Mosul, beyond the conviviality of the ice-cream parlours and the wedding feasts, anguished stories hidden but keenly felt began to emerge.

It's hard to write about war. It's hard to talk about war. Time and time again I have been told in Syria, Afghanistan, Libya and other places that you have to live war to know war. And even the scale of the atrocities, even first-hand accounts, when heard, are beyond comprehension.

Beyond comprehension too was the bombing of Baghdad. Despite all the threats, despite all the media attention, until the bombs started to fall, people here didn't believe Baghdad would be bombed. And when the bombs did begin to fall, on our television screens it seemed like any other video game. Wham. Bang. You're dead. In Baghdad it was all so different.

For those on whom the bombs were falling it was terror like no other. Kindergarten teacher Samira Dawood was one. Sitting under an avant-garde sculpture where the towering figure of Saddam Hussein once stood, she told me of the night the bombs fell. This was "Shock and Awe". A Shock and Awe that lasted for twenty-one nights.

> The sky became bright and the night became like day from the missile explosions from the fighter jets. It was a state of horror. I myself was terrified but I was pacifying both my children and hugging them. We stood in a corner of the house because they say that the corner won't collapse if an explosion happens. We remained standing and remained in that situation for two days, two consecutive days. We couldn't get anything to eat or drink. We constantly recited some verses from the Qur'an and felt scared. It was terrifying, terrifying.

Two days crouching by a pillar as the world collapses around you. With two traumatised children. With nothing to eat or drink. How do you live through that experience? When your children ask, "are we going to die?" what do you say? Two whole days without food and water.

That night back in my hotel I wanted to hear US President George W. Bush's justification for this war and all the justifications that came before him. I didn't expect to find any answers, but it was as if I needed to reinforce the chasm that exists between those who declare war and those who experience it. I wanted to hear again the platitudes that go with the declaration of war.

The settings and the optics on these occasions are all too familiar. In 1993, US President Bill Clinton addressed the American people for eleven minutes and nineteen seconds "on military action in Somalia". Dressed in a sharp suit with a crisp white shirt that had a kink in the collar and a red tie, Clinton began as his predecessor Ronald Reagan always did on such occasions with "my fellow Americans". Hands joined on the desk behind which he sits, the US flag itself partially hidden behind a row of books and a sculpture of a head whose identity is unclear, the overall effect softened by a large green plant, Clinton looks off to the side, not directly to the camera.

Gradually, the camera moves in on him and as it does his trademark narrowing of eyes, the jawline more pronounced as he gets to the centre-piece of his address, the justification for military intervention: "We came to rescue innocent people in a burning house."

Clinton's address to the nation on the 1999 military action in Kosovo was justified on similar grounds. The camera at a slightly different angle, also from the left but this time high-lighting gold cufflinks and his wedding band. The broadcast lasted thirteen minutes, seven seconds.

In 1991, two years before Clinton's address on Somalia, his immediate predecessor, George H.W. Bush, this time looking straight to camera from behind the desk in the Oval Office, the US flag off his right shoulder, addressed the US nation at the start of the 1991 Gulf War. Dispensing with "my fellow Americans", Bush began with "just two hours ago...". As the camera moves in on him, Bush characterises Kuwait as a small and helpless neighbour. "A country crushed; a people bru-talised in a cruel war". Among the objectives of the mission, Bush claimed, was to free Kuwait and restore the legitimate government of Kuwait. His address took twelve minutes and twelve seconds to deliver.

Dispensing with long justifications, a startled-looking George W. Bush took just four minutes, twenty seconds to declare war on Iraq on 20 March 2003. A date kindergarten teacher Samira Dawood will never forget.

> The invasion started at half past two precisely, a date I will never forget.

Like Clinton, George W. Bush too was wearing a crisp suit, white shirt and red tie. This time the flag is on his lapel. On the White House desk to his left is a photograph of his wife Laura and her dog Barney, and to his right a photograph of their two daughters. Clearly a family man.

Samira, a family woman, said:

I was on my own with my children. No one else. My husband was out of Baghdad. They were small in age.

Bush continued:

My fellow citizens. At this hour American and coalition forces are in the early stages of military operations to disarm Iraq, to free its people and to defend the world from grave danger.

It was not how Samira saw it.

We were caught by surprise. We were asleep in the middle of the night. The warning sirens became very loud and there was a blackout, it was frightening and my children and I, we didn't know where to go. The children cried and shivered with fear. My small daughter hid under the chair from fear and she still suffers from the trauma. In the morning there were dead bodies on the street, houses demolished, buildings destroyed.

Addressing directly the military personnel that he was sending to war, Bush continued:

The people you will liberate will witness the honourable and decent spirit of the American people. In this conflict America faces an enemy that has no regard for conventions of war or rules of morality. Saddam Hussein [has attempted] to use innocent men, women and children as shields for his own military. A final atrocity against his people. I want the world to know that every effort will be made to spare innocent civilians from harm.

Samira continues:

I was upset and my children were crying, there was no food. There was a shortage of food, Baghdad markets were deserted and all the shops were closed. Two weeks later, while still going through that suffering in the same house, we managed to organise cars in a hurry, we headed towards Al-Anbar. I saw dead bodies

lying on the street - women, men, children - and ani-
mals eating the bodies, the country turned into terror.
It was a curse not a blessing.

Bush again:

We have come to Iraq with respect for its citizens, for
their great civilisation and for the religious faith they
practice. Our nation enters this conflict reluctantly. Our
friends and allies will not live at the mercy of an outlaw
regime. We will bring freedom to others and we will pre-
vail. May God bless our country and all who defend her.

And so, the United States President continued to spin a web
of propaganda and falsehoods: falsehoods about the rationale
for war; falsehoods about the threat posed by Saddam Hussein; falsehoods about their respect for the great traditions and
history of this land. Falsehoods that were repeated by Colin
Powell and Tony Blair.

Samira was all too clear on the threadbare nature of the lies.

No, that is not the reason for the attacks, that Saddam
was a threat. We know that the Americans, Mr. Bush,
they were afraid of Saddam Hussein – he was too powerful. He had a good military. All had an interest in Iraq
because of its rich resources, its treasure. Iraq has oil
resources that can satisfy the world. We are rich in Iraq
with mineral resources, oil, even dates. There is a lot of
interest in this country; Americans occupied Iraq in our
view because it's a resource-rich state.

Playing on his much commented-upon intellectual insecu-
rities and his oft-acknowledged academic mediocrity ("I was
a C student, but hey, guess who's President?"), his predato-
ry foreign policy mandarins steamrolled him into war. Dick
Cheney and Donald Rumsfeld. The military industrial complex, as US commentator Maureen Dowd wrote, "cocked and
ready". Unrestrained, macho foreign policy taking on the
world. Grandiosity on a hubristic scale. The swagger. To the

delight of his approving supporters at the 2005 Republican National Convention in New York City, Bush declared, "Some folk look at me and see a certain swagger, in Texas we call that walking." The over-arching confidence. The recklessness. The lies. The self-interest. The naivete. And ultimately, the tragedy.

The military industrial complex. It wasn't as if successive US presidents weren't warned of its insidious, nefarious influence. President Dwight D. Eisenhower, in his parting speech in 1961 (why political leaders have to wait until they leave office to make such observations when they are least politically effectual is another question), called on the citizens of the United States to guard against "the acquisition of unwarranted influence, whether sought or unsought, by the military-industrial complex. The potential for the disastrous rise of misplaced power exists and will persist". As a former US Army Chief of Staff and Supreme Allied Commander of NATO forces, he should know.

Noam Chomsky, in his searing indictment of the reactionary quick-fix culture (devoid as he alleges of any intellectual or historical attention but one that shapes and comforts the government of the United States in its imperialist and hegemonic ambitions), blasts the craven and submissive way in which successive US presidents have, for the past 100 years, crassly conformed to the demands of that military industrial complex, which continues to have a vice-like grip on its body politic.

Chomsky argues that if Principle 111 of the Nuremberg Principles – the fact that a person who committed an act which constitutes a crime under international law, while acting as Head of State or as a responsible government official, does not relieve him of responsibility under international law – were applied, every post-World War II US president would be indictable, Eisenhower included. Chomsky cites him for the overthrow of Iran's democratically elected nationalist government of Prime Minister Mohammad Mosaddegh in 1953, and

the 1954 overthrow of Guatemala's democratically elected socialist president Jacobo Arbenz. For the record, he cites John
Kennedy ("one of the worst"), Lyndon Johnson and Richard
Nixon over Vietnam, among other sites of presidential criminality; Gerald Ford, for his endorsement of the Indonesian
invasion of what was then East Timor; Jimmy Carter, also in
relation to Indonesia; Ronald Reagan, the first president to be
condemned by the International Court of Justice for the unlawful use of force in Nicaragua; George H.W. Bush, for the Gulf
War; and Bill Clinton, for the sanctions in Iraq following the
Gulf War as well as his decision to send cruise missiles to Sudan. He could have added Libya, Syria, Iraq and Afghanistan
to Barack Obama's list, and Venezuela to Donald Trump's.

Meanwhile, back in Iraq, Bush Jr. ("you are either with us
or you are with the terrorists"), Colin Powell, Dick Cheney,
Donald Rumsfeld, Condoleezza Rice, Paul Wolfowitz, John
Bolton and all those who failed to heed Eisenhower's warnings were floundering in the quicksand of Iraq.

And when it all went horribly wrong, the recriminations.
George H.W. Bush, in typically mangled English (a trait his
son inherited), turned the screw on Cheney and Rumsfeld.
Rumsfeld, he claimed, had "a lack of humility, a lack of seeing what the other guy thinks, an iron-ass view of everything.
He's more kick-ass," while Cheney joined forces with the "real
hard-charging guys who want to fight about everything, use
force to get our way in the Middle East". As if all of this ex-
onerates his son of responsibility for the war in Iraq. The forty-third president of the United States.

George W. Bush wasn't alone in his determination to go
to war, whatever the consequences. Tony Blair stood by him,
step by step. A decision that has outraged Irada Al Jiburi, Professor of Journalism at the University of Baghdad, whom we
met at a heavily fortified hotel in Baghdad. Her struggle with

the English language did not for a moment diminish the venom with which she spat out the words.

> Of course, Blair, I'm talking about Tony Blair he is as a person, not just as a system responsible with Bush about destroying Iraq. If there is any justice in the world they have to prosecute Blair and Bush as war criminals. And they really, they really, really, really deserve that. They are responsible for about a million (lost) lives, all the victims of Iraq. They are responsible about the heritage, stolen from Iraq. Responsible for health, economy, our future, everything. It's not just people. Iraq deserve compensation about all these things.

As if to emphasise her point, she jabs her index finger in the air. Each word spoken with deliberation and no little anger. Stretching for an analogy that can reflect her rage, she continues, "How this man make a great country like Britain follow America like a homeless dog." Immediately I get its significance. Traditionally, Muslims regard dogs as impure, particularly the saliva of dogs. So to compare Blair with an unwanted dog was the worst epitaph she could summon. *Ya Kalm* literally means "you dog" and is uttered to degrade someone as being filthy, dishonest, immoral.

Anger as a response is often derided as out-of-control emotionalism, the response of the unstable, the irrational, the illogical. During the years of austerity in Ireland, economist Colm McCarthy repeated mantra-like that anger was no substitute for policy. For economists, as well as for Catholics, anger is one of the seven deadly sins.

Not everyone agrees. Academic and activist Susan George told me in 2011 that she is angry with the world, a statement that also prefaces her book, *Whose Crisis, Whose Future?*

> I am angry, perplexed and frightened: angry because so many people are suffering needlessly on account of the economic, social and ecological crisis and because the

world's leaders show no sign of bringing about genuine change.

Years later Peter McVerry, priest and homelessness activist, told me:

> As a priest you feel very angry by it all. They've made me angry. And I'm glad to be angry. And I always say when I lose my anger, I'll be no use to them. And I hope that you become angry. Become angry because we as a society have failed them.

So, when Professor Irada Al Jiburi spoke I could feel her anger, and even if I did not, she spelled it out for me.

> It's not just anger, it's bitter anger. I'm really angry. My generation are angry. Angry because a country like Iraq, what they did with our country, my country. Iraq with all the civilisation. Iraq the centre of the world in civilisation with Egypt of course. Yes, I'm angry. Really angry. Bitter angry.

> I'm tired from war, I say I'm tired. I mean we have no time to life, to live, I mean to live normal life. For my daughter, always I'm afraid about her, from kidnapping, from killing, always, dangerous. There is shortage about gas, no food, no electricity, no water, no food, no safe. This is our life. I mean, and always there is a reason to die in Iraq, by war, by embargo, by sectarian, by American, by your brother, by war, by sick, everything, always there is this reason to die, but the problem we have no reason to life in Iraq. And this is the problem.

And with justification, a justification reinforced by the Chilcot Inquiry report into the war in Iraq that took seven years to complete at a cost of £13,126,900, which was a damning indictment of Blair's decision to go to war. Confirmation, if confirmation were needed, that Irada and the Iraqi people have a right to be angry. In a press briefing Sir John Chilcot summed up the inquiry's unanimous and scathing critique of the Blair decision to go to war.

At the outset, Chilcot stated that there was no imminent threat from Saddam Hussein, ostensibly the main justification for the invasion. "We have concluded," the report stated, "that the UK chose to join the invasion of Iraq before the peaceful options for disarmament had been exhausted." This in itself was a damning indictment of both Bush and Blair. The indictment continued: "the policy on Iraq was made on the basis of flawed intelligence and assessments. They were not challenged and should have been."

Furthermore, both Bush and Blair were accused of exaggerating the threat posed by Iraq's weapons of mass destruction (WMD), "presented with a certainty that was not justified".

Chilcot also cited the inadequacy of any post-invasion preparedness. Refusing to heed specific warnings that the invasion could unfurl unforeseen conflict within Iraq, Bush and Blair ploughed ahead: "the circumstances in which it was decided that there was a legal basis for UK military action were far from satisfactory".

The report did not spare Blair's culpability: "the certainty with which Mr. Blair presented the rationale for war was not justified". His Foreign Secretary Jack Straw was deemed equally culpable: "Mr. Blair and Mr. Straw had described WMD as vast stocks and an urgent and growing threat. There was no basis for this."

As a result, Chilcot concluded: "the government failed to meet its stated objectives. The UK military role ended a long way from success ... an intervention that went badly wrong".

The Chilcot Report was a strong, uncompromising condemnation of the whole sorry saga. Important as the report was, it offers little comfort to all those who have suffered so grievously.

Iraq was forced to provide over a billion dollars to Kuwait in war reparations for its 1990 invasion of Kuwait, a debt with which generations of Iraqis will be saddled. No such reparations have been paid to Iraq by the US or British government for their invasion of Iraq.

And this military intervention was meant to win hearts and minds and free the Iraqi people from the oppression of a tyrant.

Perhaps not surprisingly, Samira looks back to the time when Saddam Hussein was President as the good times – a view not universally shared, and certainly not by the Kurds of Northern Iraq or the people of the Wetlands in Southern Iraq. "I was safe and in peace and my children were with me. You could go out in peace," she told me. And on hearing of his execution? "I cried, we all cried, most Iraqis cried, we cried for that situation we're all in and his execution." For her, Saddam Hussein was their President and she and many others we met in Baghdad deeply resented his execution.

I travelled to Iraq with Denis Halliday. Born in Dublin in 1941, UN Secretary-General Boutros Boutros-Ghali appointed Denis Halliday in 1994 as UN Assistant Secretary General for Human Resources Management. In 1997 Secretary General Kofi Annan appointed Mr. Halliday as Humanitarian Coordinator of the Oil-for-Food Programme in Iraq at Assistant Secretary General level. In August 1990 the UN Security Council, at the behest of the United States, imposed comprehensive economic sanctions against Iraq as leverage against Saddam Hussein, sanctions that continued long after the ending of the Gulf War up to 2003 and the invasion of Iraq. The sanctions leaned heavily on the Iraqi people. On Saddam Hussein and his government, they had little impact.

It has been my belief throughout this work that learning from those with first-hand experiences provides unparalleled insights. It is open university as Open University was never

imagined. Learning in homes, fields, factories. Open coun-
tryside, towns and cities. On buses, planes and occasionally
trains. Education on the go. Unparalleled insights. From the
young and the old. Women and men. And all of those who
find themselves outside this binary world. As we criss-crossed
the country, I listened as Denis talked me through the sanctions' regime and its impact, and Iraq's backstory.

> The comprehensive sanctions actually were initiated in
> 1990 by George Bush the first, and then of course after
> the war in 1991 they were continued but made more
> comprehensive, more deep, more total, and very delib-
> erately designed I think to challenge the survival of the
> country itself, by undermining medical care and health
> care, education and so on. The sanctions hit heavily, es-
> pecially children aged between one and five. Water and
> sewage installations were bombed – both illegal acts -
> and as a result people were forced to drink contami-
> nated water. It was a unique programme, open-ended,
> uniquely painful, designed to punish the people of Iraq
> in the hope that they would rise up and overthrow the
> Baghdad government. The sanctions closed down the
> banking system, international trade, international in-
> surance, the phone structure, so the export of Iraqi oil
> was no longer possible. The export of Iraqi produce and
> other items of business were stopped, so it was a com-
> plete case of economic and social isolation.

Seven years later, in 1997, and in an effort to ameliorate the
impact of the sanctions, the UN launched the Oil-for-Food programme, otherwise known as the Humanitarian Programme.
The programme was fully funded by Iraqi oil sales, which
were managed entirely by the United Nations. Selling Iraqi
oil at slightly below the international market price, about two
dollars a barrel below, the revenue went directly to the United
Nations. Thirty per cent of this revenue was given to Kuwait,
in compensation for private sector, corporate and government
damage arising from Iraq's invasion of that country. The UN

took a five per cent overhead charge for managing the programme. The balance went to Iraq, used (as Denis Halliday explained to me) to buy "simple things like tea, sugar, cooking oil, pulses, all the basis of foodstuffs of a daily nature, excluding however animal proteins, no fresh vegetables, no fresh foods, no eggs, none of these things".

At the end October 1998, some 15 months after his initial appointment, Denis Halliday resigned from the UN (the first ever resignation at the rank of ASG) to protest and expose globally what he regarded as the genocidal impact of these UN sanctions on the people and children of Iraq, who were totally innocent of the invasion of Kuwait, the supposed justification for UN Sanctions. He is of the view that after the 2003 US and British invasion, regime change was the prime motive.

> I was driven to resignation because I refused to follow Security Council instructions. Furthermore, I did not want to be complicit in the loss of Iraqi lives caused by the sanctions, which were incompatible with the spirit and word of the UN Charter. I needed to be free to speak out publicly vis-a-vis the media and to legislative bodies worldwide with a view to changing UN sanctions policy. Although in 1996 US Ambassador Albright stated killing 500,000 Iraqi children was "worth it" [i.e. removing Saddam Hussein], I found no justification whatsoever for this view.

Part of that open university learning I encountered with Denis was in Basra, close to the Kuwaiti border. Kuwait, once part of Iraq, he tells me, is a small emirate governed by the monarchial absolutism of the al-Sabah family, notwithstanding its 1962 constitution that ostensibly imposes limitations on that absolute power. The National Assembly has the power to issue motions of no confidence in ministers and prime ministers, a unique provision within Gulf States. The reality, however, is that it has never done so.

Kuwait is effectively a dictatorship. This is the "legitimate government" that George H.W. Bush sought to protect in 1990. Once part of Iraq (until it was portioned off in 1921 by Britain, France and the US following the collapse of the Ottoman Empire), many within Iraq never accepted the amputation of Kuwait, so when Saddam Hussein invaded Kuwait it seemed as if he was righting an ancient wrong. And initially, it seemed as if the United States thought so as well. This, however, was not an act of benign liberation. Saddam needed Kuwait's oil, in part to repay Iraq's heavy debt, estimated at between $80 and $100 billion incurred from the Iran-Iraq war.

Thanks to Chelsea Manning's WikiLeaks, the world learned that prior to the Kuwait invasion, then US Ambassador April Glaspie "assured Saddam of Bush's friendship". She also explicitly said that "the United States took no position on the border dispute between Iraq and Kuwait", though the summary also mentions that she made clear that the US wanted the border dispute solved peacefully. From all of this it would seem as if Saddam had at the very least an orange light from Washington, if not a green light, to invade Kuwait. He certainly did not have a red light. When Saddam did invade Kuwait, Bush changed his mind, resulting in three decades of cataclysmic war inflicted on the people of Iraq and the Middle East.

Into that cataclysmic mix came ISIS or Daesh in 2014. For those seeking escape, the children and the grandchildren of the Arabs brought to France to work in automobile factories in conditions French workers would not tolerate, the allure of ISIS is real and, for a small minority, irresistible. Their counterparts, the Caribbean people known as the "Windrush generation", arrived in Britain full of hope and optimism following the Second World War, as evoked by Andrea Levy's *Small Island*. "He told me opportunity ripened in England as abundant as fruit on Jamaican trees." The reality was all so different. "For the teeth and glasses, that was the reason so many coloured people were coming." The Jamaican experience in England was replicated by the Turkish experience in Germany, the Algerian experience in France, the Moroccan experience in Belgium and the Indonesian experience in The Netherlands.

From these troubled and troubling worlds of racism and xenophobia, ISIS offered acceptance. For the disaffected and the disenfranchised, that generation of French young people living in what the French political scientist Jérôme Fourquet characterised as atomised, Balkanised, disaggregated, dislocated, fragmented France, what *Irish Times* correspondent Lara Marlowe has called "the metamorphosis that has taken place before our eyes", ISIS held the tantalising possibility of certainty, a place of refuge and a different way of living.

For the ostracised and the shunned, ISIS also offered the possibility of revenge. And for all the class and ethnic hatreds inflicted on them this was their moment, their hour. All of which, of course, was exploited by a small group of pernicious clerics. For a whole generation of people, particularly young men of colour lost in the semi-abandoned conurbations of Paris, London and Brussels, joining ISIS was a rational choice, a concept far removed from the fanatical caricature the Western World conferred on these young recruits. Their time had come. If ISIS seemed attractive to those who perceived themselves as sinned-against in Western Europe, it equally appealed to the sinned-against within Iraq and Syria. It was as if the words of the old Jewish prophet in Deuteronomy had come to pass. "It is mine to avenge. I will repay. In due time their foot will slip, their day of disaster is near and their doom rushes upon them."

For western governments, this was an uncomfortable narrative, one that highlights the failures within their own countries. One muffled, if heard at all, by mainstream media and a silence broken only by the audacious bravery of diminutive twenty-two-year-old Chelsea Manning, then known by her former male identity as Bradley Manning, the US army

Iraq-based intelligence analyst who disclosed nearly 750,000 classified documents (the largest hoard of US state secrets in history, and the most significant leak since Daniel Ellsberg leaked the Pentagon Papers in 1971 on US political and military involvement in Vietnam), in what became known as the WikiLeaks scandal. On 28 February 2013, Manning read a 70-minute statement in military court explaining her motivation for leaking the classified government documents. An audio recording of Manning's statement was subsequently leaked and is now available on YouTube. In it, Manning says that what has happened in Iraq and Afghanistan "burdens me emotionally". Manning initially contacted *The Washington Post* and *The New York Times* but neither followed up on the story.

Manning was subsequently sentenced to a thirty-five-year prison sentence for her whistle-blowing, of which she served seven. Following a clemency decision by Barack Obama in 2017, she was released. In March 2019, Manning was back in jail for her refusal to cooperate with a grand jury investigation into WikiLeaks.

When asked by a journalist at his post-Chilcot press briefing if the war on Iraq was the catalyst for the rise of Al Qaeda, and then ISIS or Daesh as they are referred to in the Middle East, a haggard-looking and weary-sounding but defiant Blair ("I take full responsibility. I took it [the decision to go to war] in good faith") rejected the conjoining of these events. At least initially. He did, however, acknowledge in a CNN interview in 2015 that one of the consequences of the invasion of Iraq was the emergence of Islamic State, while insisting that "IS actually came to prominence from a base in Syria and not in Iraq".

Not so. On 29 June 2014, Abu Bakr al-Baghdadi (assassinated in October 2019) declared an Islamic caliphate that grabbed the world's attention and grew at spectacular speed and at a seemingly unstoppable pace. Mixing smart social media and archaic violence, new recruits came in great numbers from within the Middle East, North Africa and Europe, former member of the Irish defence forces Lisa Smith included. "I want for myself an actual caliphate," Smith told a BBC journalist in 2019. She was not alone. At its height, Daesh controlled large swathes of Syria and Iraq, approximating the size of Ireland, populated by eight million people. Contrary to how it is often represented in the media, the ISIS project was an exercise in nation-building, not just an exercise in annihilation and destruction. Annihilation was not an end in itself but a means to an end.

The caliphate operated two administrative capital cities, Mosul in Iraq and Raqqa in Syria, and demonstrated all the apparatus of statehood including issuing motor vehicle plates with the IS logo. Land distribution was codified. Records for elaborate tax collection were subsequently discovered. Its anthem declared, "My Ummah, Dawn Has Appeared – eternal glory that will not perish or disappear ... the blood of the righteous has been spilled." Clearly, though, the checks and balances and respect for human rights that we associate with well-functioning governments were non-existent.

In June 2014, having captured Mosul, ISIS issued a fourteen-point plan for all its residents. Women were forced to go veiled or stay at home. Smoking, alcohol and drugs were banned. Apostates who refused to repent would be killed. Within Mosul University, the departments of political science, human rights, fine arts, archaeology, English translation and, curiously, hotel management were all closed. (The latter unlikely to have any priority in this new world order. The tourists had long since fled.) For those who refused to bend to the caliphate rule, punishment was swift, severe and in many cases up to and including death. Death from lashes (drinking wine). Death by stoning (blasphemy, adultery and homosexuality). Death by crucifixion (highway criminality). Severing of the right hand and the left foot were also options in the latter case. Strict revolutionary "justice".

All of which, for Western audiences, were constructed and perceived as outside the human frame. And yet ISIS's methods were very much within the Judeo-Christian tradition, which in turn frames Islamic theology – the three great Abrahamic religions. Add to Deuteronomy, Romans 13.4: "If you do wrong be afraid, for rulers do not bear the sword for no reason. They are God's servants, agents of wrath to bring punishment to the wrongdoer." To what extent beheading is more barbaric than hanging, the electric chair or the lethal injection is probably too nuanced a question for those in their final moments of life. And yet few argue in favour of beheading while many argue in favour of other forms of the death penalty. George W. Bush signed the death penalty for 152 people while Governor of Texas, at the time the highest execution rate in the Western world. He also argued in favour of lowering the death penalty age to include fourteen-year-olds. The crucifixions ISIS practiced, abhorrent as they are, are also very much within the human frame as all followers of Jesus Christ can testify. They were carried out by men, once children, who grew up to carry out shocking cruelty, a cruelty that is very much part of human capability.

The means by which ISIS sought to  impose their version of the ideal caliphate were not that different from the Bush-Blair imposition of their version of the ideal Iraqi state. It's not that there's an equivalence but there were strong echoes. Both were bloody and brutal in their imposition. Both resorted to coercion. Neither consulted with the Iraqi people as to their preference. Allowing for the similarities in imposition, the outcomes are significantly different.  At its core, Sharia law is a fundamental violation of human rights in a way that western legal codes, for all their flaws, are not. Yet the scale of the ISIS killing never matched that of the Bush and Blair killing following their invasion of Iraq. As for the victims of the killing, the ISIS fighters did the killing in all its brutal, bloody and macabre execution themselves. They heard the pitiful cries of the imminently executed, their longing to live.

On the other hand, Bush and Blair and their associates ordered the killing from the comfort of a well-ventilated office, far from the anguished cries of those whose killing they had sanctioned. What unites Bush/Blair and ISIS is greater than what divides them, as the people of Mosul were to experience in all its horrors.

In 2019, Denis Halliday and I headed for Mosul. During a nine-month battle the US-backed Iraqi army retook Mosul in January 2017 in what it called a "war of annihilation" in which it carried out 34,000 air and military strikes, as a result of which 54,000 homes were destroyed in and around the city. For me this was déjà vu. Aleppo all over again. Another once great city brought to its knees. Pummeled from the sky by US forces. And as we were to learn by Australian forces too. Perhaps what's most noticeable on the ground in both places, quite apart from the obvious destruction, is the silence. Cities unlike other cities. Just abandoned. Street after street. Even the wind had died. There was just a stillness. An emptiness. A world come to an end.

We met with Amjad Saffar, who refused to leave the city during the ISIS occupation. Denis asked him what life was like before the US occupation of his country.

> I was born in Mosul, from Mosul parents, we are a deep-rooted family of Mosul, father and grandfather. Mosul is a beautiful city, one of the ancient cities. It was the top city in Iraq for cleanliness and tidiness. The old part of the city is unique in terms of its social and family closeness. Most people are connected by marriage. If an incident happens to anyone, whether it is sad or good, you would see all the neighbours come together. They delight in the happy moments and share sorrow in the sad moments. This was the reality of Mosul before the occupation.

Then came Daesh and the battle for the heart and soul of the city. On the Daesh occupation he said:

> Their treatment of people was harsh, forced group praying, punishments, whipping, for not having beards, exposure of women's eyes or women without a scarf, no means of making a living, work was stagnant. Life completely stopped. The schools closed. My children missed school terms during Daesh. It was a painful experience, you feel tied.

From all of which the liberation brought no respite. The liberation was accompanied by devastating destruction of Mosul, bridges, roads, water projects, electricity. In particular, the old part of the city, where the main conflict happened, is ninety per cent destroyed. Most of the families in the old part are poor and are not able to return. Their condition is wretched. The situation is difficult and Mosul residents are in despair.

Here is a truncated version of Amjad's personal story.

> On 13 June 2017, I received news about a strike on the Saffar family in the Shifa section of the city. The daughter of my sister Kareema arrived at my house just before one o'clock. Her first words were, "Uncle, all those present in the house are dead".

> With difficulty we managed to reach the place two days after the incident. We tried searching around and discovered that everyone inside was dead. The total death toll of that incident was thirty-four people. Most of them were family: my brother, my sister and her son, five of my cousins, their wives and children, thirty-four people in total. In just a second you lose thirty-four of your family members.

> First a missile struck the first floor and it collapsed onto the ground floor, the building collapsed on itself. In that moment my niece managed to find a small gap in the basement. With the help of neighbours she was dragged from there. Another missile struck on the same

house. I think the second missile is the one that finished them completely. The gap between the two missiles was not more than about ten minutes perhaps.

Afterwards we learned that those responsible for the strike were two Australian pilots. They claimed there were seven Daesh snipers on the roof of the house. Their claim is wrong. They would have found bodies of Daesh in the rubble. According to the forensic medical certificate there were just our martyrs, may the mercy of Allah be upon them. There was no choice but to seek refuge in Allah. In such a situation it is difficult to have strength or endurance.

Standing amongst the rubble it was impossible to imagine the carnage that unfolded. The ten-minute gap between the first and second missile strike. The agonising screams dying away to agonising groans. The dust and the dirt. What happens in those moments of a person's life? These are the crucifixion moments. Take this cup … not my will but thine be done? Jesus? Allah?

Perhaps Amjad is right. In such a situation it is difficult to have strength or endurance. For him too, and his lone surviving niece. Deep in the crevices of the human body is where the heart breaks. And sometimes, too, the heart just cracks and breaks from grief and trauma. Maybe Woody Allen got it wrong after all. The heart is not a resilient little muscle. We construct a façade to mask the pain while, as T.S. Eliot recalled, we prepare a face to meet the faces that we meet.

Perhaps that was the face we met when we met Amjad. In Iraq, I suspect, there is a lot of that.

Denis and I left Mosul that evening. The following day it all seemed surreal, eating ice cream in Al Fakma cafe in midtown Baghdad, watching the young and the not so young. And wondering what lurks beneath all that conversation, all that gaiety.

Sometimes you just have to lift the lid.

# 4

# STILL BLEEDING

## *Libya*

Perhaps it was the day that was in it. Perhaps it was the location. Perhaps it was the vehemence with which it was said. But on the day of Friday prayer in the grounds of a mosque in Tripoli, a man who had recently prayed and who spoke fluent English approached to tell us that those people could or should fuck off as far as he was concerned. It was truly shocking to hear this. Shocking and unexpected. If it were directed at us, it would be understandable. Uncomfortable, certainly, unwelcome, too, but understandable. We were foreigners, and of late foreigners had not served this country well. And it wasn't clear to whom he was referring, who "those people" were. His vehemence and anger were unsoftened by his recently recited prayer. Given his demeanor, I thought it wise not to pursue the source of his hostility. To know he was incensed with those who were around him was sufficient. A random microcosm, perhaps, of the buried anger of the people of Libya.

Prior to his outburst, we had paused outside the mosque just to get random views from those passing by. Vox pops. Perhaps it was one of the people with whom we had just spoken who sparked such a reaction. One was a trader, a farmer who had come a long way to trade. He, too, manifested disturbing

69

symptoms. In his case, anxiety. Nervous and clearly ill at ease, he too had good English. "There is no freedom of speech. You cannot speak. We are at the highest point of the dictatorship. Killings are daily. The killings are daily."

For people outside of Libya, the public execution of Muammar Qadhafi marked the end of Libya's dictatorship. For some, at least, within Libya, that was not the case. Perhaps the emotional outburst we had experienced was rooted in the belief that those who had come to trade in Tripoli were supporters of the deposed dictator, or perhaps he himself was a supporter. Latent support for Qadhafi is still a reality. In this highly splintered country, unpacking who's loyal to whom is one tough task.

It was clear that the trader wanted to talk to us, and yet was unsure about it. It was as if he was compelled to do so, as if this was his only opportunity to let people outside Libya know what was happening inside the country. And clearly he blamed the people outside Libya for the bloodshed within.

> I am now telling you all of this and I'm worried for my life. I'm nervous. I don't feel comfortable. What I'm trying to tell you, what I'm going to tell you, is considered madness. Because of this interview you are having with me now, I am a man walking into a danger zone. I don't feel secure, comfortable, stable. I mean that I cannot guarantee my life, that I will arrive home alive. There is no peace. There is no security.

Suddenly we were in a volatile and unpredictable situation. At such times curious crowds gather quickly. People take sides. And as outsiders we became the centre of attention. Given the scenario that was unfolding, we left hurriedly, as much for the sake of the distressed man as our own. But not before our translator had the presence of mind to reassure this very worried man that what he had to say would not feature in the documentary, and his face would not appear either. If, as he indicated, talking to us endangered his life, we did not want to be party to that risk. It was as if the two interjections bookended Libya's recent history. Threats and counter-threats. Anger and anxiety. Fear and loathing. Bloodshed and killing. Upended by foreigners, Libya was now a fractured, fearful country.

In trying to come to terms with Libya's recent history, inevitable comparisons with other countries mired in conflict come to mind – Tunisia, Western Sahara, Egypt, all victims of an Arab Spring that turned sour. In August 2015 we travelled to Libya in an attempt to try to understand what life was like in the post-Qadhafi country.

And Libya is a trying place. Not just for those who have lived there under forty-two years of Muammar Qadhafi's autocratic rule, but for those who have had to endure the past eight years of civil war that has further splintered what was in fact a deeply fractured state from its post-World War II creation.

Given the enormous complexities of the conflict in Libya, perhaps the fact that we found the situation difficult to comprehend is not surprising. Another Afghanistan? Another Iraq? Another Syria? And as we gazed over Tripoli, that most unlikely of comparisons, Ireland. Tripoli's skyline looked like post-Celtic Tiger Ireland haunted by years of recession. The cranes stood tall and immobile, stilled by years of conflict, albeit of a very different kind. Skeletal blocks of unfinished apartments burned by the relentless sun. And a kind of eerie silence that emerged from them. Standing as if in reproach for the failure to build a well-functioning, cohesive post-Qadhafi society.

But this is not Ireland.

And then Iraq, a government toppled at the behest of Britain and the United States; in Libya's case, a government toppled at the behest of France, Britain and the United States. Not unlike Iraq in that there were minorities within both countries which longed for such a toppling. A regime change. *Regime,* that most pejorative of words, used to describe a government not to one's liking and an excuse for its violent overthrow. The fickleness of language. And then what? Iraq required foreign boots on the ground that quickly became part of a killing machine. Here there would be no boots on the ground. Iraq had taught the foreign invader that much. The Iraqi invaders had cleared the country of any vestiges of the Ba'athist regime, and in the process had disabled critical institutions required for state reconstruction. That mistake was not to be repeated in Libya.

Here, no one was to be excluded. All those who fought for the revolution, even if they are now fighting each other and the state, are on the state payroll. It must be unique to Libya. The state – insofar as any vestiges of the state remained in any meaningful sense – was funding those who seek to overthrow it. The state as a unified entity is no more in Libya, given that it has at least two rival parliaments and three competing governments. And these armed groups (nobody here seems to like the word militias, particularly the militias themselves) are everywhere. But Libya's comparison to Iraq is superficial.

Libya is not Iraq.

Then Syria. Libya differs from Syria also, if the scale of the killing is anything to go by. And that scale, like everything else here in Libya, is much contested. Inflating casualty numbers is a key plank in the competition for victimhood and international support. As in other conflicts, propaganda is an important tool in the quest for the war's justifications. Disaggregating levels of conflict deaths and injuries from deaths and injuries through generalised violence is particularly difficult. And ultimately it is not about numbers. There isn't after all "an acceptable level of violence", as former British Home Secretary Reginald Maudling declared in 1971 in the context of Northern Ireland.

But Libya is not Syria.

Still in the throes of conflict, Libya is navigating a restless course between its various tribes, its east-west divide, and between the many contesting claimants of the true spirit of the revolution. Meanwhile those outside Libya who were so quick to call for change have fled. The diplomats have gone. The embassies are empty. However, the Italian flag still flies over a deserted building.

And despite its Mediterranean coastline the tourists too have stayed away, as have most journalists. There are a few of the latter who have stayed the course, Irish journalist Mary Fitzgerald among them. We were beneficiaries of her deep understanding of Libyan politics. And there was a real sense of Libya being tired of foreigners with their "we know what's best for Libya" attitude. Despite their deeply entrenched differences, most factions in Libya were agreed on that. But for all that deep distrust of outsiders, we were treated with great courtesy. Even on the street when we cautiously stepped out, we were either ignored or welcomed.

Libya may now be an open wound. Under Colonel Muammar Qadhafi, Libya was a closed wound, a repressive state, nowhere more so than in the now-abandoned Abu Salim prison. For years Abu Salim housed political prisoners. These were usually incarcerated without warrants and held incommunicado and in deplorable conditions. Torture was endemic. Detainees were allowed limited access to their families, denied medical treatment and deprived of any recreational activities or outdoor space for long periods. On 28 June 1996, prisoners staged a riot calling for better conditions and for their cases to be processed. Negotiations with senior government officials, including intelligence chief and Qadhafi's brother-in-law and chief enforcer Abdullah al-Senussi, followed. Then soldiers arrived and herded the prisoners into courtyards. The soldiers then threw grenades at the prisoners, shooting those attempting to flee. Within two days 1,200 prisoners had been mercilessly slaughtered. Family members were not informed of their deaths until twelve years later. Long after this massacre took place, families continued to send food and clothes to their close relatives, not knowing they were all dead. The soldiers took the food parcels, clothes and other gifts for themselves.

Protests over the following years by women demanding justice for relatives who had died in the Abu Salim massacre prepared the ground for wider demonstrations against Qadhafi in February 2011. So also did the arrest in the same month of Fathi Tarbel, a young Benghazi lawyer who represented the Abu Salim families (and who lost three relatives himself). His arrest sparked rallies by lawyers and judges who joined the families in demanding his release. Thus two days ahead of a planned "Day of Rage" inspired by the events in Egypt and Tunisia, Benghazi erupted in demonstrations that later tipped over into armed uprising.

Once underway, revenge for what was considered Qadhafi's worst atrocity was central to the revolution's narrative. As one Benghazi protestor put it in late February 2011: "The Abu Salim massacre is the deepest wound in our country and we want vengeance."

Several armed groups were named after those killed in 1996. When rebel fighters poured into Tripoli in August 2011, they used rocks and metal bars to smash the locks off cell doors at Abu Salim, freeing thousands of inmates, most of whom immediately joined the revolution.

On the day we arrived in Abu Salim in 2015, a strange silence enveloped the compound. The now abandoned prison remains encased behind a twenty-foot high wall. The rusting hulk of a watchtower still dominates the enclosure. As we approach, on the eight-metre-high concrete perimeter slabs, six cartoon-like scenes depicting the horror that unfolded inside are on display: the first a soldier shooting a blindfolded and kneeling handcuffed figure while another lies on the ground. Another is an illustration of a soldier whipping two kneeling figures while the foot of another soldier is aimed at one victim's chest. A third shows a gun being fired at a line of captives. Inside the main open area that runs for about fifty metres in length and twenty in width, nature has begun to obliterate the unnatural and vile atrocities that took place here. Greenery is shrouding concrete slabs. Further on, all the cell doors are thrown open revealing debris from the regime scattered about inside.

Cardiff-educated engineer, father of two and Islamic scholar Mohammed Busidra, imprisoned without charge for twenty-one years in Abu Salim for speaking out against the Qadhafi regime, was one of just five who survived that morning's massacre of 28 June 1996. He took us into a cage-like inner courtyard that ran for about 20 x 10 metres and which was covered over by a metal grid. It was here that the killings took place. "Unspeakable crimes took place here," he tells me, "ones that no human being should have to experience. Men were beaten, starved, sodomised. And killed." Mohammed Busidra recollected for us what unfolded on that fateful morning:

> At five o'clock in the morning all the men were corralled into this cage. The soldiers stood atop one of the walls. One line. Shooting. They started shooting for three hours. I remember the sound of the bullets and the screaming. It went on for hours. It is a sound I will never forget, 1,270 people were killed, 28th of June 1996. It's a very deep wound and still bleeding.

Presumed dead, he survived, but not the routine torture that was the norm within the prison. Subjected to mock hangings, naked in freezing conditions, often suspended by his hands for hours from the ceiling, he took us to his cell measuring no more than ten metres by ten where, along with twenty others, he spent eleven years. But for the remaining ten years of the twenty-one year incarceration he was kept in solitary confinement. With the aid of a light from his mobile phone, he took us down to his cell along a series of steps past walls which were now covered in anti-Qadhafi graffiti. "During those years the main problem was the absence of light," he tells me. "All was darkness. And they told us, 'you will stay here until you forget your names' because they called us by numbers. I was Number 7." It bears repeating. Ten years in a cell on his own in total darkness. That's 3,650 days and nights.

From there, he took us to the torture room. What appeared to be a bed frame stood to one side with tattered bits of clothing: a once-white vest, a now-discoloured singlet vest, a striped t-shirt, a greenish-blue bed-sheet which was discoloured with what might have been blood or faeces randomly tied to the bars. Other bits of clothing were strewn around the room. A rope dangled on one end of the bed. Standing beside the place of torture he explained what happened.

> They forced you to lie down and make your feet under the metal bar and they start beating you. When you move your feet, they would be cut by that metal bar. The moment you get unconscious they throw you on the floor. And on the floor they will look for the injuries to pour salt on them.

Now Abu Salim is a second-hand car depot. Crushed cars crushing out the ghosts of its past. But across the city in Hadba lies Libya's highest security prison. Some of those who sanctioned the atrocities are held within this prison, including Qadhafi's brother-in-law Abdullah al-Senussi, sentenced to death in 2015 along with Qadhafi's son Saif al-Islam, following a trial condemned by the United Nations as seriously flawed. Former Abu Salim prisoner Fadel al-Thin-ay is the assistant governor here. His brother and his uncle were among the 1,200 killed in the Abu Salim massacre.

Why a Western television crew were allowed such access still puzzles me. In what passes for normal states, access for a foreign television crew to the highest security prison in the country would be most unlikely to say the least. In a fractured state, luck and stumbling across the right person can unlock possibilities, as occurred on this occasion. Libya is a fractured state. And sometimes you just roll your luck.

We were given unprecedented access to Hadba prison. Fadel al-Thin-ay took us straight to the block that held those directly connected to the Abu Salim massacre. As we walked the corridors, prisoners glanced out through the post-box-sized opening on their locked doors. Returned glances indicated three or four middle-aged men in each cell, which appeared to be no more than six to eight feet in size. "But of course these prisoners, including Abdullah al-Senussi, are treated differently to how they used to treat prisoners," he assured me.

That may very well be the case, but the legality of their detention was challenged by a 2018 Office of the United Nations High Commission for Human Rights Report, which found that the detention of twelve senior figures in the Qhadafi government (regime was the word used) was arbitrary and denied the detainees their right to a fair trial, as was the detention of seventy-seven individuals accused of involvement in the 1996 Abu Salim prison killings. By the time that report was published, many of the detainees had been transferred from Hadba to Ain Zara prison, from which a mass break-out involving 400 detainees took place in September 2018. I have no idea how many of the people we met on the day we arrived in Hadba were involved in the break-out.

In Area 2 a group of about a dozen, all in regulation white t-shirts, blue shirts and trousers – with one exception – were sitting or walking around a walled-in area about the size of a basketball court, covered over with a closely webbed steel grid. All grey-haired men in their sixties or seventies. This was their half-hour time in the sun. Some were reading, others praying. As soon as they saw us entering, they stood to attention. All I was told was that they were Qadhafi loyalists. I greeted each one as they stood. One, Ali Ahmed Abu Sowan, agreed to talk. "During the 2011 events, I presented a religious programme on television and I talked about the danger of deviating from the line drawn by the governor (Qadhafi)," he told me. Fearful that a rebellion would result in bloodshed and corruption, he opposed the overthrow of Qadhafi and was now incarcerated for trying to protect his country. That was his story as he related it to us. As he spoke, he fingered his prayer beads.

The only man not in regulation blue uniform, for reasons I did not get an opportunity to ask about, spoke fluent English and, much to my astonishment, told me that he had been to Ireland several times in the 1980s when he was Minister for Planning and Finance. When asked what it was like to work for Colonel Qadhafi he told me that he wasn't very much in favour of militarism and dictatorship. On the issue of human rights, he acknowledged that there were some problems. At this point, concerned with the direction of our discussion, the prison staff intervened and cut short our conversation.

To suggest that Qadhafi had some problems with human rights was an understatement, if not a complete misrepresentation. Quite apart from the massacres at Abu Salim, Qadhafi's crimes against his own people were brutal and systematic. Crimes that contravened not only international law, but also Libya's own criminal code. Over four decades the internal state security infrastructure menaced the population, creating a climate of fear, and acting with impunity, including summary executions, widespread disappearances and torture.

Political courts and "black hole" prisons, suppression of cultural rights, and discriminatory policies against minorities were commonplace. Qadhafi's crimes were intentional, including public and often televised executions of political opponents. The 1984 hanging of Al-Sadek Hamed Al-Shuwehdy in the basketball stadium in Benghazi was the first execution under Qadhafi and the first to be broadcast on television. Thousands of school children and students were bussed in to witness the macabre sight and sounds of the pleadings of Mr. Al-Shuwehdy as he was dragged in fear and anguish to the gallows.

A not-altogether-dissimilar fate befell Qadhafi himself twenty-seven years later. Following the February 2011 protests in Benghazi and Abdullah al-Senussi's ordered arrest of Fathi Tarbel, the human rights attorney who represented the Abu Salim relatives, Qadhafi's regime began to disintegrate. Former allies fled. Cornered, Qadhafi railed against his opponents, threatening "to cleanse Libya inch by inch, house by house, home by home, street by street, alley by alley, one by one until the country is cleansed from filth and impurity". He called on his supporters to "chase away the (Benghazi) rats and terrorists" who were daring to rise up against him and who were plunging the country into civil war. It was a turning point in the revolution. Son and putative heir Saif al-Islam promised reform while threatening wholesale slaughter. Chaos ensued. Nobody was in charge.

At that time Mohammed Bashein was a seventeen-year-old student who had returned to Libya with his family seven years earlier. Born and raised in Salford, Manchester, he told me of those early war days in his proud Manc accent. "There were people calling out for revolution on Facebook, Twitter and on the internet," he told me. Mohammed joined the resistance.

So too did Ahmud Azzabi, Mohammed's childhood friend. Mohammed has grainy images of Ahmud on his phone. A baby-faced, giddy, fifteen-year-old smiles directly to the camera. Beside him another boy dressed in what would pass for golf gear, complete with baseball cap, smiles broadly too. War babies. In his left hand he holds a Kalashnikov. In the background stands another with an RPG, a rocket-propelled grenade. At fifteen Ahmud was able to use a 14.5-metre anti-aircraft missile, Mohammed says. He was a really good kid according to Mohammed, who was not much more than a kid himself.

Fifteen-year-old Ahmud was fighting in the Nafusa mountains when other boys his age were doing their homework, playing football, sleeping peacefully in their beds. Ahmud was, Mohammed said, "a joyful lad, a really brave kid, we played football together". The photograph tells that story, the story of a joyful lad. A kid certainly. Brave? Probably. But probably scared too. Hungry? Homesick? Who wouldn't be, despite having two of his brothers fight along with him, one of whom was also killed. After all, he was a fighter in a war. Perhaps at times he longed for home, for the comfort of his own bed, for the company of his family. But in war, kids need to be brave. And longing for home comforts needs to be hidden away, from oneself as much as from others.

Ahmud died in the battle to take Bab Alazizia, Qadhafi's last home in Tripoli before he fled the city. It was almost the last battle of Tripoli. But in the intensity of battle there is little time for emotion.

> It was a dynamic time. He was a fighter so there is a sense that it could happen to any one of us. There isn't much time to reflect. Of course it was a sad day, but death was everywhere and you can't really think about one death in a battle. But yes, people cried. It was a really really sad day for us. Now people call him a martyr.

For years I have been conscious of the frequency with which martyrdom is invoked. Not just here in Libya. Martyrdom. Its power and its emotion. Its lure and its legitimisation. With deeply held religious resonance, the martyr myth runs deep in war mythology, particularly in the Middle East. And it has a distinct resonance for Muslims dating back to the death (martyrdom) of Iman Husayn ibn Ali, the grandson of the Prophet Mohammed at the Battle of Karbala (Iraq) in the year 680, an event that is still commemorated to this day. It's not, however, unique to Islam; think Saint Stephen, the first Christian martyr. Acknowledgement of the saintliness of martyrdom continues within the Catholic Church today with the canonisation of El Salvadorian Bishop Óscar Romero in 2018.

Ireland is not immune to the trend of retrospective recognition, as Irish people know. In Ireland, martyrdom has a strong allure. Fenians Allen, Larkin and O'Brien, the Manchester martyrs – coincidently the birthplace of Mohammed Bashein – hanged in front of an estimated 10,000 people on 23 November 1867 and memorialised in their home town of Kilrush in West Clare, close to where I was born. Numerous others who would be anointed by martyrdom were to follow: Robert Emmet, Joseph Mary Plunkett, Thomas Ashe, Kevin Barry and Bobby Sands, to name but five.

Martyrdom. It celebrates. It elevates. It memorialises the dead. But it also politicises and propagandises. It frames and reframes. It invokes heroism, sacrifice and the subjugation of the self. It becomes the embodiment of the abstract: freedom, nationalism, communism, the nation state, even God. It's the suicide bomber, the child soldier, the romantic and idealist, the unsure and the unseen.

What or how much Ahmud knew or understood about Libya's politics, Qadhafi's excesses, or of the international machinations is unknown. What made him take up a gun?

Was he recruited or was he perhaps an atypical teenager who knew the risks but was prepared to take them on in an effort to overthrow Qadhafi? I asked Mohammed these questions. "Who knows?" he simply replies. It was a disconcerting response. But perhaps Mohammed's shrugged response encapsulates war. Who knows why human beings kill and injure each other in the way they do? Who knows?

Nor do I know if he would have been aware of the US and NATO missile attack on a house in Tripoli that killed Qadhafi's youngest son and three of his grandchildren, children aged between twelve months and four years. Or that Belgium, Denmark, Norway, Italy, Sweden and Canada played supportive roles in the destruction of his country.

I have no idea how much Ahmud knew about the politics of Libya. My guess is he knew nothing of the international players who catapulted Libya into the morass in which it is still mired in 2019. Knew nothing about the US, British and French UN-mandated air attack over Libya. Probably never heard of former French President Nicolas Sarkozy, allegedly the recipient of Qadhafi's largesse during his 2007 presidential bid. Probably never heard of British Premier David Cameron who declared with confidence at a Conservative party conference, "On Libya, our strategy is clear...". As if. I know that Ahmud did not live long enough to hear US President Barack Obama's quasi-apology for what has become of Libya, when he declared that failing to plan for the aftermath of his country's intervention in Libya was the worst mistake of his presidency.

My guess is that he never learned of the squabble over the number of casualties in the early stages of the war. Figures that ranged from 1,000 to 10,000. Because he was one of them.

On the 23 August 2011, at the age of fifteen, Ahmud Azzabi was killed by a sniper.

*Abdul Miamat, whose seven brothers were killed in Afghanistan's many wars, Jalalabad, Afghanistan.*

*Abdul Miamat's brother Mohammed who was thirty years of age when he was killed, Jalalabad, Afghanistan.*

*Malalai Joya, politician and human rights
activist Kabul, Afghanistan.*

*Basira Sultani, with her two-year-old son. Her husband and
brother-in-law were killed in Kabul, Afghanistan.*

*Edmilson Silva Filomeno, São Paulo, Brazil.*

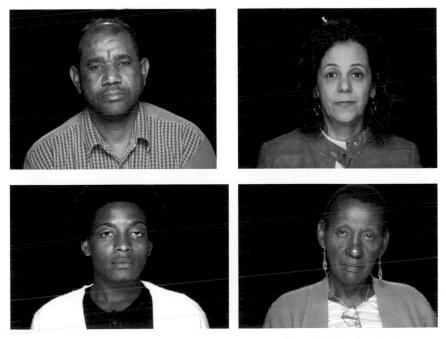

*Clockwork from top left: Amaro Jorge de Silva, Valdenia Paulino,
Zilda Maria de Paula and Yasmin Cristina da Silva Efigenio,
São Paulo, Brazil.*

*Guilherme de Oliveira*
*Mascarenhas, São Paulo, Brazil.*

*Herbert Douglas Ribeiro da Silva,*
*São Paulo, Brazil.*

*Mikael dos Santos, São Paulo, Brazil.*

*Starting over in Aleppo, Syria.*

*Denis Halliday with Amjad Ali Mohamed al-Saffar in Mosul, Iraq.*

*Peadar King with Denis Halliday in Mosul, Iraq.*

*Mohammed Bashein, Tripoli, Libya.*

*Misrata, Libya.*

*Mohammed Busidra in Abu Salim prison
with photographs of victims, Tripoli, Libya.*

*The Mexican-USA border close to Ciudad Juárez.*

*Billboard on the wall of Ciudad Juárez, Mexico, looking for Carmen Castillo's daughter Mónica, one of the disappeared.*

Later that year, on 20 October, Qadhafi too was killed. Brutally so. As if there is any other way. Filmed too. His death still plays out on the internet. As does his dead body.

We visited Misrata, Libya's third largest city, located between Tripoli and Sirte. The latter is Qadhafi's birthplace and place of execution where his desecrated body was showcased in a storeroom in a shopping centre that drew crowds of people, children included. Like Benghazi in the east, Misrata played a critical role in his overthrow. Hundreds of people were killed there. Still standing, a delusional symbol of defiance, is a gold-coloured sculpture of a Libyan fist crushing a US fighter jet. Ultimately, though, it was the country that was crushed. Close by, a museum tells a very different story. Uncensored scenes of the macabre events that unfolded here are on show. Images of bloodied corpses, frantic medics, distraught relatives. In addition, portrait photographs of "martyrs" line the walls.

People walk silently and reverently past. Less reverently, as they enter the museum, is a wall hanging bearing Qadhafi's image which has now become a door mat on which people stop to wipe their shoes. Showing the sole of the shoe has long been an insult in Arab culture. As an insult to President George H.W. Bush following the first Gulf War, a mosaic of his face was laid on the floor of the Al-Rashid Hotel in Baghdad. Anyone entering the lobby would have to walk over his face to get into the hotel. The mosaic was subsequently destroyed by US soldiers in 2003 and replaced with an image of Saddam Hussein. In the Misrata museum, not only did people walk on the floor mat but stood there for some moments, both feet placed firmly on Qadhafi's image.

As for Mohammed's own involvement in the overthrow of Qadhafi, he has no regrets.

People have to know that the Libyan revolution didn't start with arms. In the first two weeks of the revolution

83

people didn't have guns. Qadhafi was killing people who were only protesting. I don't regret using a gun against Qadhafi. It was the only way to get rid of him.

The chaos that characterised the fall and execution of Qadhafi continues to mar the country. Beneath Qadhafi's chimera of placidity were a large number of social, economic, political, tribal, regional and ethnic problems that were hidden for the four decades of his rule. Controls over trafficking across Libya's 4,348 kilometre borders had been limited, capricious and often corrupt, but not necessarily ineffective.

The conflict has seen the replacement of state authority by local armed groups and *ad hoc* authorities, especially in the south. Divided by tribe, geography and shifting political alliances, a plethora of militias are competing for power and influence. Efforts to co-opt armed groups into a unified military force merely resulted in state-funded militias fighting and further destabilising the state. Since the collapse of the state, trafficked migrants stream into the country, almost half a million (423,394) from thirty-eight countries, the majority of whom are from Sub-Saharan Africa, according to a 2017 United Nations report.

The power struggle that is threatening to tear Libya apart is fought not just by Libyans. Factions within each camp are supported by external backers and foes of political Islam, particularly Qatar, Egypt and the United Arab Emirates. Since 2014, ISIS has gained a foothold in Libya, especially in Qadhafi's former stronghold of Sirte. Tripoli, too, has not escaped. A police captain, Mohammed El Daki, told me of one incident he encountered at a checkpoint. A driver detonated a bomb, killing himself. "Four people were 'martyred' and three wounded," he told me. For ISIS, the detonator of the bomb was the martyr. "They casually slaughter," he says, "and have no fear of God." What happened has really marked him, he says. Not surprisingly. Death leaves its mark.

Any danger for us is fleeting and short-lived, if at all. We get to leave. But most stay, among them Mohammed Bashein, our Mancunian contact. Now twenty-five years of age, he is determined to remain. "You can't turn back the clock. We have so many things to fix. We didn't see that coming." Mohammed Busidra too. For him there is no escaping the past. Of Abu Salim he says: "It's a very deep wound and still bleeding." Libyans still bleeding. And as for those we met outside a mosque in Tripoli after Friday prayers?

Still angry. Still volatile. Still fearful.

# 5

# BE AFRAID

## *Mexico*

A freight train makes its way along the US side of the border with Mexico. On the Mexican side, a solitary cross marks the spot where two young men were killed. Their crime: smuggling people across the border. Their punishment: death by stoning. Their killers: linked, by all accounts, to the drug cartels. Anyone messing with their turf is dealt with remorselessly.

"That day we didn't have any money," the mother of one of the young men killed tells me. "My son's friend asked for help to bring people across the border. He was to get 150 pesos [at the time the equivalent of €9.00] for helping. The next day he didn't return, so we went looking for him. We asked around but nobody could tell us anything." Later he was found. Dead. Killed by stoning. "We think the biggest rock was thrown at my son. And we think that's when he died, when it hit his skull."

She spoke to us on strict guarantees of anonymity, filmed in silhouette against an open door with a lace curtain blowing gently to and fro. At her request, we distorted her voice on screen. It was to become part of what we did in Juarez. Speaking out carries great risks. When asked if she knew who her son's killer was, she simply replied: "Yes, but we are afraid to confront that person. He is a member of a drug cartel."

Her son was a *coyote*, the colloquial Spanish-Mexican term for people who smuggle contraband, usually drugs, and migrants across the border. Fearing that individual amateur *coyotes* are more likely to attract the attention of US border control guards if caught, the more established criminal gangs move quickly to stamp out any competition. Those who threaten their turf, their profits, are mercilessly killed. The border is their terrain, their domain, and it is jealously guarded. For migrants who hope to cross it, this is the third deadliest corridor in the world. The Mediterranean is the most dangerous.

The 3,000-odd-kilometre-long border that stretches from the Gulf of Mexico in the east to the Pacific coast in the west is the most crossed border in the world. It's also the most infamous. In its path three major cities have grown: Albuquerque in New Mexico, El Paso in Texas, and across the border Ciudad Juarez in Mexico. The Rio Grande forms almost two-thirds of the border (1,931 kilometres) as it winds its way through arid, semi-desert scrubland and canyon, beginning in the snow-capped peaks of Colorado's San Juan Mountains through West Texas to the Gulf of Mexico. It's a harsh, unforgiving landscape. An open, dry, thirst-inducing barren land for those making the crossing. Hot too. And freezing cold at night-time. June 2017 and a record-breaking blistering 124 degrees Fahrenheit (51°C). Winter lows fall below 32°F (0°C).

Spanning 193,000 square kilometres is the Sonoran Desert with its sparse water supply and scant plant life. On the US side of the border, individuals organise and regularly replenish informal water stations at great personal risk to themselves. On the Mexican side, various organisations and concerned citizens post posters warning people against crossing the desert. "No Vaya Ud! No Hay Suficiente Agua! No Vale la Pena!" "Don't go! There's not enough water! It's not worth it!"

Many who refuse to heed the warning pay the ultimate price. The desert, a death sentence. Just how many die, nobody knows for sure. According to the United Nations Migration Agency, 398 died in 2016 and 412 in 2017. These are regarded as minimum figures only. Taunted by death, confronted by the fear of capture (341,084 in 2017 and 611,689 in 2016), the determination to set out for what many hope will be a deliverance from poverty and violence, and the possibility of the American dream, is urging many towards their death, step by painful step.

Those who fear the desert try the river. Dangerous it may be with strong currents, up to 30 kilometres per hour, and it's cold all year round, but for desperate people it looks too inviting to be ignored. And some of the crossing points are enticingly close to the Promised Land.

As I write (25 June 2019), a haunting image of twenty-five-year-old Oscar Alberto Martínez Ramírez and his nearly two-year-old daughter Valerie, lying face down on the Rio Grande, is circulated worldwide. Taken by journalist Julia Le Duc and first published by Mexican newspaper *La Jornada*, the image brings to mind another grim reality, that of the death of three-year-old Alan Kurdi, the toddler drowned off the Turkish coast in 2015. In the Rio Grande photograph, little Valerie's arm is wrapped around her father's neck in her final moments, clinging on to her Dad. It is an achingly poignant and disturbing image. Their bodies were discovered near Matamoros, Mexico, across from Brownsville, Texas, less than a mile from an international border bridge. Apparently, the father successfully brought his daughter to the US side and went back to collect his wife. Seeing her father swim away from her, Valerie panicked and re-entered the water. Desperately trying to save her, they were both drowned.

The great Rio Grande river, enticing people to their death. Now the river itself is also under threat. The year 2000 was the first year it did not reach the Gulf of Mexico. Increasing temperatures and a decline in flow due to climate change have dramatically reduced the river's water volume and threatens the ecosystem that supports an estimated 10 million people and more than 400 species of native fish, wildlife and plants. Ironically, this makes it all the more appealing for those trying to cross as it reduces the risk of drowning and increases the likelihood of a successful crossing. But it was a different type of threat that brought us to Juarez, a city of 1.3 million that was, between 2008 and 2012, known as the most dangerous city in the world.

In 2013, I travelled to Juarez flying via El Paso, a city that gave its name to a western spaghetti film company and a prescient 1949 film of the same name in which a vigilante group seeks to bring law and order to the town in which the judge is a drunk, the sheriff corrupt and the town is run by a crooked landowner. We didn't stop but made our way relatively easily across a heavily fortified border to Juarez. Typically, 20,000 pedestrians cross this border point every day, along with 35,000 cars and 2,500 cargo trucks. In 2017, the US Department of Transportation estimated that 41 million northbound non-commercial crossings from Juarez to El Paso took place. Our waiting time was less than an hour. Juarez is not the only point of crossing between Mexico and the US. In total, an estimated one million people and $1.5 billion worth of goods cross every day along the entire border.

The death of the young *coyote* who was killed while aiding people to cross illegally into the United States was not an aberration. This was not an uncommon occurrence, notwithstanding the Trump-inspired racially charged and politically expedient brouhaha about illegal entry into the United States through its southern border. The numbers have declined sharply since the high point which occurred towards the end of the 1990s. In 2006 there were 851,000 illegal crossings while in 2016 that had dropped to 62,000. In 2017 they were at their lowest level since 1971. What has increased is the number of "family units" making the crossing. In May 2019, US authorities detained more than 85,000 "family unit" members, an average of nearly 2,800 per day, at the border. Border arrests typically surge in the spring, when demand for US farm labour grows, then subsides during peak summer months.

Juarez is one of the most written-about cities in the world, a *cause célèbre* for artists (including Irish artist Brian Maguire), playwrights, poets, film-makers, academics and others. People are drawn not just to what has unfolded in Juarez over the past twenty-five years but how local and international cultural representations of the violence have shaped our understanding of the political, judicial, societal and gender structures that have produced these crimes.

And the crimes are relentless, brutal in their intent and macabre in their execution. In the two days prior to our arrival, twelve people were killed in Juarez. In the seven years prior to our arrival, 70,000 people had been killed, and some put that estimate at 100,000 people. And it was not just the number but the manner in which people were killed. Torture. Mutilation. Dismemberment. Even public lynching. Killings on a scale beyond human comprehension. But killings nonetheless, executed by humans. Mexico is a country ravaged by homicide – 33,341 in 2018, a record rise of thirty-three per cent over its 2017 figure of 25,036.

Between 2013 and the start of 2019 there was a forty per cent increase in the country's homicide rate. It is estimated that between 1997 and 2018, at least 400,000 people died from violence committed by organised crime, some would say with the complicity of the Mexican state institutions.

Australia-born parish priest Fr Kevin Mullins had been working in Juarez for eleven years prior to our arrival. His parish runs to within half a kilometre of the border. He has an interesting personal story. Despite his name he has no blood connection to Ireland. Adopted by an Irish family in Australia, he was given the name Kevin. At seventeen years of age he decided he wanted to become a Catholic priest. There was a problem. He was born "illegitimate", and prior to the Second Vatican Council an "illegitimate boy" could not be ordained. A compromise was reached. He could enrol, but if he was to continue to ordination he would have to get special Vatican approval before his ordination could be sanctioned. He embarked on his studies for the priesthood but days before he was due to be ordained, a major crisis occurred. Even though everything was in place for his ordination, it was realised at the last moment that Vatican clearance had not been sought or granted.

Kevin was expecting to be ordained following seven years of study. His family and friends were likewise expecting that he would be ordained. Frantic efforts were made to contact the Vatican as the countdown to ordination neared. Permission arrived in the nick of time. He was aware of none of this at the time. Over the course of the film shoot we developed a warm friendship. Kevin was generous with his time and introduced us to many people including the mother of the young *coyote* killed crossing the border.

"What was it like to join an organisation that didn't really want you?" I later ventured to ask him.

"Well I didn't know at the time. Had I..." and he just smiled.

I thought to push him on it, and then thought the better of it. He was, and remains, a most gracious man.

And he too had seen terrible things.

> I've seen people dismembered in twelve pieces, their body parts scattered throughout the colonias. It is shocking, disgraceful, nauseous. It is sickening. I remember one woman coming to me saying, 'I have found the body of my husband but not his head'.

Later I was to learn the significance of the dismember-ment. If the tongue is cut out, it means they talked too much – a snitch, or *churpo*. A man who squealed on the clan has his finger cut off and maybe put in his mouth. Castration was the punishment for having slept with or looked at the woman of another man in the business. Proprietorship of women is fun-damental to machismo culture. Severed arms could mean that you stole from your consignment, severed legs that you tried to walk away from the cartel. Decapitation is another thing altogether: it is simply a statement of power.

Thinking back to the death of the young *coyote* he said:

> I remember being very sickened. When we got down there the police had already taken away the bodies. But there was still a lot of DNA on the rocks. We bur-ied that and washed the rocks. The funeral mass was held in our parish. One of the caskets was open. The other wasn't because the damage done to the other person was so severe.

Those other people. Non-people. Expendable people. Young men who do not matter, except to their families of course. And their grief at the death of their children is as vis-ceral as that of any other family. Othered in language too. The people mules and the drug mules.

Vilified, too, are the young men – and it's mostly young men – caught up in the violent, murky world of drug traffick-ing south of the border. Easily caricatured. Easily maligned. Easily stigmatised. Sociopaths. Psychopaths. The relentless tabloidisation of these young people's lives. Screaming head-lines. Monsters. Evil. Fiendish. Drug-crazed. And not just in Mexico. A British study reported that drug users were most likely to be condemned in the tabloid press, where about a fifth of remarks about users were condemnatory. What was particularly interesting in the study was that young drug us-ers and drug-using parents were much, much more likely than other users (professionals, celebrity/public figures) to be condemned by newspapers. Curiously, the English regional press was more likely to be empathetic.

Despite all the evidence to the contrary, despite all the deaths, all the brutality, the lure of the drug trade is overwhelming, particularly for those who feel there are so few options. Somewhat archaically, Kevin describes the temptations and the consequences for "gentlemen between the ages of fifteen and twenty-five".

"It's seductive. You get good money, lots of women, good food, good booze. Three years. And then you're dead."

I was anxious to hear from a cartel/gang member in Mexico. With the help of Kevin and local fixer/photojournalist Julián Cardona, who has been documenting the city since the early 1990s, one young man agreed to speak to us, again on the basis that his identity would be protected. Not surprisingly, gang members are notoriously reluctant to talk to the media.

We were dropped off at a barrio and guided by Julián, who was on the phone all the time, and walked through a network of streets, through a house and into another back street until we came to another house, and were taken to a shed at the back. We set up the gear and then a young man joined us. Heavily disguised with dark glasses, baseball cap pulled down on his head and a bandana across his face and nose, we could only guess at his age, which we presumed to be mid-thirties. Later I learned that he was thirty-nine years old.

"I don't have a family. I've been alone since I was a boy," he began. "My Mama died when I was young. I was six years old. I never met my Dad. My childhood was very sad ... full of drugs. I started with marijuana, and later, when I grew older, I started using heroin. I was twelve."

He was eight years old when he first handled a gun.

I was eight. I met with two friends and we went out on the street and carried out a mugging. My friends carried the gun but then gave it to me and I was the one to shoot it. I gave him three, four shots and then we took what he carried. No, he didn't die. I think he was left disabled.

I asked what it was like to shoot someone, to which he simply said, "horrible, but I had to do it". From the mugging they got a mobile phone, three rings and 200 pesos – less than €10.00. A life.

Later he joined another gang and, as he told me, he "started to do worse things".

> There was a gang war. We were knifing them, having gun fights, from one area to another. When I was fourteen, I remember we killed a guy. Between the three of us we stabbed him about twenty times. Even when he was no longer moving and lying on the ground, we kept stabbing him.

There was no shortage of killing instruments.

> I was familiar with the 9mm, the 45. I was familiar with AK-47s as well. We had them too. The 22mm. Flick knives. Big knives too. We had those as well. Well, at the time, everyone knew that it was war.

As he got older, his involvement in gang warfare deepened.

> Eventually I was involved in kidnapping opposing gang members. We would hand them over to our comrades. I had to ensure that nobody saw what they were doing.

And what they were doing was merciless, beyond most people's comprehension but not beyond human capability. He described in graphic detail one such torturing and killing.

> I heard the noises inside. They were savage. They cried out horribly. They groaned. They cried. It gave me goose bumps but if I wasn't prepared to put up with it,

then I feared that the same thing would happen to me. They could kill me at any moment as well. They had me. There were gangs who tortured and cut off heads. Nearly everything one gang was doing, the other did back.

The gangs were not the only ones capable of such brutality. So were the police. Our witness was once caught by the police while robbing a car.

> The federales arrived, they grabbed me at the corner as I was robbing a car. They grabbed me and got me for crack. And then they brought me to this place, a house on its own. They put me in a bag. They hit my feet with a club until they were completely purple. They shocked my balls … my tongue … my lips. The torture went on repeatedly for about eight hours. They hit me on the feet with the club until they left me, until they left me for dead. They thought that I had gone, that I had died, but thanks be to God, here I am. Still.

In 2007, the newly elected President Felipe Calderón (2006-2012) launched a fiercely aggressive police and military offensive. The "war on drugs" became an indiscriminate war on the streets. A marauding army and police force and even more violent cartels fought for control of Juarez and its lucrative drug trade. Others, too, wanted some of the action: judges, city officials, local politicians and a whole host of others who were also complicit in the spiralling violence. According to a US 2018 Congressional Report, an estimated 150,000 killings have taken place since Calderón declared war on the country's drug cartels. Things just got worse, as our thirty-nine-year-old key informant told me.

> When the army was here, the federales and all that, I saw that it was worse, everything got worse. More gangs started to emerge. Crime increased with those around.

At the height of all the killings, confidence in the police was at an all-time low. Corruption reached the highest levels. In 2008 Ricardo Gutierrez Vargas, the head of Interpol in Mexico, was arrested along with a top government anti-drugs adviser. Both were charged with taking money from the cartels.

An April 2011 Human Rights Watch report alleged "strong evidence of police involvement and lacklustre investigations", a view supported by Amnesty International. Their report claimed arbitrary detention, torture, excessive use of force and forced disappearance by municipal, state and federal police agencies.

One of the stand-out features of the killings in Juarez, and one that has attracted much local and international commentary, is the number of women who have been killed, the killing of women simply because they are women. The phenomenon of female homicides in Ciudad Juárez is called in Spanish the *feminicidios* ("femicides") and *las muertas de Juárez* ("the dead women of Juárez"). The number of female dead is not clear, but the incidence of femicide between 2003 and 2018 is anywhere from 400 to possibly as high as 1,000, with hundreds more missing. However, many local residents believe that the true count of *los feminicidios* stands at an estimated 5,000 victims. The murders of these young women were accompanied by horrifying and gratuitous sexual violence. Femicide statistics within Mexico are truly shocking. On average, seven women are killed each day as a result of gender violence, a rate fifteen times higher than the world's average. Husbands, boyfriends or family members commit sixty-six per cent of femicide attacks.

The Juárez killings began around 1993. Many victims were teenage students, poor and working-class young women. According to an Amnesty International 2003 report, the majority of the victims were less than eighteen years old. Almost half of them were subject to sexual violence beyond the basic act of rape. Many had bite marks, stab wounds, ligature and strangulation marks on their necks. Some had their breasts severely mutilated. Autopsies determined that some of the missing girls were kept alive for a few weeks before being murdered. Investigators believe the girls were held captive and repeatedly raped and tortured before being murdered. Posters plastered on city walls bear testimony to the scale of the killing.

I attended a press conference of parents of the disappeared. Some held photographs of their daughters. Some had t-shirts with images of their daughters. All had similar stories.

My name is Evangelina Arce, mother of Silvia Arce, who disappeared 11 March 1998. She's been missing for fifteen years. We still don't know anything. The police never did anything.

My name is Olga Esparza and I'm the mother of Monica Janeth Anís. It's been four years since my daughter disappeared. She was last seen inside the university. I dream of my daughter. She comes to me and says, 'Mama, I'm here', with her books, with her bag. 'I'm here and I'm not leaving'.

On this day, 25 March 2009, our daughter, Monica Janeth Anís Esparza disappeared. Eighteen years old, she was a student at the University of Juarez. She was last seen inside the Institute of Business and Social Sciences. Four years ago, my life and the life of my family were turned upside down.

Olga Esparza Anís [and her husband whose name I did not get] are the parents of Moní, who disappeared on 27 March 2009. They say that men don't cry because we're macho. But we do cry. I cry for my daughter. I miss my daughter. She had many dreams, but what she really wanted was to go to Spain on a student exchange.

I'm Norma Laguna, mother of Idalí Juache Laguna. I'm forty-two years old. My daughter disappeared on 23 February 2010. She was going to town on a family visit. She left the station at one for the visit, and we don't know any more after the station. When she disappeared she was nineteen years old. Since my daughter disappeared, I've been looking for her. I've gone with many people who help look for my daughter, but I haven't found an answer yet.

One woman told me after the meeting that she has been searching for her daughter since 1993.

Afterwards I spoke at length to one of the women, sitting on a park bench with her husband, who didn't utter a word during the ninety-minute conversation. Holding a bottle of water in his hands from which he didn't drink, he never made eye contact with his wife, who recounted the disappearance of their daughter. Staring at the same spot in the distance, it seemed as if he were numbed by the weight of what he knew only too well.

> My name is Carmen Castillo. I'm fifty-two years old. I'm the mother of Monica Liliana Delgado Castillo. I arrived home and I arrived to darkness. The house was dark. 'Moni, Moni'. She wasn't home. She was at home one day and then she disappeared.

She disappeared on Monday 18 October 2010. The investigation went nowhere. Then in September 2011, the District Attorney's office contacted her.

> We're here to tell you that we found your daughter... but not as we would have liked.

Her daughter's body was found 58 kilometres from Juarez.

> They dumped my daughter like you would dump an animal.

Moni was a fanatical football follower and a huge fan of the Santos Laguna team. Later, in her home, her mother showed me all the football paraphernalia that still adorned her room. Here Carmen told of another killing, that of her neighbour.

> I have a neighbour. Someone killed her little girl. The little girl was only thirteen years old. They raped her, killed her and disposed of her body.

Of the thirty-two countries where femicide most frequently occurs, seventeen are in Latin America. Mexico, ranked sixth in the world for crimes against women, has seen a rise in femicide of forty-six per cent since 2013. In 2015, the United Nations declared femicide a pandemic in Mexico.

Perhaps the most potent and poignant symbol of the young women who have disappeared are the pink crosses that puncture the desert landscape, places that briefly held the bodies of the murdered. Pink, the quintessential "feminine" colour, saturating this arid landscape. Like the bodies they have come to represent, some of the crosses have crumbled into the desert sand.

As the rate of killings began to rise, some of the officials responsible for investigation and prosecution began employing a discourse that, in effect, blamed the victim for the crime. The victims wore short skirts, went out dancing, were "easy" or "sluts out roaming the streets at night-time, were prostitutes". This moralistic explanation/justification is commonplace. In 1995, a television advertisement exhorted women not to dress provocatively.

Some point to the highly charged atmosphere, the self-destructiveness of the drug trade and the emotional toll it takes on men, distancing themselves from their own humanity, destroying their sense of empathy and any possibility of finding common cause with the women in their lives. There are myriad explanations but few answers. Neoliberalism. Hegemonic masculinity. US imperialism. State collapse. State take-over. State corruption. Social media. The normalisation of violence. Violence as a spectacle. The dead responsible for their own deaths. The desert itself is blamed – this wild, ungovernable space where the norms that bind a society together are lost in the sands of time.

One feature that has garnered much attention and is favoured by photojournalist Julián Cardona is the rise of the *maquiladoras,* the official name of Mexico's sweatshops, the proliferation of which was furthered by the 1993 North American Free Trade Agreement (NAFTA). The mass production factories located on the Mexican side of the border manufacture everything from electronics to pharmaceuticals to auto parts and household goods. Among the many transnational companies currently operating in Juarez are Lear, Johnson and Johnson, Honeywell, Avon Automotive, Delphi, Siemens, Emerson and Foxconn. While the *maquiladoras* were originally intended to employ men, managers soon realised that it was in fact young women who made the perfect employees. They are considered more docile and obedient, and their young nimble fingers are deemed better suited to the repetitive work. By the 1980s, about 90 per cent of workers were women.

In the *maquiladoras,* workers are forced to put in mandatory overtime on top of nine-hour days (that stretch to twelve hours when an average one-and-a-half-hour bus ride on each side is factored in). Workers are regularly exposed to toxic chemicals and dangerous machinery without adequate safety equipment. Sexual harassment and abuse are rampant. Women have virtually no choice but to submit to ongoing sexual harassment as well as actual abuse and rape to hold on to and advance in their jobs. Since the government mandates sixty days of paid leave for pregnant women, females are forced to take pregnancy tests and anyone who is pregnant is not hired.

Far from the site of the *maquiladoras* I met with some of the women who work there. "It's not well paid. They kill you for nothing and they pay you very little," one young woman tells me. "I don't want to continue working there."

Another young woman told me:

> When I go to work it's so dark, well yes, I'm afraid. Well, because the streets are empty. That some mad man will grab me, that they will kidnap me and whatever happened to the other girls will happen to me.

Routine harassment of young women is an everyday experience, sometimes with explicit threats.

> Going into town is uncomfortable. They're whistling and shouting at you. They say, 'come here, don't you know what will happen to you if you are alone'. They grab you and won't let you go and say: 'be afraid'.

"Juarez," Julián told me, "was once known as an idyllic postcard border town but its sudden growth set the stage for a future of violence. The city was growing in a chaotic way." Migrants flocked to Juarez in search of work, resulting in the growth of the sprawling shantytowns, called *colonias*, one of which Fr Kevin walked me through on my first day. About 255,000 people work directly in Juarez's 330 *maquiladoras*, almost all of which are foreign owned. The *colonias* are home to human suffering, exploitation and endurance.

I asked Kevin what kept him going. "Three things," he replied. "I pray the rosary twice a day. I walk up that mountain you can see there," and then somewhat mischievously, he said, "and I smoke eight cigarettes a day". What keeps the bereaved parents of Juarez going? The desire to see justice for their daughters. The workers of the *maquiladoras?* There is no choice. And the young men, the members of the gangs? Well, as Fr Kevin so succinctly explained, initially it's the good money, lots of women, good food, good booze. And then trying to ensure that you are not counted among the dead.

The war on drugs has been an unmitigated disaster. Even Bill Clinton recognises that. Too late. He has moved on. The 19th US Surgeon General Dr Vivek H. Murthy (2014-2017) described the forty-odd-year-old war as a failure. "We cannot prosecute and incarcerate our way out of the problem." Former Canadian Health Minister Dr. Jane Philpott has also deemed the war on drugs a failure. Guatemalan President Otto Pérez Molina declared in 2013 that the war on drugs had brought Latin American nations to their knees. And early in 2019 Mexican President Andrés Manuel López Obrador declared an end to his country's war on drugs. On that latter declaration, the jury is still out.

Everyone in Juarez seems to be a loser: the city itself, its young women, its young men and their grieving parents. Older people too. People are thrashing around looking for a way out. Meanwhile the "war on drugs" rumbles on while the solution to the migrant crisis is to cut people off, to build a "great big beautiful" wall.

And the vast majority of the world's nations refuse to acknowledge a simple truth: that in this harsh, unforgiving world some form of escape, however transitory, is needed for sanity's sake. And sometimes that form of escapism comes in the form of psycho-active substances. It has ever been thus.

In 2016, I attended the United Nations General Assembly Special Session on Narcotic Drugs (UNGASS) in New York. What struck me most was the belligerent tone. The self-righteous attitude. The "war on drugs". Despite all the evidence, the war continues. The Resolution adopted by the General Assembly on 19 April 2016 included the following:

> We underscore that the Single Convention on Narcotic Drugs of 1961 as amended by the 1972 Protocol, the Convention on Psychotropic Substances of 1971, the United Nations Convention against Illicit Traffic in Narcotic Drugs and Psychotropic Substances of 1988 and other relevant international instruments constitute the cornerstone of the international drug control system.

The Resolution reaffirms the UN determination to tackle the world drug problem "and to actively promote a society free of drug abuse", something that it has spectacularly failed to do up to now.

If, as Albert Einstein is widely credited with saying, "The definition of insanity is doing the same thing over and over again, but expecting different results", then there was plenty of insanity on display at the UN. There was to be no change. Prohibitionists had won, at least at the official level. There were, however, some dissident voices, among them Uruguay (see page 216).

In the meantime, the killing, the torture, the pain, the disappearances, the grief, the fear, the exhaustion, the incomprehension of it all remains a feature of life in Juarez. With reason, the people of this border city continue to live fearful lives with the "be afraid" warning ringing in their ears.

# 6

# WE ARE NOT DOOMED

## *Palestine/Israel*

They could have been a couple in love. And perhaps they were, in their own way. Rami Elhahan and Bassam Aramin, men in their fifties or sixties. All the tell-tale signs were there. The eyes. The slightest of smiles. And then unexpectedly their arms reach across each other's shoulders and briefly rest there, then pause. Their eyes drop, and both briefly fall silent. A distance emerges. A solitariness. A shadowed darkness. And then with heads raised they continue.

I watch from a distance and know what is coming. If this is love, and I've no doubt it is, it is born out of a terrible, terrible grief. A shared grief. Rami's story I had heard the previous day. He was an ex-combatant, a dedicated fighter for a Zionist Israel in the 1973 Yom Kippur war, a war he now deeply regrets being part of. And one that has left him embittered, empty and traumatised, a beaten and battered man. His late father, a Holocaust survivor, lost most of his family in Europe's extermination camps. Israel was his place of safety, his place of refuge. "I am a Zionist Jew," he tells the American audience who have come to hear him and Bassam speak. "But before everything else I am a human being." A pause and he continues. "My fourteen-year-old daughter Smadar was killed by a Palestinian suicide bomber."

Bassam shifts uneasily in his seat, his mobile phone pressed between his praying hands. "I am a Palestinian Arab," he begins and immediately I sense he is pacing himself. Then a breath. "My ten-year-old daughter Abir was killed by an Israeli soldier."

Yehya Fawzi Abu Hishmeh is not long for this world, and he knows it. His largely immobile frame takes up half of the sofa on which he lounges. Wrapped in a shawl, still in his pyjamas, it is unlikely he will be going out today, or any day soon. Until, that is, that fateful day comes, the day of the Grim Reaper. His eighty-four years on this planet sit heavily on him. Despite his infirmity, he welcomes us into his home, located on the first floor of an uncertainly constructed tower block in the Bourj el-Barajneh Refugee Camp in Lebanon's capital city, Beirut. The weakened body has not weakened the voice which is gravelly strong, and commanding. "Come in," he waves. "Come in, come in." With us is his physician and chess-obsessed old friend Dr. Mohammed al-Khatib. They are happy to see each other. Old stories bind them. Old sores too, sores that have never gone away. Deceit. Displacement. Dislocation. Dispossession. Yehya was thirteen years of age when he was forced to leave Palestine. Mohammed just two.

Like many people of their age there is a sense of lost time. Where did all those years go? And what has become of us now? Refugees for decades of our lives, lives dominated by a past that refuses to go away. And that momentous moment in 1948 when hundreds of thousands of Palestinians were expelled from their homeland on the pretext that it was for their own safety, that in a matter of days, weeks at worst, they could return.

They never did.

Cautious people, those who owned their homes took their deeds, their keys too. Other than that, they left pretty much everything – they were coming back after all. Yehya Fawzi

Abu Hishmeh was one of the cautious. Not only did his family take the deeds and the key, but he took land maps that clearly identify his holding.

All of these he produces for me, tied in the original cord, now ever so fragile, flimsy but recognisable things. Not just the deeds to his home and the map of his land, but bill headings, receipts, all the paraphernalia of a cautious businessman. "This is the map of my property in its entirety." And then he says he wants to show me something else, his grandfather's home where he lived, a shoe box size exact replica. "I was born in this house." He lifts the lid and points to the bedroom where he slept as a child and the room he moved to during summer's heat, a room with a balcony where night-time winds cooled summer bodies. As he leans in towards the model, the years fall away and he is a boy again. And for the briefest of moments, there is a sense that this aged man can feel the breeze again on his once taut body.

A home in Jaffa, a six-hour journey away. But a lifetime away, never to be seen again.

In a community centre in Jerusalem people listening to Rami Elhahan and Bassam Aramin perceptibly lean forward, silence in the room, empathy for the two men. A hard and bitter agony it is for them. I notice one listening man weeping. Awe and wonder. Disbelief from those listening that they could be so forgiving.

"My name is Rami Elhahan, I'm sixty-nine years old, a graphic designer, living in Jerusalem, born in Jerusalem, seventh generation. I'm a Jew, I'm an Israeli, and before anything else I am a human being," he begins. "For the last twenty years I'm a member of the Parents Circle, the Israeli Palestinian Bereaved Families for Reconciliation and Peace, probably the only organisation on earth that does not seek new members."

There is a sense that their stories have been told before. But if so, their authenticity and taut tension have not diminished.

As was the case with the mother I had met in East Jerusalem earlier in the week. Suha Abu Khadarsits. Her impeccable, charcoal-coloured coat that envelops her body was buttoned to the chin with a matching grey scarf around her neck. A long sofa runs the length of two walls of her living room, a room adorned with photographic images of her dead son. A golden-coloured Qur'an is the only other stand-out adornment.

Sixteen-year-old Mohammed Abu Khdeir, younger in one photograph with spiked gelled hair, eyes alight and a broad smile. Youthful joy. In another he was older with a baseball cap, and in another testing his strength in a hand-wrestle with a friend, followed by one with the now ubiquitous close-shaved buzz-cut. A child growing into a teenager, a teenager who never grew into an adult. Images frozen in time.

Sitting straight-backed, a tissue clutched between her hands that rarely stray from her lap, hers is a story she too has told before, many times. A story she never tires of telling. A story she wants heard. The ending of the life of her sixteen-year-old boy who was kidnapped and burned to death. Sixteen years of age ... burned ... to ... death. Killed by a twenty-nine-year-old man and two underage accomplices, and a police force that sought to destroy the evidence. Despite the frequent repetition of her story, the emotion is overpowering. We stop, switch off the camera and her head is bowed; she is alone.

Another woman. This time in Beirut. Zahra Nahar.

"My heart bleeds when I think of that day." It was as if each uttered word added another layer of pain to an already deeply pained face, a pain, it seems, that is as visceral now as when first experienced twenty-six years ago. A lifetime of bearing pain, with nothing to assuage it, nothing to soften or suppress the memory. Not the boxes of medicine stacked beside her. Not the tightly gripped prayer beads moving endlessly between her thumb and forefinger. Pain beyond belief. Beyond words of consolation.

And the torrent of words that poured out of her did not bring relief, ending with her headscarf covering her face. There was no need to translate this raw emotion. There was no pause for translation. That came later.

Seventy-year-old Zahra Nahar was witness to the 1982 Shatila massacre in Beirut in which her husband and fourteen-year-old son were killed, her daughter doused with acid. A massacre that was a by-product of what the Israelis call the War of Independence and the Arabs call the War of *al-Nakba*, or The Catastrophe, which began with the forced violent expulsion of between 700,000 and 800,000 Palestinians from their homeland in 1948. Following this expulsion of Palestinians, Jewish people moved into the newly emptied homes, farms and businesses, beginning the process of creating a Jewish state for a Jewish people. And now, four generations and seventy years later, the Palestinian people live in a state of permanent temporariness, a limbo people caught in a no-man's land.

For forty continuous hours between sunset on Thursday, 16 September, and midday Saturday, 18 September 1982, one of the most infamous and barbaric massacres of the late twentieth century took place here in the Shatila refugee camp in Beirut. Photographs taken in the immediate aftermath of the bloodbath that has left Zahra and countless others drowning in grief demonstrate the depth of the depravity that unfolded during those tumultuous hours.

> Precisely it was on Friday 17 December 1982 at 10:30 in the morning. I was looking for my husband. Dead. Dead. Dead. Everywhere. All the murdered bodies were men. Many were cut open. Their legs and arms broken. Tortured. Killed. Slaughtered. I continued to look for my husband, my father, my brother, my grandfather, and my fourteen-year-old son at that time. I kept searching amongst the dead bodies. The murdered bodies were piled up.

I searched in the shelters and trenches. I searched in the underground pipes for my son and husband. But all I could see is dead bodies covering the ground. I walked amongst the dead bodies. I held these murdered men with my bare hands.

The numbers killed and injured were contested by all sides, but that is irrelevant; individual grief can never be defined by numbers. "What real differences do numbers make?" asks Bayan Nuwayhed al-Hout, a Palestinian academic who has written what many regard as the most authoritative account of the Shatila massacre, *Sabra and Shatila September 1982*. "Suppose we were to say one figure and another," she says.

> Suppose we were to say the number of victims was 1,000 rather than 3,000, or just 300 rather than 1,000? Would that reduce or minimise the hateful nature of the crimes of torture and killing of unarmed innocent people? Would that wash away all that blood, all that death?

In addition to the brutality of the killing, the mutilation and the dismemberment which Zahra stumbled through in her account of the massacre, for the victims and survivors there is the searing knowledge that this killing was deliberate. Not a frenzied killing, even though it may have become that, but a cold, calculated, deliberate, pre-planned killing that targeted the Palestinian refugees who, under duress, had fled their homeland thirty-four years previously. And as subsequent events revealed, no Palestinian was responsible for what was the actual trigger of the massacre, the 1982 full-scale invasion of Lebanon by the Israeli army and the assassination of the pro-Israeli Lebanese president-elect Bachir Gemayel, who died along with twenty-six others including his four-year-old daughter Maya, when a bomb shattered the headquarters of his Lebanese Christian Phalangist Party.

A subsequent Israeli inquiry into the Shatila massacre, headed by Israeli Supreme Court Justice Yitzak Kahen, found that Israel was *indirectly* (my emphasis) responsible and that then Israeli Defense Minister (later Prime Minister) Ariel Sharon bore personal responsibility for the massacre. It is a finding that Palestinians reject. For the people of Beirut, Israel was *directly* responsible. Its army facilitated the assault by the Phalange militia (supporters of Gemayel) on the defenceless refugees in the camp.

But all that nuanced language of indirect responsibility seems like a distant, dispassionate place from the heart-breaking words of grief as Zahra and I stand on the fourth floor outside her tiny damp apartment into which are squeezed two bedrooms, a kitchen, bathroom and living room. On the landing of the fragile block from which a web of electrical cables dangle above the narrow alleyways in which she lives and rarely leaves, she points to several of the killing locations. She tells of the corpses upon corpses she witnessed within the 1.5 square kilometre refugee camp, now home to anything between 10,000 and 22,000 people, all of whom live in squalid, polluted, vastly overcrowded, impoverished conditions.

Inside, her son, in his early thirties, unemployed like so many of his lost generation, takes down a faded photograph of his dead father and brother which had been hanging beside a copy of the Holy Qur'an. Zahra sits with the photograph on her lap and gently rubs their cheeks. Words have deserted her.

There is nothing more to be said.

Depravity, too, was evidenced in the killing of sixteen-year-old Mohammed Abu Khdeir.

> My son Mohammed was killed on 2 July 2014. It was the beginning of Ramadan month, the fourth day. Mohammed went out to pray morning prayers in the mosque. He had just eaten Suhoor [an Islamic term referring to the meal prior to fasting] at around 2:30 a.m. Two Israeli settlers, as claimed in court afterwards, approached

him, and asked about directions to Tel Aviv road. As Mohammed was showing the two Israeli settlers directions to Tel Aviv road, they kidnapped him. They hit Mohammed on his head, shoved him in the car and took him away to Deir Yassin area. They brought fuel. The Israeli settlers poured fuel on Mohammed and set my son on fire. Autopsy has proved that Mohammed was set on fire while alive. He wasn't dead when the Israeli settlers burnt him.

And yet more depravity in the killing of Smadari Elhahan.

On 4 September 1997, two Palestinian suicide bombers blew themselves up in Behhooda Street in the centre of Jerusalem, killing five people that day, including three little girls. One of these little girls was my fourteen-year-old, Smadari.

It was Thursday afternoon, and the beginning of a very long and very cold night which continues until today. It was the first day of school, she was on her way to buy new school books. I was on my way to the airport. My wife called me and she said someone saw Smadari go down the mall, and I immediately understood that, you keep hoping that maybe this time this finger will not turn towards you, this time, and then you find yourself running in the streets trying to find her. She completely disappeared. You go from one hospital to another, from police station to police station. Many long and frustrating hours until eventually later that night you find yourself in the morgue and this finger is stuck right between your eyes and you see this sight which you will never, ever be able to forget for the rest of your life.

I asked Rami Elhahan if it is possible to describe his grief, to put words on it.

It's not something that you can describe, it's devastating, it's a feeling that you cannot get rid of it. It's one wound that will never heal, and it fills you twenty-four hours a day, fifty-nine seconds of every minute. You don't recover from it, you are full with anger, you are full with frustration, you are full with deep emotions and the only question remain to be answered is what are you going to do with this energy. The energy is a nuclear energy, you can use it in order to bring darkness and revenge and you can use it to try and bring some hope.

Inevitably, the questions move from the personal to the political. Who's to blame? One state or two? Bantuanisation or Balkanisation? Federation or Confederation? "Give me one state, two states or 10,000 states," Rami had told me earlier, "and we won't stop the hate." Other than in a conflicted, confrontational context, Rami had never met a Palestinian until he was forty-nine years of age. Now he and Bassam want to talk about love, reconciliation, forgiveness, ease, respect. Things that need to be heard within the partisan echo-chamber of this conflicted land. Things that can never be legislated for no matter how many states one creates. So, too, do other members of the Israeli Palestinian Bereaved Families for Reconciliation and Peace, that organisation that does not want any new members. They too want to talk about love and forgiveness. Peace. An escape from all the killing, from all the hatred.

Peace. Justice too. Recognition. And accountability. For the 1948 *al-Nakba*. For the young men sent out on suicide missions. For the Shatila massacre.

Robert Fisk is a multi-award-winning Middle East correspondent who over a forty-year period has covered the war in Syria and Lebanon, five Israeli invasions, the Iran-Iraq war, the Soviet invasion of Afghanistan, the Algerian civil war, Saddam Hussein's invasion of Kuwait, the Bosnian and Kosovo wars, the American invasion and occupation of Iraq, the 2011 Arab revolution and the Troubles in the Northern Ireland. In an interview with him for the online journal *Policy and Practice*, I asked him to explain the origins of *al-Nakba*.

The Palestinians were driven off, driven from their homes, or fled from their homes in what is now Israel, during the war of 1948/49 when the Israeli state was established and the refugees were living on the land which is now Israel. They, of course, call it Palestine and that was their property. They lived on it, they had the deeds to it, they owned it and they were citizens of a mandate, British mandate before the Second World War called Palestine, which of course was composed, too, of both Jews and Arabs. Most of the people of Palestine historically are Arabs and were, indeed, when the original British Balfour declaration said that the British would support a Jewish homeland in Palestine.

So those Palestinians who fled their homes either because of massacres or through sheer fear, fled northwards, say from Galilee, and the Galilean Palestinians ended up in Lebanon, in the south of Lebanon, in Beirut itself in large numbers and in the Bekaa Valley in eastern Lebanon, and they believed of course when they arrived, the original refugees, that in a matter of days or weeks they would return to their homes in Palestine which is why they kept their land deeds, the keys to their front doors. They were going away for a few days, locked the front door, left everything intact inside their houses, thinking they were going to go back when the war was over.

They never did return.

Among those who did not return was ninety-year-old Abedullah Talib Salhani who told me about his life in Palestine before he was forced out of his homeland.

I worked as a farmer in Palestine herding sheep. I had eighty-four sheep. Some were very young. The sheep belonged to me. I had a small land property. My house was also perfect for me and my family. I had olive trees too. I had around 60 olive trees which I planted with my own hands. Looking after my olive trees and having olive oil from them meant the world to me. Because I had only a small number of the olive trees, I used to do the work myself. I used to pick the olives, squeeze them, and bring the oil home to use for cooking.

For the past seventy years, Abedullah has lived in Shatila refugee camp. Now he sits on a white plastic chair outside his home. Still agile, he makes his way to the mosque for daily prayers. Otherwise he sits and watches. He deeply regrets leaving Palestine. He, too, expected that in a matter of weeks he would return.

> The Israelis came to our village and told us: "We need you to leave for one week, and then you will return. They told us not to take our belongings with us. They said: "Leave everything in place because you will return in one week."

Weeks became months. Years became decades.

> When I sit outside the house, I weep over my situation. I wish I had stayed and died in my country and didn't come to Lebanon.

Death too shadows the conversation between Yehya Fawzi Abu Hishmeh and Mohammed al-Khatib, two old men confronting the inevitable.

> Mohammed: We're old now. And death is inevitable.

> Yehya: Yes, of course.

> Mohammed: Do you know what my will is going to be about? My will is that once Palestine is free, I would like my body [bones] to be reburied in my home country. So, I can rest in my grave. Wouldn't you love to be buried in your home country?

> Yehya: Of course. I would love that.

> Mohammed: You want your body to return and be buried in your grandfather's house in Palestine?

> Yehya: Yes. That's what I want. It is difficult though.

Mohammed: No, it's not. Even after 100 years, you request from your children that they move your body to Palestine.

Yehya: That's my wish. First and foremost, I would want to live and die in Jaffa, Palestine. I wouldn't mind being buried there at all. My father died in Palestine and he is buried there in the Alsheikh area. Palestine is our country from the river to the sea.

Mohammed: Exactly, that's it.

Yehya did not get his wish, at least not yet. The Grim Reaper called shortly after I met with him and he is buried in Lebanon. Time and time again, I have witnessed that desire to be buried in the homeland. Perhaps he knew he wouldn't. He must have known. What the next 100 years will hold remains to be seen.

I met with the eighty-four-year-old Yehya, seventy-two-year-old Mohammed, ninety-year-old Abedullah and seventy-year-old Zahra Nahar in Palestinian refugee camps in Beirut in November 2018. Their lives are marked by prolonged injustice which shows no sign of abating.

The following February, I travelled to Palestine/Israel. Prior to my arrival, the voices emanating from Palestine/Israel were altogether different. A cacophony of discordant voices was gathering apace in the run-up to the 9 April 2019 elections. Hard, piercing, shrill voices.

As harsh and unyielding as the 507 kilometres of walls that have spoiled this holiest of lands. The walls of Bethlehem. The walls of Ramallah. The walls of Jerusalem. Walls on which the words of that most reviled of Shakespeare's characters, the Jew Shylock, are paraphrased: "We all bleed." Voices as harsh as a young Jewish settler teacher who told me that they, the Palestinians, don't think the same we do, they don't feel the same we do. The telling is in the *they*. A Canadian-born campaigner for the increasingly marginalised Labor party tells me: "We won the war in sixty-seven and we are entitled to the spoils of war." But of the walls that divide this city he says, "the walls depress me. The walls show that we have failed as human beings." On the military presence he says it makes him feel secure, the ubiquitous highly weaponised military which is everywhere. At checkpoints. At roadblocks.

Another Canadian, a young man no more than twenty-one in military uniform, had come to Israel to help protect the Jewish people, he told me. He probably shouldn't have. Soldiers shouldn't talk unless they are quizzing you. One-way traffic. But he was probably bored, standing on his own in the Palestinian city of Hebron, weighed down with God knows what on his back. Another young man caught in the maelstrom of war. Later we saw each other at a distance and waved. Just two human beings, just two passers-by.

Meanwhile, erstwhile enemies Rami and Bassam sit side-by-side in this holiest of lands. The land of Abraham, who through Isaac is regarded as the biological ancestor of the people of Israel. The land of Ibrahim, who through Ishmael is regarded as the biological ancestor of Muslims. The land of Christianity, for whom Abraham is their father-in-faith. This bleak and blighted land. A land filled with despair.

And with the slimmest slivers of hope, forlorn hope maybe, but hope nonetheless. And I came in search of hope. Hope comes from the margins, never from the centre. Those who know the pain of suffering. Those who have felt the killing. Those for whom war is anything but an abstraction. Those who know war's barbarity, abomination, shattering.

Within Palestine/Israel there are people, as elsewhere in the world, who refuse to countenance that war is an inevitability.

"Ever since I joined the Parents Circle, and ever since then," Rami Elhahan told me, "I devote my life to express this one message, we are not doomed, it's not our destiny to keep on killing each other."

It's startling that it needs to be said, that we need to be reminded of it. And he is not alone.

Engagement with social justice and human rights work has been central to the life of fifty-nine-year-old Rabbi Arik Asherman for the past twenty-three-and-a-half years, he tells me. An ardent critic of the Israeli government, he has consistently challenged what he regards as the false religious ideology that the land of Palestine/Israel belongs exclusively to the Jewish people. Rabbi Asherman does not mince his words. The assertion by religious Jews that it is their God-given obligation to redeem, to settle the land by any means possible and to make sure that it can never be returned to the Palestinian people, "is a slap in the face to God". Arik Asherman knew from an early age that he wanted to be a Rabbi. Born in Pennsylvania in the United States, he learned early on from his parents, from his rabbis, from his teachers and from his community that a basic part of what it means to be a Jew, to be a human being, is to be concerned about universal human rights and social justice. Not surprisingly, his conversation is infused with Biblical references.

> Basically Rabbi human rights, Detoyzig, it starts with this idea what we learn in the very first chapter of the Bible, in chapter 1, verse 27 of Genesis, that human beings are created in God's image, it doesn't say just the Jews are created in God's image, it doesn't say just the wealthy are created in God's image, it makes a point of saying that both men and women are created in God's image, and therefore if we truly believe that, then we have to honour and protect that image of God in every human being, and that means working for everybody's human rights. We work for Israeli Jewish human rights, social economic justice, people in need of public housing, we work for Palestinian human rights. My Zionism says I have as much of a right to be here as do Palestinians. I am exercising my right of return from 2000 years ago let's say, to be here. My Zionism also says I

can't ask for myself anything, any rights. I cannot say that I have a right to return here because I, as a Jew, have a right to return and say that Palestinians do not have the same right. I have no right to say that Palestinians, for the sake of peace, forgo your right of return. I have to recognise that right of return for Palestinians. We're saying to our fellow Israelis, we know that you are good and decent people, we know that you aspire to be just, but you need a reality check.

It is a belief not widely shared within the rabbinic fold, a view for which he has attracted much adverse criticism and physical attack on his person and on his home.

Our demagogues talk about the fact that we are somehow traitors, and among religious Jews in particular, someone who like myself is a religious Jew, is the greatest traitor of the traitors. I often get told "take off your kippa, take off your religious head-covering. How can you pretend you're a religious Jew and protect non-Jews?" I do what I do as a rabbi, as a Jew, as an Israeli, as a Zionist, and I believe that our obligation as Jews is to act according to our highest Jewish values which start with the idea that every human being is created in God's image.

For now, the demagogues are in the ascendancy as they have been for most of the existence of the state of Israel. But now more than ever. In claiming this geographically small piece of territory, about three times smaller than Ireland, a centuries-old historical connection is invariably evoked. In his invocation, English-born former Chief Rabbi of Ireland (1979-1985) David Rosen adopts an almost mystical other-worldly persona. It's as if there is no one else in the room with him.

To be able to live in the land for which thousands of years, well centuries, of Jewish prayers and hopes and dreams could only fanaticise about, and I can live here and I can look out from my window and see on the

118

Mount of Olives where my parents are buried and my grand-parents are buried and when generations of Jews have only been able to dream about the possibility of being there, and to live in this land and to enjoy all its gifts, and its beauty and its inhabitants is an incredible privilege.

"I wouldn't want to live anywhere else," he says looking me straight in the eye. "I couldn't even imagine myself having to put my roots down anywhere else other than this place for which I feel such an incredible civilisation and spiritual connection."

"There didn't have to be a conflict here," he tells me. In theory it could have been done amicably to the needs of all the peoples.

There is a Jewish National Liberation Movement that is called Zionism, and there is a Palestinian National Liberation Movement. These are two peoples that have these attachments to the land, historical, cultural, religious in different ways, that if you like, are competing for the same territory, and if they would have been wise, and if maybe one day they will be wise, they will learn how to share this territory so that two nations and three religions may flourish in this land.

David Rosen is no demagogue.

As he spoke, I thought of Dr. Mohammed al-Khatib, of Yehya Fawzi Abu Hishmeh, Abedullah Talib Salhani, Zahra Nahar, Suha Abu Khadarsits and the many people of Shatila and Bourj el-Barajneh refugee camps. I thought about the injustice of their lives. They, too, would have loved to look out on the Mount of Olives. They, too, would have loved to look out on the land where their parents and grandparents are buried. They, too, would have loved the opportunity to enjoy all of its gifts, all of its beauty, a gift they would never experience.

I asked him about the chess-obsessed Dr. Mohammed al-Khatib. About Yehya Fawzi Abu Hishmeh, whose last days

119

on this earth were clearly imminent. About the sheep and olive farmer Abedullah Talib Salhani. About Zahra Nahar who witnessed the Shatila massacre. About Suha Abu Khadarsits whose son was burned alive. And all the other people who were expelled, cast aside. That and the human cost to the three million Palestinians partly living in the apartheid state of Israel (a characterisation, incidentally, Rosen curtly rejected), and the effective blockade of an additional two million Palestinians in the Gaza Strip, Israel's non-citizens. To that Rabbi Rosen said:

> There's a terrible injustice that people who are connected to this land cannot come back to it, and that injustice has to be addressed through a peaceful resolution of the conflict.

But that injustice prevails and shows no sign of resolution. The opposite, in fact, is the case. And as for the unequivocal right of return for Palestinians, and the need for the Israeli state to be held accountable for its refusal to grant that right, Rosen appeared to blame the Palestinians.

> So, from the Israeli perspective it's only violence that's preventing the possibility of Palestinians flourishing … from the Israeli perspective it's only because they are not able to prevent the violence.

And as if in any doubt, Benjamin Netanyahu, close to being Israel's longest serving Prime Minister, declared in the lead-in to the 2019 April elections that Israel is "not a state of all its citizens" and that "Israel is the nation-state of the Jewish people – and them alone". Benjamin Netanyahu ramping up inflammatory anti-Palestinian demagoguery. Netanyahu's Jewish state for a Jewish people.

Another demagogue, another country. South Africa's P.W. Botha:

> I am one of those who believe that there is no permanent home for even a section of the Bantu in the white

area of South Africa, and the destiny of South Africa depends on this essential point. If the principle of permanent residence for the black man in the area of the white is accepted, then it is the beginning of the end of civilisation as we know it in this country.

And closer to home, the North of Ireland's first Prime Minister James Craig: "Ours is a Protestant government for a Protestant people." All for short-term electoral gain.

Voices from the past. Voices from the present.

Donald Trump is Netanyahu's staunch collaborator in exclusionary politics. So too are Hungary's Viktor Orban, Italy's Matteo Salvini, Marine Le Pen of France, Turkey's Recep Tayyip Erdoğan, Narendra Modi of India, Brazil's Jair Bolsonaro, British Prime Minister Boris Johnson and many more. A 2019 study commissioned by *The Guardian* and undertaken by a group of European scholars (Team Populism) concluded that the number of populist leaders has more than doubled since the early 2000s.

These are grudge politicians, with their skewed nationalism and distorted history. What Tikhon Dzyadko told me in Russia equally applies to Israel. The distortion of history, none more so than the memorialisation of the Holocaust.

Take, for example, Jewish Argentinian-born fifty-nine-year-old Eitan Bronstein Aparicio, Co-Director of Decolonizer, an organisation that seeks to expose and challenge the colonial nature of the Israeli state. Bronstein consistently argues, controversially I suggested to him, that successive Israeli governments distort and abuse the memory of the Holocaust. A distortion that has led to a justification for a Jewish-only state.

"I think Israel is abusing the memory of the Holocaust," he said to me. It is a minority view, but he is not alone in stating it. Political science professor Norman Finkelstein, the son of Holocaust survivors, in his book *The Holocaust Industry: Reflections on the Exploitation of Jewish Suffering*, claims that the

Nazi genocide has been distorted and robbed of its true moral lessons, and instead has been put to use as an "indispensable ideological weapon" and used to justify Israel's criminal assault upon the Palestinian population and international law. Finkelstein was banned from entering Israel for ten years for his views, and fired from his teaching position at DePaul University in the United States.

"We have to struggle to separate the Holocaust from the State," Bronstein argues, "to really struggle, that the State of Israel would not have anything to do with the Holocaust. Israel uses and misuses the Holocaust to further its exclusionary nationalistic project."

Rather than foment narrow oppositional nationalistic fervour, Bronstein argues that the Holocaust ought to be a reminder of the brutality of narrow "othering" nationalistic ideas.

"The lessons from the Holocaust should be that we oppose those ideas and practices of rejecting the other, that we oppose violent brutal nationalism, racism and all those forms of hating the other." Instead, he argues, over the intervening decades the Holocaust has been instrumentalised as a nationalistic project by a succession of leading Israeli politicians, one that ignores the festering wound of *al-Nakba* and the plight of the Palestinian people both within Palestine/Israel and in the many refugee camps throughout Lebanon and Syria.

And yet there are many within Palestine/Israel who refuse to be cowed, who refuse to be bullied, who refuse to be silenced and who reject the politics of exclusion.

Among them are those who have an intimate knowledge of war, ex-combatants, including former Palestinian freedom fighter Usam Alleat (although he still considers himself a freedom fighter, but now by force of argument, not the force of a gun) and former Israeli soldier Udi Gore. "Combatants for Peace," Udi told me, "is a grass roots organisation that is run together by Palestinians and Israelis and promotes a non-violent solution to the conflict. This is our mission: to stop the circle of violence, and to say there is another way and we want to work together to achieve it."

Like their older counterparts, there is a warmth between them, an ease, a playfulness. There is gentle ribbing while sitting side-by-side on a wall under a tree on the outskirts of Jerusalem. Who's the terrorist? Who's the occupier? All the old language turned on its head. Accusations subverted, all with a seriousness of purpose. And the chance to tell their stories, stories not easily experienced or easily told. The first Intifada.[1] Started in 1987 and lasted five years. The second Intifada. The third Intifada. The night raids. The deeply ingrained resentments. The seething anger. The underlying hatred. "I hated Jews, and I hated Israel," Usam Alleat told me. Udi nods understandingly as Usam talks about the slow realisation that hatred is a zero-sum game, eating away at the soul, corrupting the heart, convulsing the body. The hatred finally gave way.

The reality is that hatred sits comfortably within the majority Jewish population in Israel. As one man told me, "we won the war," shrugging his shoulders. It may be one of the most militarised and walled states in the world, a price the majority of the Jewish population in Israel are prepared to pay, which is an indication, Udi says, of how deeply traumatised the country is. For talking to Usam, for attempting a reconciliation with Palestinians, people perceive Udi as a traitor, he tells me.

"I'm not afraid of them." This former Israeli soldier has proved his patriotism.

> I'm living here, I'm working here, I have the right to struggle for the future of this country. The interests of the Palestinian people and the Israeli people are the same. Peaceful compromise is the oxygen for the two

---

[1] Intifada literally means "shaking off" but more commonly refers to armed Palestinian uprisings against the Jewish takeover of their land. There have been three (1987-1993, 2000-2005 and 2008-2009).

peoples living here. So, what I'm doing is, in my eyes, certainly not treason. It's the patriotic thing to do.

The Middle East. Palestine and Israel. A conflict that has dominated world headlines since the expulsion of the Palestinian people and the establishment of the state of Israel in 1948. Successive US presidents have sought to establish their political legacy by brokering a deal, such as Jimmy Carter's 1978 Camp David accord involving Egyptian president Anwar Sadat and Menachem Begin, and Bill Clinton's 1993 Oslo Peace Accord, marked with a historic handshake between Palestinian leader Yasser Arafat and Israeli Prime Minister Yitzhak Rabin. Yet the accord failed to address three fundamental questions: the rights of Palestinian refugees to return to the homes their families fled in 1948, the future of the settlements, and East Jerusalem.

In 2019, Donald Trump floated an offer, the deal of the century, a $50 billion aid package dismissed as a shameless bribe. "It's absolutely foolish to believe you can have economics without sound politics," former British Prime Minister Tony Blair and one-time peace envoy in the Middle East remarked. Not that Blair has much traction in the region.

It is a dead deal even before it is fully launched.

In this uncertain world, there are some certainties. There was, as Robert Fisk told me, "a place called Palestine, and that is the problem for the Israelis and for the world – there was a place called Palestine".

And the Palestinians and their descendants who were forced out have the right to return, a right enshrined in international law and reaffirmed time and time again. Resolution 194 (III) was passed by the UN general Assembly in 1948 and affirmed and reaffirmed by the UN more than 135 times. Resolution 2535 recognises "that the problem of Palestine Arab refugees has arisen from the denial of their inalienable rights under the Charter of the United Nations and the Universal Declaration of Human Rights".

Other key UN resolutions include 393, 2452, and 3236, which further strengthen the Right of Return as "indispensable for the solution of the question of Palestine". What is often forgotten, particularly within Israel, is that Israel's admission as a member to the UN was made conditional on its implementation of resolution 194, a resolution Israel has disregarded on the basis that, according to the Israeli government, compliance would undermine the Jewish character of Israel.

Another certainty is that there are seven million Jewish people in Palestine/Israel, some fourth, fifth, sixth, seventh generation, and these seven million people have the right to remain.

How to reconcile the rights of Palestinians and the rights of Israelis is the conundrum that has bested political leaders for the past seventy years. A one-state or two-state solution? A two-state solution, Fisk argues, is a fantasy now. It would seem as if he is right. And one state is also a fantasy because it won't happen.

"It is an utterly depressing and bleak scenario," I suggest.

"It's an untold tragedy," he replied. "One which will continue long after we're gone from the world, and all the survivors will be memories too."

"Give me 10,000 states," Rami Elhahan says, "and you won't solve it." It is a view shared by Rabbi Arik Asherman. "I couldn't care less between a one or a two or a ten-state solution."

I didn't ask Dr. Mohammed al-Khatib. And I didn't ask Yehya Fawzi Abu Hishmeh, Abedullah Talib Salhani or Zahra Nahar. For them and the hundreds of thousands of displaced Palestinians the only question they want answered is when can they return? But return to what? To a walled-in existence?

To routinie searches by an army they do not recognise? To a life not all that dissimilar to the one they are currently living?

Unless and until…

Unless and until Jewish leaders listen to Rami Elhahan and Udi Gore, and Arab leaders listen to Bassam Aramin and Usam Alleat. Unless and until Arab leaders listen to Rami Elhahan and Udi Gore and Jewish leaders listen to Bassam Aramin and Usam Alleat, and to all those bereaved parents aching for peace, aching for reconciliation, aching for some respite from all the killing, from all the grief.

As my conversation ends with Rami, there is one more thing he wants to say.

> Ever since then [the death of his daughter] I devote my life to go everywhere possible to talk to anyone possible, to convey the very basic and very simple message which says "we are not doomed". This is not our destiny to keep on killing each other in this holy land of ours forever. We can change it. We can break once and for all this endless cycle of violence and revenge and retaliation and the only way to do it is simply by talking to each other. It will not stop unless we talk.

As of now there is no sense of that aspiration becoming a reality.

Would that it were otherwise.

# 7

# A WOMAN IS HANGED IN UVAROVKA

## *Russia*

A ll through my childhood, Russia or the Soviet Union was an outcast state — a dark, sinister place that not only weighed heavily on the world, but whose government weighed heavily on its people. A people characterised as recalcitrant, sullen, dour. A beaten people. A crushed people. Oppressed and suppressed. That, at least, was the hegemonic narrative we in the West had been fed for generations. A narrative with little equivocation, understanding or empathy.

The dualism of the West versus the East. One good, the other evil, particularly as personified by the Kennedy–Khrushchev stand-off. One smiling, good-looking, Irish and Catholic. The other bald, stern, atheistic. One an open, liberal democrat, the other a cold, closed communist. Essentially, what we were exposed to was a caricature of a place and a caricature of a people.

Russia has always been another place, a vast sprawling country that remains a mystery for most Western people, a distant and undiscovered place. With its eleven different time zones, it stretches from Finland to Japan and has an uneasy border with Europe to the West. Once the bedrock of the both reviled and revered Soviet Union, until its sudden and unexpected collapse in 1991, for decades the spectre of the Cold

War hung over this vast space, its system of government and its people. For all that, Russia is close: Moscow is closer to us than New York. But that physical closeness masks a great cultural gulf that has, to this day, not been bridged.

Such early formulations, which were underpinned by Catholic Church dogma, vilified communism and anything or anybody associated with it. *Divini Redemptoris*, the Papal Encyclical of Pope Pius XI on atheistic communism, summarised its threat as "a Bolshevistic and atheistic Communism ... a modern revolution that threatens everywhere, and it exceeds in amplitude and violence anything yet experienced in the preceding persecutions launched against the Church". There is no equivalent encyclical for western imperialism in Africa or Latin America, although Popes Leo XIII, John Paul II and Francis have heavily criticized the excesses of capitalism.

The call for the conversion of Russia – as ostensibly told by the Mother of Jesus to the three children of Fatima on 13 July 1917, just five months after the establishment of the Russian Provisional Government and the dismantlement of the Tsarist autocracy – heralded the Catholic Church's antagonistic engagement with the nascent USSR state. One of the visionaries, Sister Lucy, is quoted as saying: "She (Jesus' mother) said that Russia will be the instrument of chastisement chosen by heaven to punish the whole world if we do not beforehand obtain the conversion of Russia."

The Leonine Prayers, composed originally by Pope Leo XIII and subsequently reinforced by Pope Pius XI and Pope Pius XII, and for which there was a 300-day indulgence, were among the instruments adopted to the cause of the conversion of Russia. Consisting of three Hail Marys, the *Salve Regina* (Hail, Holy Queen) and the Prayer of St. Michael the Archangel – the latter with its strikingly evocative imagery ("these most crafty enemies ... inebriated with gall and bitterness [for] the Church, the spouse of the Immaculate Lamb ... have laid impious hands on her most sacred possessions") – the Leonine Prayer urged the faithful to pray for Russia. Russia and Soviet communism, the long promised/threatened Armageddon.

Enough. Enough to reinforce the willfulness, the mendacity of the Russian people and all communists with their imperious designs on and threat to the Western way of life.

These were the prayers of my childhood. Not the whole of the Prayer of St. Michael but the much more succinct "for the conversion of Russia, pray for us", "Saviour of the world, save Russia".

And then in my teenage years I became aware of another narrative. One that idolised the Soviet Union. The model state. The worker. Contented. Fulfilled. Equal. Women and men. Altruistic and selfless. The hewers of wood and the drawers of water, to borrow a Biblical phrase, that most unlikely of courses for Soviet communism. United in a common purpose. Reaching for the utopian dream. All given expression in what became known as socialist realism, an art characterised by a reverential depiction of the emancipated proletariat, the rural and the urban, women and men who toiled selflessly for the glorification of the communist dream. A dream that also captivated western intelligentsia.

Among them was Irish Nobel Laureate George Bernard Shaw. Shaw described criticism of Stalin's rule as "inflammatory irresponsibility". For English historian Eric Hobsbawm, the 1956 invasion of Hungary, however agonizing, was a necessary counter-revolutionary act. US singer and civil rights activist Paul Robeson declared Soviet audiences "were the finest in the world" and the Soviet Union was "the only nation in the world where racial discrimination is prohibited".

In 1924 Irish Labour leader Jim Larkin attended the Comintern congress in Moscow and was elected to its executive committee, while the writer Liam O'Flaherty tried to launch a Soviet in Dublin. In Limerick's Markets Field on May Day 1918, a 10,000-strong crowd passed a motion of solidarity with the Russian revolution.

From within the Soviet Union came a different story. Fyodor Dostoevsky vividly described the horror of pre-communist Russia, just as Alexander Solzhenitsyn portrayed the hollowness of the Soviet utopia a century later.

And then, in my adult years, another wave of unrelenting vilification of the Soviet Union from without. Ronald Reagan declared that "the Soviet Union is an evil empire and Soviet communism is the focus of evil in the modern world". For Margaret Thatcher the Soviet Union was "a country the produces what no one wants to buy, and whose workers receive wages that they cannot use to buy the things they want".

For years I had wanted to visit the Soviet Union. As a teenage student of Leaving Certificate history I was fascinated by the fall of the Romanov dynasty in 1917, the death of Nicholas II and the emergence of the Bolshevik Revolution. All of which captured the imagination of a teenage boy carefully ensconced in a lower middle-class west-of-Ireland boarding school, far away from any fall-out from such revolutionary fervour. Then the later introduction to Boris Pasternak's epic civil-war novel *Doctor Zhivago* and David Lean's masterful cinematic interpretation added another layer of fascination with this distant place.

The arrival of Mikhail Gorbachev, famously caricatured by Martyn Turner of *The Irish Times* with the hammer and sickle embossed on his forehead in the shape of his stand-out birthmark, seemed to herald the redemption of the Soviet Union. Two words, *glasnost* and *perestroika*, openness and reconstruction, two words that framed the policies of the final leader of the Soviet Union. But words were not enough to save the Soviet Union. What happened subsequent to its demise, I had travelled to witness. If the Soviet Union had been an enigma, this was my opportunity to try to understand what had fascinated me for so many years. In 2015 I got there.

Meeting twenty-seven-year-old Tikhon Dzyadko, one of Moscow's foremost radio and television journalists and Deputy Editor of RAIN TV, in one of only three nationwide independent media outlets in Russia, put paid, momentarily at least, to any equivocation I might have about Russia or the Soviet Union.

"I love Russia," he began. "I love living here. My family are here. My three kids. The problem is that there are not so many things to be proud of in Russia." And then unexpectedly: "Russia is a very cruel country. And all the history of Russia is very cruel. Sometimes it is very tough to live here and think about it."

"The history of Russia is very cruel" is as forthright a statement about one's own country as one is likely to hear. The only thing that unites this vast, sprawling country is, according to Tikhon, the memory of the Great Patriotic War. And on to that memory the current political elite in Russia, he believes, have grafted their own orthodoxy, their own siege mentality. From that orthodoxy no deviation is allowed. Tikhon elaborated as follows:

> If you look at what Russia is telling [people] about the Great Patriotic War, they are telling [us] Russia is great. Why [is] Russia great? Because Russia won the war. This was seventy years ago, but we won the war and this victory is used to explain everything. I think the problem is, there is no nation idea to unite all the people. All they have is the same language. And the same passports. The least thing that unites Russian people is the victory in the Great Patriotic War. If you not agree with the politics of the state you will hear that you are a fascist. This is how it works in the propaganda. The Great Patriotic War is exploited for current political gain by Russian President Vladimir Putin.

It was a view I would hear later in Palestine/Israel: how the state misrepresents and abuses its own history to serve current political needs.

And as every Russian student knows, its literature is testimony to Russia's past as a history of invasion. While Tolstoy, whose home in Yasnaya Polyana I visited on a cold, wet day, might have been a friend of the Russian peasantry, his home had all the hallmarks of the bourgeoisie. Years previously I had struggled to read and never finished his *War and Peace* masterpiece. But one scene I still remember. Prince Andrew is lying on the ground wounded: within the chaos, silence and a zen-like moment of existential cosmic awareness. A stand-out scene for most readers and commentators, I was subsequently to learn. A brief reprieve from the relentless carnage and what must have been howls of anguish from the dying and those who craved the relief of death.

> Above him was nothing, nothing but the sky – the lofty sky, not a clear sky but infinitely lofty, with grey clouds sweeping across... How can it be that I have never seen that lofty sky before? Oh how happy I am to have found it at last. Yes, it's all vanity, it's all an illusion, everything except that infinite sky.

Beautiful. War and Peace. And then there's Tchaikovsky's *1812 Overture* that incorporates brief snippets of *La Marseillaise* (the French national anthem), traditional Russian folk music, the church bells of Uspensky cathedral and, of course, the distinctive cannon blast written to celebrate Russia's defeat of Napoleon's army in 1812.

Napoleon's invasion of Russia is listed among the most lethal military operations in world history. Estimates as to how many were killed and injured in the whole of the Napoleonic wars vary from a staggering 3,250,000 to 6,500,000. These same estimates put the number of Russian soldiers killed at between 400,000 and more than 540,000.

In the First World War it is estimated that 30 per cent of all military deaths were Russian, a total of 1,811,000.

And then there's the Great Patriotic War. For Russian people the Second World War, or the Great Patriotic War (*Velikaia Otechestvennaia voina*, VOV), as it is referred to within Russia – the term first used in the state newspaper *Pravda* on 23 June 1941 – is the great touchstone event in its history, the memory of which runs deep. And with good reason: 24 million Soviet people died in the Great Patriotic War.

Starting in 1941, the Soviet Union bore the brunt of the Nazi war machine and arguably played the most important role in the defeat of Hitler. By one calculation, for every single US soldier killed fighting the Germans, 80 Soviet soldiers died doing the same. For Russians, the Siege of Leningrad from 8 September 1941 to 27 January 1944 was their stand-out battle. Nearly two-and-a-half years of horrific suffering. A battle that stopped the German advance into the Soviet Union and which many believe marked the turning of the tide of war in favour of the Allies. More than two million soldiers fought in close quarters and nearly two million people were killed, including tens of thousands of civilians. It was perhaps the bloodiest battle in modern warfare.

Tikhon Dzyadko was right. The history of Russia is very cruel. A country that has had to endure a succession of invasions. A country that has known what it's like to live with war. A country that had to rely on its own resources. A country where no Papal encyclical came to its defense. This is a country whose history is drenched in blood.

Eighty-five-year-old Serafimove Kazakova was witness to the Great Patriotic War. As she sits in her one-roomed Soviet-built apartment she talks openly of that time. Her story is Russia's story. She witnessed the German occupation of her home town of Mozhaisk 100 kilometres south of Moscow, the closest the German army came to Russia's capital. Serafimove remembers the day the German army arrived on 13 October 1941.

"I was a thirteen-year-old girl full of curiosity," she tells me as she describes how the Germans went from house to house in search of anyone that might look Jewish. "The Germans were here for three months from November 1941 to January 1942. Of course, people were very much afraid. They didn't know what could happen to us." Not surprisingly, prior to the arrival of the German army the rumour mill was in overdrive in Mozhaisk. "Before the Germans reached here, they occupied Ukraine and people heard rumours of what had taken place there." Knowing what was to come, people were terrified. Some fled.

What surprised me most about Serafimove's recollections was not just the make-up of the German army, as she was to explain, but the manner in which the first Germans arrived. "There were army reconnaissance people coming into our house dressed in white camouflage. They came on skis. Then they blew up our church, the explosion hit our windows and they were broken."

Serafimove went on to describe the composition of the German army.

"There were not only Germans in the army, there were Czechs, Finns and others." Young men, conscripts, for the most part, subject to insidious Nazi propaganda. Under orders in a strange land. Fearful young men unaccustomed to the local language, geography or topography. In the steppes of Russia in the dead of winter. Circumstances conspired to turn these young men into killers. Once-warm young men who had known love turned cold, indifferent to human suffering. Racists now. Anti-Semitic, too, willing to carry out the most heinous of crimes. They were, Serafimove remarked, "different people of different character with different attitudes towards us. They behaved really badly."

And the chief targets were Jews and people who looked Jewish. Serafimove described how these young men went from house to house in search of Jews.

> The Germans came with a lamp because there was no light in the village so they were searching houses, taking lamps from the houses and going from one house to another with these lamps. There was one lady in the village and the Germans were chasing her – I don't know what they wanted from her, probably something bad. They came like this to the house where we stayed and they were searching, coming up to each person with a lamp looking at their faces and my sister had dark hair, they came up to her and put a light to her face and they obviously decided it was not her.

Despite the fear and despite the enormous risks, some Soviet people made great efforts to protect their neighbours, their friends. Knowing the danger, knowing the consequences.

> The woman they were looking for, the landlady, was able to hide her on top of the stove and later when the Germans searched the house she escaped and hid in a haystack.

Later she heard a woman was hanged in neighbouring Uvarovka. Whether she was the same woman taken away from Mozhaisk in the dead of night or not, Serafimove cannot remember. It matters little.

A woman was hanged.

The Great Patriot War marks the high point of the Soviet Union, its Herculean moment, the Siege of Leningrad its finest hour. To this day that heroism is celebrated every year. The Soviet Union stood tall and firm against fascism and won. A special 60th anniversary commemorative medal of the Great Patriotic War was created by Russian President Vladimir Putin in 2004. Serafimove proudly shows us her medal awarded to participants in the war, along with a photograph of the day she received it of which she is immensely proud. "I feel pride because even though I was only thirteen years old I went to the hospital to provide some assistance. It was my small contribution to the main cause. When every Victory Day approaches there's always a letter of greeting from the President." She reaches for the letter and reads…

> Respected Serafimove Mikhailovna please accept our hearty greetings on the 69th anniversary of the Great Victory. This holiday is forever recorded in the history of the country and into the fate of every Russian citizen. From deep in my heart I wish you health, well-being and happiness. President of the Russian Federation, Vladimir Putin.

"I consider Victory Day to be the greatest holiday because we protected our country. I am proud of my contribution, however small it might be, and I am proud for my country – I feel pride for our people", Serafimove says as she carefully stores away Putin's letter.

It is a cynical gesture, Tikhon Dzyadko argues, yet more manipulation of the masses. He has a different narrative. Prior to my arrival in Russia, RAIN TV questioned whether it was necessary to defend Leningrad from the Nazis at the expense of 750,000 lives (some estimates put the number of deaths as high as 1.1 million) of civilians blockaded in the city with scarcely any food for 872 days. Hunger and cold stalked the city. Dogs, cats, horses, rats, birds gradually disappeared as the population sought food from whatever source. Sawdust mixed with flour to make bread, soup from leather, people even turned to eating the dead. The streets were lined with corpses as the Soviet winter made the digging of graves by the hungry and the weak impossible. To this day the siege of Leningrad remains a potent symbol of Soviet/Russian resistance to Western encroachment and imperialism. Any questioning of what happened in Leningrad is quickly slapped down.

Putin's spokesman Dmitry Peskov accused RAIN of disrespecting the suffering of the Soviet people and moved against the station. RAIN still exists but was forced to rescind its Leningrad commentary. Any questioning of Russian orthodoxy carries great risks. "There's a meeting in the Kremlin once a week," Tikhon claims, "and during these meetings the guys in the administration they tell how to cover incidents. This doesn't mean that in each media there is a guy with a gun who is standing behind the editor in chief, but these editors in chief they understand what they can do and what they can't do."

Tikhon's view of what happened during the Great Patriotic War is not shared by Serafimove. "In my soul I am a communist." After the war she returned to school, trained as an accountant, and for a time worked as a receptionist in a centre that distributed potatoes from the collective farms. Later she worked for the Moscow Energy Company. These were the good times that Serafimove remembers.

> The good thing about these times was we had our own industry. There were plants, there were factories, we had our own clothes-making factories, a plant for graphic printing. People were given apartments. For example, I got this apartment for free. I remember at weekends, at holidays we used to go to pick potatoes, to work on weekends on collective farms to help the people there. We did it with pleasure.

And then it all came crashing down. The abrupt switch from a centrally planned economy to a neoliberal one caught everyone in the Soviet Union off-guard, except for the tiny minority that gobbled up state enterprises. It was, to borrow a phrase, a shock doctrine that left people reeling and pauperised whole sectors of the Russian populace.

> We used to have everything here before. Everything is closed down now. There are no jobs here. They started privatising enterprises. Everything belonged to the

state, and all of sudden it was all privatised. People now go to Moscow for work. In my time there were plants here in Mozhaisk. Previously after graduating from the institute a job was provided for you. And nowadays my grandson has graduated from university and he now has to look for a job himself. I had to help my daughter to pay for my grandson's education, to cover food and clothes. My grandson studied in Moscow and lived in a hostel there. And I had to help them. There was a time when all this was free.

Personal freedom has also been lost, according to Serafimove. "It was not like that before," her conversational mantra.

It's no longer safe as it once was to walk the streets. Russia's children taken from the country. It was not like that before. You could go out any time, day or night, and now all of this has changed. Our children are being adopted in America, abandoned children, and it was not like that before. There were no millionaires, no billionaires at that time. It shouldn't be like this.

There were other deprivations. She could no longer enjoy her beloved caviar. "Of course, I don't eat black caviar now and I even do not remember the taste, but in previous times I could afford it," she wistfully muses. "It was sold in shops before the war and I could buy it, but now I can't."

Before I left, I told Serafimove that as a child in Ireland we used to pray for the conversion of Russia. She looked puzzled, perhaps even hurt. I had to explain that it was presumed that communism and religious belief were incompatible, that religious practice was banned and that all churches were destroyed, priests sent to the gulags. While it was true, she told me, that party members were prohibited from openly practicing religion, people found a way.

Many baptised children and if someone died there was a religious ceremony. I baptised my own children and nobody said anything to me about it. The people did

what they wanted according to our tradition, and I
think that God helps me and I was able to live to this
age because I believe in God.

Perhaps Irish prayers were more powerful than the ideological superstructure that governed communist Russia. Or
perhaps, just perhaps, our prayers were superfluous. Russia
didn't need them after all.

Suddenly Serafimove said: "I said a lot. I think that's
enough," and brought the interview to a conclusion. On the way
out I asked who was the Soviet Union's greatest leader. Without hesitation she said "Stalin". And then, as an afterthought,
General Zhukov. Heroes she credits with the reconstruction
of the Soviet Union. Born into extreme poverty, Zhukov was
the Commanding General of the entire Red Army during the
Great Patriotic War and is considered by many within Russia
to be the greatest military mind in their entire history. A sculpture by Vyacheslav Klykov of him astride a horse on a granite
pedestal trampling over Nazi banners, weighing 100 tons, was
unveiled in 1995 close to Red Square in the centre of Moscow.

But I have one last request for Serafimove. Would she take
me to the Tomb of the Unknown Soldier in Mozhaisk? Before
she agrees, there is one task she has to complete. This diminutive, white-haired, eighty-five-year-old communist woman
must put on her lipstick.

> Now I will comb my hair and put on my lipstick. I never
> used lipstick in the past but once one of my colleagues
> asked me, "why don't you use lipstick?" So, I decided
> to use it and after I did it once I continued to do it all
> the time. Now I have my lipstick on and I am beautiful
> now. Now my lips are red. Now I have become more
> beautiful, that's very good.

We drive the short distance to the war memorial, the Monument to the Soldier-Liberator, his hands raised high above the
city. In his right hand he holds a machine gun. An estimated

50,000 Soviet soldiers died here. A wall of memory holds the names of more than 2,500 Mozhais who fought on the fronts and died during the war years. Among them Serafimove locates the name of the director of her school. In their memory the Eternal Flame burns, before which Serafimove stands reverentially mouthing prayers. Here, too, is a sculpture in the style of Soviet realism: a woman and a man striding forward, hammer and sickle held aloft. Around Serafimove two boys cycle by, indifferent to her presence and, it would appear, to the historical significance of the place.

And so, the generational polarised perception of recent Russian/Soviet history is played out. The arch-critical young journalist concerned about the manipulation of history and the restrictions of the press, freedom of expression and political activity. The older woman nostalgic for the more heroic past, to a time of plenty.

Back in Moscow, Gorky Central Park café is in full flow, even if the prices are exorbitant. Young people and families stroll in the sunshine, beach volleyball played by the young and the energetic. It has all the appearances of an open, relaxed, tolerant society. But even here, aspects of Russian life are hidden. For LGBT people in particular, since the 2013 law that prohibited the "propaganda of non-traditional sexual relations", their oppression is real.

Having shed the shackles of communism in December 1991, Russia decriminalised homosexual relationships in 1993, the same year it was decriminalised in Ireland. While decriminalisation – whenever and wherever it happens – is a watershed moment, it doesn't of course change deeply ingrained and hostile attitudes. Russia, particularly in its deeply conservative heartland, remains a cold place for gays and lesbians, as well as for bisexual, transgender and intersex individuals.

But it was the 2013 law that prohibited the "propaganda of non-traditional sexual relations among minors in a manner that distributes information aimed at the formation among minors of non-traditional sexual attitudes, attractiveness to non-traditional sexual relations, misperceptions of the social equivalence of traditional and non-traditional sexual relations, or imposing information about non-traditional sexual relations that evokes interest in such relations" that caused such an outcry.

The controversy was still rumbling on as I headed to Russia in 2015. Anxious to ascertain what impact that law was having on the LGBT community, I met with two of its members. While we met openly in Gorky Park it was like hiding in plain sight. We could have been speaking about any subject, no one took any notice. However, we had to promise that only blurred images and distorted voices could be used in the broadcast film.

There has been widespread hysteria and homophobia in the last number of years, one of the LGBT spokespersons told me. "I'm afraid for my own life, for my wellbeing, for my security," the woman said, "and that's why I decided I don't want to admit it openly. I'm considered a freak, even though I'm a human being, like anyone else."

Later I thought of the soldier liberator in Mozhaisk. For these two young people there was no sense of liberation. And as far as Tikhon Dzyadko is concerned, neither the defeat of Nazism nor the collapse of communism has brought liberation to the Russian people. Just another repressive regime. First the Tsars, then the communists, and now the oligarchs. The Empire's new clothes.

According to the *Guinness Book of Records*, World War II, or the Great Patriotic War, has the unenviable distinction of having the highest number of casualties – estimated at 56.4 million people, of whom 24 million were Soviet citizens. Russia's cruel history. One death is a tragedy, a millions deaths is a statistic, Stalin is purported to have said.

And in conversation with Serafimove, one tragic death stands out. A soldier or a group of soldiers from the German Nazi army approach a house in Mozhaisk, 100 kilometres from Moscow, in the winter of 1941-42. A woman is taken away. Nothing is known of her or her family. Only the fear and dread she experienced that night can be guessed. She must have guessed her fate. Did she go quietly or was she dragged kicking and screaming, her husband and children helpless to intervene? Did the neighbours cling to their own children, shushing them inside bolted doors? Did anyone subsequently ask of her fate?

And what about her captors? Were these young men also fearful or emboldened by their own power, the arbitrators of who lives and who dies? What became of them in the long march back to Germany across the Soviet steppes, if they made it that far? Were they too among the countless dead? Did they grow old in a prosperous West Germany or were they to suffer in the inaptly named German Democratic Republic?

Nobody even knows for sure if the captured woman in Mozhaisk was the same woman who was hanged in neighbouring Uvarovka. Had she the time or the inclination to contemplate the sky before her death? Did she pray before her death? The former unlikely, I would have thought. The latter in Communist Soviet Union? Are there atheists at the gallows?

What we do know is that none of the memorialising will bring her back. None of the grandiosity associated with war's aftermath. None of the elegance of Tolstoy. None of the high drama of Tchaikovsky. None of the sculpted triumphalism of Vyacheslav Klykov. None of the Putin parchments.

Perhaps the truth lies far from the site of her death, in Pegeen Mike's observation in John Millington Synge's *The Playboy of the Western World,* written in 1907 — the same year that the Russian Tsarists tried unsuccessfully to turn back the tide of history by dissolving the second Duma or parliament that included eighteen Bolshevik deputies. In Synge's play, Christy Mahon, he with "a mighty spirit in him and a gamy heart", boasts of killing his father and his willingness to "face a foxy divil – on the flags of hell", and to stand up to "the loosed khaki cut-throats, or the walkin dead" is eventually revealed for his cowardice. Stripped of Christy's imaginative heroism, Pegeen Mike confronts him.

> … a strange man is a marvel, with his mighty talk; but what's a squabble in your back yard, and the blow of a loy, have taught me that there's a great gap between a gallous story and a dirty deed.

A stranger calls to Mozhaisk. A woman is taken from her home. A woman was hanged in Uvarovka. A life was ended. A dirty deed.

Decades later, a woman sits pensively among all the triumphalism of war's victory. A woman who knows war. Serafiimove says almost imperceptibly, "They should stop all these wars." An old Russian woman speaks – from experience.

As for Tikhon's assertion that Russia is a cruel place, well…

# 8

# A Bomb Goes Off in Africa

## *Somalia*

This infernal heat and worse to come. The disappearing rain, less and less each year. The sun-dried earth cracks open a little wider each year. Emergency-built houses stand sentinel-like, row after row. Houses with hot tin roofs and sides too. Except when it's cold and heat is needed, then they bleed heat. Cold comfort. Other hovel-homes are a kaleidoscopic patchwork of rags and plastic. Sticks too. And little else, inside or out. Mats and a few cooking pots. That's it.

Life. Luuq, Somalia.

Large groups of women, men and children seek refuge under sparse trees. Sixty thousand in total, spread across a couple of square kilometres. There is little talk. Women sit. Men wander. Children are still, eyes wide. Many look on in incomprehension. How has it come to this?

And then the seeming inescapability of war. A war without winners. Was it ever thus, except for those who declare war? And the ever-present threat of famine. Not that this country hasn't known past famines. Death stalks this land. Baby deaths. Child deaths. Teenage deaths. Mother deaths. Father deaths. Fighter deaths. Victim deaths. Passers-by deaths. The ghosts of past famines, past wars that refuse to go away, 1992 and then in 2011/2012. And today in Mogadishu, a city in lockdown. Nobody is allowed to move. Car-less streets for a population of 2.5 million people, a quarter of the country's inhabitants.

This is Somalia in 2018.

It is 14 October 2017. A truck stuffed with a hundred kilograms of military-grade and homemade explosives. A driver triggers his own death on one of the busiest junctions in all of Mogadishu, now renamed the 14 October Junction. Detonated next to a fuel tanker and a minibus full of schoolchildren. Carnage of unprecedented proportions. The biggest bomb in all of Africa. Ever. The deadliest bomb attack in all of Somalia's bloody history. Six hundred lives extinguished, many incinerated beyond recognition, the injured beyond counting.

This was the world's worst terrorist attack since 9/11, yet on the Richter scale of global news it barely registers. A bomb explodes in Africa... Six hundred people dead...

> Something terrible happened here. It was a busy time, 3.30. Six hundred people were killed here at this junction. In 2017. In one day. It was a truck bomb. It was afternoon. At this time. And the truck bomb exploded inside the road. Then the situation changed in minutes. On what happened that day, you can't talk. Even myself I can't say what I saw that day. Everything was scattered. Levelled to the ground. People died everywhere. They were scattered. The bombs were flying. The bodies were dying. Body parts flying. Really it was terrible. Really it was just a disaster.

Sunday, 9 September 2018. Along with Ahmedweli Hussain, a young local TV and radio journalist, I stood at the exact spot where the bomb exploded. Apart from some still-shattered buildings, some open spaces where buildings once stood, it was as it was minutes before the 14 October bomb exploded. Snarled traffic. Toyota Hiluzes bulldozing their way through. Red three-wheeled *tuc-tuc* taxis competing for space. And customers. School-going children. Office workers. Business people. Burka-wearing women. People jay-walking. People hawking goods.

A Mogadishu day.

We arrived at the scene in an armoured vehicle, the first time I had travelled in one. This, I was told, could withstand an RPG (rocket-propelled grenade). Being there was not just a threat for Ken O'Mahony and myself but for an ill-at-ease Ahmedweli Hussain and for all those who happened to be passing. A threat they were not taking lightly, and with good reason. "The security risk in Mogadishu is very high. It is very high. This is dangerous," he told me. "I feel insecure. When in Somalia, you should feel insecure. You might be targeted easily. As a westerner you will not survive. We cannot stay long."

We didn't. Perhaps ten to fifteen minutes.

On the way, Ahmedweli in his faultless English continued:

> At the time of the explosion we were broadcasting our news programme. That programme was live. I heard definite explosion. The situation changed in minutes. I thought that we are under attack. There was destruction everywhere. Parts of the radio station, windows were broken. Mirrors scattered everywhere. At least three of my colleagues were injured. Screaming for help.

> After a few minutes I arrived at the scene of the truck bomb. It was really terrible. Outside of our studio everywhere you can see parts of human bodies flying broken. People were blown into the air. And the body parts fell like rain on the other people. The road was packed with by-standers and cars. Really it was just a disaster.

> The scene I have visited was unspeakable. I can't say any word about that day. Everyone was calling for help. People were screaming. Blood everywhere. There is no tragedy worse than what I have seen. People were coming to the dead bodies of their relatives. Can't recognise

146

*Udi Gore and Usam Alleat, Jerusalem, Palestine/Israel.*

*Eitan Bronstein, Tel Aviv, Palestine/Israel.*

*Zahra Nahar, Beirut, Lebanon.*

*Abedullah Talib Salhani,*
*Beirut, Lebanon.*

*Dr Mohammed al-Khatib,*
*Beirut, Lebanon.*

*Bassam Aramin and Rami Elhahan, Palestine/Israel.*

*Tikhon Dzyadko, Moscow, Russia.*

*Statue of Joseph Stalin in Muzeon Park also known as*
*Fallen Monument Park or Park of Fallen Heroes, Moscow, Russia.*

*Soviet utopianism.*

*Serafimove Kazakova,
Mozhaisk, Russia.*

*A group of displaced women in Luuq, Somalia.*

*Peadar King with the late Minister for Constitutional Affairs, Abdurahman Hosh Jibril, in Mogadishu, Somalia.*

*Somali radio and television journalist Ahmedweli Hussain.*

*Nuurto Abdi Hassan, Luuq, Somalia.*

*Kristin Douglas, Jeju Island, South Korea.*

*Protesters on Jeju Island, South Korea.*

*Tangerine farmer Jung Young-hee, Jeju Island, South Korea.*

*Yang Yoon-mo, Professor of Film Studies at*
*Seoul Institute of the Arts, Jeju Island, South Korea.*

*Aluel Kuol, Bor, South Sudan.*

*Arem Alier, Bor, South Sudan.*

*Ateny Wel Alier, Bor, South Sudan.*

them. Can't recognise them as humans. Some people hold the body covered with blood. Even you can't recognise them as a human being. What I have seen that day is still fresh in my mind. I remember…

And his voice trails off…

The next morning some relatives were arguing over the bodies. Some say "this is my son". "No, it is our son." Someone else coming saying: "No, it's our uncle." Because no-one can recognise the bodies of their loved ones who were killed. Yes. Some victims were panned beyond recognition. It was a disaster. Really it was a disaster. Thousands of people gathered at the hospital. Thousands of people gathered at the scene. People were crying. Children were crying looking for their parents. Parents were crying looking for their children.

Back in the television station, he shows me footage from the aftermath of the bomb. In the opening shot are smouldering, still burning, tangled buildings. As the camera draws back, black clouds fill the sky. A lone man appears, hands on head. Incredulity. Bafflement. Horror. Not for the first time, the horror, the horror. Another man stands, hands on head. People scrabbling among the debris. Bodies pulled from the rubble and carried on makeshift stretchers. One eyewitness says to camera, "These are the scenes the eyes cannot bear to look at."

I continue to search through the footage.

Evening time, as the sun sets, the fires still burn and long-shadowed relatives go from mutilated corpse to mutilated corpse. Some of the dead faces are covered. People lift a cloth, look, and walk on. Other dead bodies are just lying there with no one to attend to them. And then, body parts beyond recognition. Another man comes into view. He too, hands on head.

The truck lying on its side, astonishingly still intact for the most part.

> I heard the bomb. Even after hours, I couldn't hear anything because it was just a deafening big explosion. People died everywhere. Everything was scattered. There was blood everywhere. Even the human bodies. You see bones. Hair. Legs. Body parts were flying. Flying everywhere.

> Even after six months you can't stay here because of the smell. Still smelling the people when it rains. And a year later you are still finding body parts. That day was a terrible day.

And then there were the injured.

> I was shocked. People started to scream. The wounded people. They were coming and they were screaming. They were lying down. Please take me to the hospital. They were coming fractured. I remember one of our friends: he was a journalist. He was fractured. He was walking on one leg. He was screaming. Please open the gate. It's me. It's me. One of my colleagues who was sitting there. He just fell down. Was just him. Voom. He was bleeding.

> So, it was a dark afternoon. A dark afternoon.

> The scene I visited was unspeakable. I can't say any word about that day. Everyone was calling for help.

> There is no tragedy worse than what I have seen.

Situated in the Horn of Africa along the Gulf of Aden and the Indian Ocean with access to the Red Sea and the Suez Canal, Somalia gained its independence in 1960, when the former British and Italian colonies of the State of Somaliland and the Trust Territory of Somalia united to form the Somali Republic, a union that never gelled. Forty years after independence, the still feudalised country spiralled into near total collapse.

Clan-based militias, dire economic policies, widespread corruption and a costly territorial war with Ethiopia upended the country. Land-grabbing, looting of food and resources, and repeated population displacements resulted in a large-scale famine in 1992 during which an estimated 240,000 people lost their lives.

Out of the chaos the Al-Qaeda-aligned Al Shabaab emerged. Throughout 2007 and 2008, as Al Shabaab gained control over vast areas of Somalia, the crisis deepened. A humanitarian crisis ensued.

Drought added another layer to an already crisis-ridden country.

From 2016 to 2018, three successive below-average rainy seasons resulted in crop failure, widespread livestock deaths and loss of assets, causing large-scale population displacements, hunger and malnutrition. In 2018, unexpected heavy rains and the cyclone Sagar led to widespread flooding and damage to infrastructure and shelter, as well as an increase in water-borne diseases. In 2017 there were 79,172 cholera cases including 1,159 associated deaths.

Estimates (2018) from the United Nations Office for the Coordination of Humanitarian Affairs (UNOCHA) put the number of people in need of urgent humanitarian assistance at 4.2 million. In addition, there are 2 million internally displaced people across the whole of Somalia, out of a total population of approximately 12 million.

The humanitarian crisis in Somalia is, according to UNOCHA, among the most complex and long-standing emergencies in the world. The social costs of war have been enormous, leaving Somalia with some of the lowest human development indicators in the world. To a very large extent, and notwithstanding the recent efforts at political stabilisation, Somalia remains a crisis-ridden, ungoverned space, its capital city Mogadishu a traumatised space.

Prior to going to Somalia in December 2018, no one I spoke to had heard of the Mogadishu massacre. Not one. Not the people who normally take an interest in such things. Most had, however, heard of *Black Hawk Down* and the killing of eighteen US soldiers. Given the personal, cultural and historical connections that exist between Ireland and the United States, it is of course unreasonable to compare what happened in 9/11 New York to what happened in Mogadishu. Mogadishu is a world away from the vast majority of Irish people.

But what happened in Mogadishu was no less traumatic for all those involved than what happened in New York. And the absence of coverage is indicative of the Eurocentric, western-focused prism of mainstream media.

In that world, Africa does not count.

It's 11 September as I write. The anniversary of that other massacre. Eighteen years have passed. Today 9/11 features on the first page of the RTÉ News webpage. Yesterday, the *Irish Independent* headlined: "Rocket blast at US embassy in Kabul on anniversary of 9/11". The *Irish Examiner* ran an almost identical headline: "Rocket blast at US embassy in Afghanistan on anniversary of 9/11".

Following the Mogadishu massacre, *The Irish Times* carried three stories on "the most powerful bomb" ... "creating an enormous fireball" ... "biggest blast ever witnessed in Somalia's capital". In the third story it put the death toll at "more than 300". That figure was never revised upwards. And no further articles appeared.

Coverage in Britain was equally sparse. *The Guardian* headlined the atrocity on its front page with a photograph of the bomb site, "Somalia reeling as terrorist attacks leaves 500 casualties". BBC Radio 4's *Today* did an interview with Anne Soy, their senior Africa correspondent at 06.13 hours. On subsequent bulletins, nothing. None of the other broadsheet English papers, *The Times*, *The Telegraph*, put the bombing on their front pages. *The Independent* covered the bombing in its News-World-Africa section emphasising the United States link to the atrocity rather than the human catastrophe that unfolded. The US is mentioned three times, US President Donald Trump, once. *Metro,* the free tabloid newspaper, referenced the Mogadishu bombing in its World Bites section while headlining with Taylor Swift eating a kebab.

However, by Monday 16 October, one journalist, *The Independent*'s Will Gore, challenged western media's neglect of the massacre. "Why is the press reporting on Hurricane Ophelia but not the worst ever terrorist attack?" he asked.

> Saturday's truck bomb in the Somalian capital, Mogadishu, received moderately little attention … If such an attack took place … anywhere else in the West – it would plainly have taken centre stage for weeks.

> Somalia, indeed, is far down the list of nations we might think of in that bracket of troubled places. We know all about Syria and Iraq; and quite a lot about Libya. Yemen is next in line; and of course, the kidnapping of 276 (Nigerian) schoolgirls by Boko Haram…

> If we think much of Somalia it is probably in connection with pirates … the US in 1992 and 1993 – mainly because one battle during the international effort to bring order to Somalia was immortalised in the film Black Hawk Down.

Gore writes with a nuanced pen. It's not that the "relatively wealthy, predominantly white, Westerners don't care about relatively poor, mostly non-white foreigners in war-torn or disease-ridden places a long way away", he argues. Human suffering weighs heavily on most human beings. But most are sheltered from the reality of human suffering. A sheltering provided, for the most part, by mainstream media, content to blow hard on the frailties and foibles of people closer to home along with the inevitable preoccupation with the weather.

Gore wonders if "we should pay a little more attention to difficult political situations in far-flung parts of the world; and
rather less to the potential consequences of a system of mod-
erate low pressure in the Atlantic, no matter how much hot air
it produces". It was an important and pertinent question, and
one that I have often considered.

On 8 July 2011, I was watching the RTÉ Nine O'Clock
news. Nothing unusual about that. About five items in, there
was a report on a plane crash in the Democratic Republic of
the Congo (DRC) in which forty-eight people lost their lives.
Forty-eight people. A story picked up by many media in the
US, Europe, Britain and Ireland. For the families involved, tre-
mendous sadness and loss. The story struck a chord. People
die in much larger numbers all over Africa and are never reported. And the DRC has been, for nearly all of its existence,
awash with death.

Eight years earlier *The Irish Times* reported on another
plane crash.

> More than 120 passengers were sucked out of a trans-
> port plane to their deaths when its massive rear cargo
> door burst open at 33,000 feet over the Democratic Re-
> public of Congo. The aircraft was carrying up to 200
> policemen and their families across war torn Congo,
> formerly Zaire, on Thursday night.

The article provides details of the plane (the Russian-built
Ilyushin 76), its logo (emblazoned with Ukrainian Cargo Air-
lines on its fuselage), the altitude at which the plane was flying at the time of the accident (33,000 feet), when the accident
happened (forty-five minutes in), the nationality of the pilots
(Russian and Ukranian), details of the survivors (nine), their
condition (traumatised), the plane's destination (Lubumbashi)
and its main economic activity (diamonds). All that and the
age-old trope of war-torn Congo.

All these technical details, meticulously recorded, in "war-torn Congo". Of the causes, extent and reality of war-torn Congo? Nothing. Of the millions of Congolese whose lives has been sucked out of them, shivering to their death as a result of the incessant war, in "war-torn Congo"? Not a mention.

According to studies by the US-based aid agency International Rescue Committee (IRC), some 5.4 million people died in the DRC between August 1998 and April 2007 from violence and war-related hunger and illness. By any yardstick it is an astounding figure – 5.4 million people who were killed or have died as a result of the ongoing conflict in the Democratic Republic of the Congo. It bears repeating. Between August 1998 and April 2007, 5.4 million people died from violence and war-related hunger and illness. The IRC estimate that as many as 45,000 people died every month in 2007. This is the deadliest conflict since World War Two in what has now become known as Africa's First World War or Africa's Great War.

The reality is that very few people have heard about what is happening in the DRC. A plane crashes in the Democratic Republic of the Congo and forty-eight people are killed – a story worth telling. Five-and-a-half million people killed over a ten-year period – a story ignored. Nothing. Forty-five thousand people died every month in 2007 – nothing.

On Friday, 16 March 2012, I flew from the DRC capital Kinshasa to Goma. In many respects that flight epitomised the great divide that exists within the DRC and beyond. Disproportionate number of white people, burly businessmen with bulging briefcases, women dripping with gold. The all-pervasive presence of senior army figures with sycophantic subservient foot soldiers to do their bidding. Pretty similar to the passenger list of the Russian-built Ilyushin 76. Except it was carrying not army personnel but up to 200 policemen and their families.

Not surprisingly, there were no street hawkers on board, no subsistence farmers, not one of the tens of thousands of people who visibly carry the physical burdens of the country's endemic poverty. Not one of the people who carry the wounds of the conflict that has blighted the country ever since the Belgians first set foot in the Congo region during the great scramble for Africa in the 1870s.

Perhaps therein lies a clue to the world's media coverage, that and the fetishisation of plane crashes. People who fly are for the most part middle-class, individuals with whom the media can identify.

Incidentally, according to the Geneva-based Bureau of Aircraft Archives, 159,718 people have died from civilian aircraft accidents between 1918 and 2018. That is less than three percent of the number of war-related deaths in the DRC.

In a piece entitled "Retreating from the World" for the *American Jerusalem Review* (December/January 2011), Jodi Enda argues that "many mainstream news outlets have turned their backs on the world". John Schidlovsky of the US-based International Reporting Project (2012), in an article entitled "International News Coverage – A Vanishing Species", has written:

> ... to shortchange, or to ignore, what is happening in Africa, Asia, Europe, Latin America or the Middle East while we focus so obsessively on the bumps and slumps of the latest political poll is to court disaster. The existence of a public that is uninformed, or under-informed, on global issues is an open invitation to the government to make missteps in foreign policy that can cost lives and dollars.

And then there remains the observation from the late revered broadcaster Edward R. Murrow, to whom a plaque bearing the inscription "he set standards of excellence that remain unsurpassed" is still on display in the CBS headquarters in New York City.

In a speech to the US Radio and Television News Directors Conference in 1958, Murrow declared:

I do not advocate that we turn television into a 27-inch wailing wall, where longhairs constantly moan about the state of our culture and our defense. But I would like to see it reflect occasionally the hard, unyielding realities of the world in which we live. I would like to see it done inside the existing framework, and I would like to see the doing of it redound to the credit of those who finance and program [sic] it. This instrument can teach, it can illuminate; yes, and it can even inspire. But it can do so only to the extent that humans are determined to use it to those ends.

Jazira One is the largest displaced people's camp in Luuq, close to the Kenyan and Ethiopian borders, home to tens of thousands of internally displaced people (IDPs). Here there was no shortage of evidence of the "hard, unyielding realities of the world in which we live". Hard and unyielding, too, was the climate which tens of thousands of people had to endure. A place of intense, hellish heat, no relieving breeze, in open unsheltered spaces.

Except at night. The hellish cold.

The years have taken their toll on fifty-two-year-old Ibrahim Abdi Mohamed, chief of Jiroon clan. So, too, has the incessant heat.

In the rainy season we used to get the feel of a fresh breeze, but now that fresh breeze lasts only while it's actually raining and when the rain stops you would think the dry season has come around again.

But it's war and death that preoccupied Ibrahim. "It is war that has brought us here," he tells me. "And it is war that has kept me here for the past seven years."

Ibrahim worked for an NGO, a dangerous occupation in Somalia. It is seen, by some, as collaboration with foreign infidels, traitors, and therefore legitimate targets.

His brother was also targeted.

155

My brother was twenty years old. He worked with me as staff with an NGO. For that he was killed. Killed before he got married. He was twenty years old.

I dropped him in the town centre. He had a milk jerrycan for his children. They killed him in front of me. I carried his bleeding body.

Following his brother's death Ibrahim fled, abandoning his wife and children in Wajid. It seemed as if he needed to justify his actions to me, as if he instinctively read or felt a sub-text in my expression. "You abandoned your family to save your own skin." Perhaps it is something he has wrestled with all these years. Perhaps it is something he has heard repeatedly. Looking me straight in the eye, he somewhat plaintively said: "You can understand my situation at that time, how I felt at that moment." The reality is that his situation was so far removed from my own world that it was not possible for me to know how he felt at that moment. Understand his world? His dilemma is beyond understanding, beyond comprehension. And perhaps his family was safer in his absence.

As I too was working with an NGO and Al Shabaab would kill those who work with NGOs. So, I hid and ran away from my children. I left Wajid at night in secret and in a hurry and a donkey was waiting in the bush. I took the donkey and we journeyed through the night and the following day as well. We passed through the bushes up to Dolow, and Dolow seemed not good so we returned here. It took us two nights and two days between Wajid and Luuq. That's ninety kilometres.

That's it.

There were other deaths. Many other deaths.

They don't like the NGOs. Anyone who works for them they kill. They decapitated a man. They displayed him in public by putting his head on his abdomen and when we saw that we ran.

He was not alone in his dilemma.

Of the many displaced persons I met in Luuq, running was a common theme. Running from war. Running from drought. Running from starvation.

In Luuq, I spent a morning talking to a group of women. They were eager conversationalists, unperturbed by the camera and all the paraphernalia that goes with making a documentary, undistracted by the curious children that had gathered around them. When asked if the children wouldn't mind standing out-of-shot, the women translated our requests in not quite the same tone. Instantly the children scattered. Formidable women.

Among them was Nuurto Abdi Hassan, strikingly beautiful in her bottle green hijab over a bright-pink dress that just skirted the dry, dusty ground, the hijab trimmed with a mustard band. Stand-out rings on her fingers. A Casio watch on her wrist, hands covered in henna designs. In the background was a woman draped in an astonishingly beautifully layered light blue head-to-toe dress. All this in a displacement camp of hastily constructed flimsy huts. Even in what appears to be the worst of circumstances, beauty matters.

Nuurto Abdi Hassan:

> Henna is used for beautification purposes and it smooths the legs and takes away the dry cracks. It is used as decoration on the legs and hands – decoration starts from the neck. Henna is about the cleanliness of the woman. It is done on legs and cures the dry cracks. It makes the legs and hands attractive – henna is one of the items that enhances the beauty of a woman, similar to bracelets and rings. First is to go to the female clothes market and when you are at the market you look for the cloth of your choice which enhances your figure. Whatever your preference or choice is, you buy it.

Beauty but hardship too.

> I had twelve children. Four died and the fifth was a miscarriage. Four died and eight are alive. I delivered all four alive. Most of my children died from vomiting and diarrhea.

Nuurto Abdi Hassan and her family travelled for three days and three nights on a donkey and cart. She and her family had managed to continue living in her home community in Goobato. Drought finally drove them out. "Thirst, hunger and bad drought is what I fled from."

> While we were on the way, do you know the little dik-dik? Small antelope. We chased and captured it. Slaughtered it and cooked it on the fire. The meat and the stock were given to the children. That is how we made it to Luuq.

It was a journey not without risks.

> Women are more vulnerable in war. There are men who rape women or kill them and men who don't. Men, they either die or run away, kill or get killed. Vulnerable women will get caught on their seat or caught while trying to hide and get raped or killed.

There were other risks too. Forced female genital mutilation. Nuurto does not spare me the details.

> The pharaonic circumcision and the religious/prescribed one are different – the pharaonic one is more harmful. If a girl undergoes the pharaonic one, she will find difficulty with periods and delivering and the husband will find it difficult to penetrate.

Cultural norms. Coercive norms too. With the rise of Al Shabaab, women's lives are subject to even more prohibition, more surveillance, more prescription. Nuurto was fourteen years old when she first started wearing the hijab. I could not but notice that children as young as three and four were now wearing it. When asked why the change, she simply said, "Al Shabaab".

Al Shabaab.

Back in Mogadishu, I met with the gentle, eloquent and softly-spoken Minister for Constitutional Affairs, Abdurahman Hosh Jibril. Shortly after we met, Abdurahman died at the age of sixty-three following a short illness after attending his daughter's wedding in Dubai. Born in Somalia, he graduated in sociology and law at Osgoode Hall Law School, York University, Toronto, Canada. His law practice in Canada specialised in refugee and immigration law, labour law and human rights law. In 2011, he returned to Somalia to help in the exercise of nation-building. Abdurahman was hosting a conference on the relationship between regional authorities and the central government within a new constitutional framework when I met him in the Peace Hotel, on the perimeter of Mogadishu's Green Zone. I approached him during a break in their deliberations and asked for an interview. Readily agreeing, he asked when it would suit me. I was anxious to understand who were Al Shabaab as well as his general sense of the security in the country.

His is an unvarnished version of recent Somali history.

> We are having a challenge because we are engaged with a virulent form of terrorism that has been messing up this country for the past fifteen years. We came out of civil war, and when the civil war happened, the government collapsed, all the institutions collapsed. And then these terrorists came with an unauthentic form of Islam, which is really alien to the Somali culture, to the Somali religion.

The context is in marked contrast to western perception, five words the critical difference: "An unauthentic form of Islam". That one word, unauthentic, subtly but importantly distinguishes it from the limited western coverage of the

Mogadishu bomb, significantly different from *The Irish Times* description of "the Islamist militant group Al Shabaab".

An adjective: a world of difference.

It is a practice *The Irish Times* has maintained. "Islamist gunmen attack beachside café in Mogadishu" (21 January 2016). "Five Islamist militants attacked a hotel at dawn in the Somali capital Mogadishu" (1 November 2015). "Islamists have forced their way into a hotel in Somalia" (27 March 2015).

*The Irish Independent* is no different. "The Horn of Africa nation continues to struggle to counter the Islamic extremist group" (25 March 2018). "The al Qaida-linked al-Shabaab … the Islamic extremist group" (16 October 2017).

A Google search of "Islamic extremism" garners 9,500,000 results in forty-two seconds.

Islam and gunmen. Islam and militants. Islam and extremism. The slow drip-drip messaging. Islam as the other. The threat. The danger.

Somalia's now deceased Minister for Constitutional Affairs had an altogether different perspective, one that did not minimise what is happening to his country, a country gripped by "a virulent kind of terrorism. Alien to Somali culture".

Aligned to and influenced by Al Qaeda, rooted in the Soviet-Afghan war, its expansion aided and abetted by the US-led invasion of Afghanistan and Iraq, Al Shabaab offered a sense of identity and belonging for the disaffected young men of Somalia. Young, vulnerable, easily manipulated kids.

Al Shabaab, "an Al Qaeda-linked Islamist movement made up of young kids many of whom were trained in Afghanistan and Pakistan", is how the Minister described the organisation. They got in contact with Al Qaeda. They were trained, they came back and they set up this movement.

*Ex nihilo nihil fit*, the Latin phrase that owes its origins to pre-Socratic Greek philosophy. Nothing comes from nothing. Shakespeare's King Lear said "Nothing will become of nothing", a variation of Parmenides' dictum. As it is with Al Shabaab. Without Al Qaeda there would be no Al Shabaab. Without the Soviet invasion of Afghanistan there would be no Al Qaeda. Without the US support for the mujahideen during the Soviet occupation of Afghanistan, it is possible Al Qaeda would never have come into existence. We simply don't know. The *what ifs* of history.

In the western narratives these are inconvenient contexts, best ignored. The reductionist "Islamic extremism" is a much simpler handle. The young men caught up in the slaughtering are easily caricatured. And western media, including Irish media, are willing accomplices.

Direct US involvement in Somalia also contributed to the rise of Al Shabaab, argues Abdurahman. In December 1992, the United States launched the UN Security Council-backed Operation Restore Hope. Notwithstanding former US Secretary of State Henry Kissinger's 1974 observation that "to give food aid to a country just because they are starving is a pretty weak reason", the mission was constructed as a life-saving humanitarian operation. It did not work out like that. Culminating in a whole series of engagements with Somali insurgents dubbed "skinnies" and "sammies", eighteen US soldiers were killed, seventy-three wounded, the highest US casualty numbers since the Vietnam War. Less well remembered are the one Malaysian soldier and the one Pakistani soldier who died. Lives remembered. Lives avenged. Lives forgotten. Following the loss of American lives, just-elected US President Bill Clinton pulled US troops from Somalia. Kissinger was proved right. In the view of Minister Jibril, Somalia was abandoned.

> I would say we were abandoned in 1994 when President Clinton pulled out the forces under Operation Restore Hope when 18 Americans were killed. I was living in Canada at the time. I was arguing at that time on TV and everywhere that Americans should not leave. If they leave, they will leave a vacuum. And that's exactly

what happened. That vacuum was filled by Al Shabaab, international criminals, pirates, all of them. Evil forces like to fill a vacuum.

Despite it all, Jibril never lost hope. He is "irrepressibly optimistic about the future of his country," wrote David Schultz, a former colleague from his Canadian university days who sent me an email following his viewing of the documentary we made in Somalia.

> Along with representatives from the regions, Chamber of Commerce, the Minister for Finance, Minister for Petroleum, Somali economists, the IMF, university professors, civil society groups, we have been discussing what kind of fiscal/federal model that fits our unique culture, geographic area in the context that we are in and so we are discussing taxation, revenue, customs, resource allocation, things like that.

The bricks and mortar of state building. The dull stuff. The absolutely vital stuff. State building in the most adverse of circumstances.

Now Abdurahman Hosh Jibril is dead. Sorely missed. Somalia's great loss. So too is Hassan Adan Isak. Hanged. On the first anniversary of the Mogadishu bomb. Convicted for detonating the deadliest bomb in Somalia's history.

Another Somali death. A bomb goes off in Africa.

And the effect of it all on the people of Somalia, I wonder? "Outrage", Jibril says. For the first time I notice the tone changes, the voice steeled. And then the voice softens again, more reflective. "It really shook the psyche of the Somali public. People who were killed were innocent bystanders, school children, prominent businessmen..." as his voice trails off and he looks away.

Six hundred people dead. Tens of thousands languish in displacement camps. No let-up on the hellish heat.

And a world that barely notices.

# 9

# Jeju's Aching Heart

## *South Korea*

Sister Stella Soh has an unusual distinction in South Korea: she is the first nun in the country's 200 years of Catholic connection to be convicted of criminal activity. The sixty-eight-year-old Benedictine is one of a determined group of protestors opposed to the Jeju Civilian-Military Complex Port in the village of Gangjeong on the island of Jeju off the lower tip of South Korea. For her and the other protestors the Civilian-Military Port is an oxymoron, a transparent cloak that fails to cover the real intent of the base. This is a military base, built to serve US military expansionism and to thwart Chinese expansionism.

Sister Stella's crime? Peaceful protest against a base that was designed to host the US navy and boost US presence in the region at a time when all eyes are on China's growth as a global power. "Yankees go home," she shouts defiantly in the driving rain as tornado-driven, white-water waves crash against the volcanic rocks on the seashore. "They are afraid to put me in prison. They are afraid of the international reaction. But I'm happy to go to prison to stop this base."

In that she failed. Doubly. In her attempt to go to jail and in her attempt to stop the military base.

At seven o'clock every morning, a disparate group – some religious, some not, some South Korean, some not – gather in protest and prayer outside the base. They gather to participate in the Buddhism-inspired 100-bow ritual that takes forty minutes to complete.

Most mornings in Gangjeong, I stood and watched as prayer mats were rolled out while an old pre-recorded prayer crackles into life. In deep and silent prayer, they prostrate themselves on the ground directly opposite the heavily guarded gate through which concrete-laden trucks pass. Even on the wettest of mornings, they gather. With hands joined and in bare feet as rain trickles down their faces, these are moments of deep reverence.

> I promise not to be swayed by the false notion that I can attain true happiness by placing my hopes and aspirations in the pursuit of material possessions.
>
> I endeavour to listen deeply to the movements of my heart and to those of the world around me in helping to build a world where peace truly reigns.
>
> It is with gratitude and deep respect that I acknowledge the preciousness of nature.

All this was in stark contrast to the violence of the destruction all around them.

It is difficult not to be moved by the sight of these praying protestors. Their serenity. Their simplicity. Their prayerfulness. And then that jarring thought. That this is all foolishness. Looking on, that's how it seemed. All that prayer. Reminders of nothing more than our own impotence. Another reminder, too, of a meeting in the distant past.

English peace activist Bruce Kent, then a practising Catholic priest, attended a Campaign for Nuclear Disarmament public meeting in Ireland. Asked if prayer could bring disarmament, he stumbled. I noticed. My once deeply embedded Catholicism told me prayer moves mountains. If ever there was a challenge to the prayerful, this was it.

Here on this island of Jeju, the challenge is mountainous. Deeper than mountains. This military industrial complex that rides rough-shod over all our lives. Rides rough-shod over all that prayer. But here the words of T.S. Eliot echo: "Prayer is more than an order of words, the conscious occupation of the praying mind, or the sound of the voice praying." How T.S. Eliot resonated on those early wet mornings. Perhaps it wasn't foolishness after all. Perhaps?

Meanwhile, watching, were stern-looking private security guards. Glacial. Armed. Severe in their expressionlessness. Later at 12 o'clock, Catholic mass is celebrated at the gate. Delaying tactics. Followed by the prayer of the rosary, also prolonging the prayerful protest. Priests and nuns sit on white plastic chairs around a makeshift altar, among them Sr. Stella and Irish priest Pat Cunningham. As the trucks approach, four guards physically remove each participant in the mass to one side. No eye contact is made. No words are spoken. This is a well-rehearsed choreographed response. Years of practice. The trucks make their way.

For those for whom mass does not call, a very different kind of protest.

They too come to protest, join hands, dance and sing in front of the gate. Some of the prayerful remain on. Each ritual seamlessly flowing one into the other. It is a joyful and sometimes noisy postscript to the earlier sombre protest, that whispering sceptic in full voice that this too is all foolishness. Until some people stand in front of a truck and the atmosphere suddenly changes. Each protestor is quickly isolated, surrounded by guards and whisked away. Protestors know this only too well. Their response, too, is well choreographed. The intention is to delay, delay a truck. Cumulatively these moments of delay count. And the counting costs.

"Personally, I think it is very important to take every opportunity available to stand in front of the cement truck,"

Kristin Douglas tells me. Douglas, an international peace activist, travelled in solidarity with the people of Gangjeong from another US military base in Hawaii where she lives.

> Because it slows down the process of building this base. And for every five minutes it takes to move me, or to move another person, or to move a nun, or to move a Father, it's going to take that much longer for a warship to pull into port. They all add up and it feels good to be part of an effort that slows down the march of the military machine here.

The delaying tactics didn't work. But it cost an additional 27.5 billion won ($23.8 million) according to the South Korean navy, which was allegedly incurred due to "the fourteen-month delay in the port's construction period owing to illegal obstruction of operations".

Not the outcome the protestors wished for, but some consolation nonetheless. That was until the navy sought to recoup the bill from them.

Where once soft corals grew and where halibut and squid swam, now stands a huge sprawling concrete slab corralled against local objectors by a three-metre-high steel fence, patrolled by an army of police and private security personnel. Built by the construction wing of the electronics giant Samsung and wholly owned by the South Korean government, the base was critical to US President Barack Obama's tilt towards Asia. Obama told the Australian parliament in November 2011:

> As a Pacific nation, the United States will play a larger and long-term role in shaping this region and its future ... I have directed my national security team to make our presence and mission in the Asia Pacific a top priority... As we plan and budget for the future, we will allocate the resources necessary to maintain our strong military presence in this region. Our enduring interests in the region demand our enduring presence in the region.

And it is that very policy shift that concerns those who oppose this base. That, along with the other footholds that the US military has established in the region stretching from Diego Garcia in the Indian Ocean, from which 2,000 people were forcefully removed in the 1960s and 1970s to Darwin in Australia, the Pacific island of Guam, the Philippines, Thailand, Singapore, Okinawa in Japan and South Korea in order to accommodate a US military base.

And South Korea has the distinction of having the largest overseas US military base in the world. Opened in June 2018, Pyeongtaek military base is expected to house nearly 45,000 troops, contractors, and family members by 2022. A *Time* magazine article reported that in addition to 2.5 kilometres of runway:

> … the base includes a 310,000 square foot shopping complex [where] soldiers in fatigues eat Popeye's chicken and drink from Arby's cups in a food hall where a wall mural reads: 'Our customers are heroes'. The base could be a suburban slice of Anytown USA, laid over Pyeoungtaek's rice paddies. The more than 650 buildings being built or renovated across a land area about the size of central Washington DC include four schools and five churches, a hospital, the largest gym of any overseas base, a bowling alley, and an 18-hole golf course.

Big, but clearly not big enough for US strategic military needs. They need Jeju too.

"The primary purpose of US military bases in Asia," according to Dr. Jung Young-sin of the Social Science Faculty, Jeju National University, "is to check China's expansion." China's economy is expected to exceed that of the United States by 2030. China will also have a very strong military as its economy grows. "The US fears that," Dr. Young-sin told me, "and wants to prevent China from replacing the US as the dominant power in the region. The reality is this Jeju naval base will escalate tension and political conflict in this area, between the US and China and between China and South Korea."

The United States maintains nearly 800 overseas military bases in more than 80 countries and territories. With 83 military bases, South Korea has the third highest number outside of the United States – Germany has 181 and Japan has 122. Maintaining these bases, according to David Vine, Associate Professor of Sociology at American University, Washington DC, cost the US taxpayer $160-$200 billion in 2014. In 2016, there were 24,189 US personnel stationed in South Korea. Vine estimates that the additional cost to the United States of each soldier serving overseas ranges between $10,000 and $40,000.

Jeju is a small volcanic island, 73 kilometres from west to east, 31 kilometres from north to south, and 130 kilometres from the southern coast of South Korea. Listed by UNESCO in 2007 as a World Heritage Site – South Korea's only such site – its moniker is the island of three Ws: wind, women and water. Traditionally, the island has had more women than men (109,907 men and 138,984 women, just after the end of the Korean war in 1953) due to the cumulative effect of the kidnapping and deportation of men by the victorious Japanese Imperial Army in 1910 to work in mines and factories in Japan and Manchuria, the loss of men in the Korean War, and prior to that the loss of men to fishing. In the 1870s there were only 83 men for every 100 women, an imbalance now corrected. Once a honeypot for tourists and in particular South Korean honeymooners (in 2017, a staggering 64,991 flights flew, 178 every day, between the South Korean capital Seoul and Jeju, a distance of 455 kilometres), the island now has an altogether different notoriety. Writing in the *New York Times* in 2011, US political activist Gloria Steinem described the beauty of, and the threat to, the island:

> Jeju isn't called the most beautiful place on earth for nothing. Ancient volcanoes have become snow-covered

peaks with pure mountain streams running down to volcanic beaches and reefs of soft coral. In between are green hills covered with wildflowers, mandarin orange groves, nutmeg forests, tea plantations and rare orchids growing wild. UNESCO, the United Nation's educational, scientific and cultural organisation, has designated Jeju Island a world natural heritage site. Now, a naval base is about to destroy a crucial stretch of the coast of Jeju, and will do this to dock and service destroyers with sophisticated ballistic missile defense systems and space war applications. This naval base is not only an environmental disaster on an island … it may be a globally dangerous provocation besides.

This is not the first tragedy to befall Jeju Island. An earlier tragedy has its origins in the 1950-1953 Korean War that many commentators believe heralded the beginning of the twentieth century Cold War between the United States and the Soviet Union, and commonly referred to as "the Forgotten War", side-lined by what was to unfold later in Vietnam. Forgotten, for the most part not just within the academy but within popular culture with one or two exceptions.

The TV series *M\*A\*S\*H* (1972-1983, winner of eight Golden Globes, six People's Choice awards and fourteen Emmys), voted in the United States in 2012 the second best TV show of all time and considered by Howard Fishman in *The New Yorker* as "the gold standard for quality programming in its day", exceptional in its focus on Korea, revealed trenchant truths within its comic genre on the reality of that war. Here was the absurdity of not just the Korean War but all war, hidden in full view. With its boy-man high-jinks humour and every day and sometimes brutal misogyny, "each morning seems to bring some fresh hell, a reminder that the nightmare is real, and that there is no end in sight", Fishman wrote. Its final episode, then the most watched television series of all time, had over 100 million people in the United States tuned in.

In 1970, Robert Altman directed a much more graphic film version of *M\*A\*S\*H* while retaining its slapstick shtick. The film opens with a helicopter rising over the Korean mountains. Initially it's not clearly evident but as the camera zooms in, a mutilated human body is revealed, its bloody arm dangling in the air, four fingers silhouetted against the greying sky. Alive and hanging in there. Other helicopters begin to fill the screen. The opening sequence runs for two minutes and forty-six seconds, an inordinately long time by contemporary standards. Towards the end of the opening scene, chaos ensues, the injured man loaded onto a stretcher almost topples off as medical orderlies trip over each other. With music by Johnny Mandel and lyrics by Mike Altman the opening is a film in itself.

> Through early morning fog I see, visions of the things to be
> The pains that are withheld from me, I realise and I can see
> That suicide is painless, it brings on many changes,
> And I can take or leave it if I please

And then there was Joan Joan Baez's bleak incomprehension at the loss of a son in John Prine's "Hello in There" from her 1975 *Diamonds & Rust* album.

> We had an apartment in the city
> Me and Loretta liked living there
> Well, it'd been years since the kids had grown…
> A life of their own left us alone
> We lost Davy in the Korean war,
> Still don't know what for, don't matter anymore…
> Me and Loretta don't talk much more
> She sits and stares through the back-door screen…

In his *Irish Times* review (2019) of Ji-min Lee's book *Marilyn and Me*, Desmond Traynor puts the death toll from the Korean War at between three and four million people; as many as 70 per cent were civilians. Roughly 25 per cent of North Korea's pre-war population was killed. In his book on the Korean

War historian Max Hastings also counted the cost: The United States lost 54,246 military personnel, just short of the 58,193 killed in Vietnam. More than four times the number of British soldiers were killed in Korea (1,078) than were killed in the Falklands War. China.org reported that 180,000 Chinese died in the conflict but others suggest that it may have been as high as 600,000. Mao Tse-tung's son was among those killed.

Jeju suffered some horrific atrocities during the war for its pro-communist stance and for its opposition to the division of Korea that for many morphed into an independence struggle. Villages were burned and civilians slaughtered in a period that lasted the duration of the Korean War. A 2019 UN Symposium on Human Rights and Jeju concluded that between 1948 and 1954 "numerous people suffered from illegitimate arrest and imprisonment, torture, execution, arson and forced evacuation due to the ideological confrontation and the resulting violent madness". In what is sometimes referred to in Korea as "our Srebrenica" an estimated 30,000 people were killed, one tenth of the entire island population.

In 2003 President Noh Moo-hyun issued an official apology to the Jeju victims, and eleven years later 3 April was designated a national Memorial Day. On 1 January 2005, the president came to Jeju and declared the island an International Island of Peace.

Nine years later, on 27 July 2014, I arrived on the island of Jeju.

By then the hugely controversial and much contested construction of the Jeju Civilian-Military Complex Port was well under way. For many, this was the supreme irony, the South Korean government constructing a military base that would accommodate the US navy on an island that lost so many of its people opposing US involvement in the Korean War while simultaneously declaring Jeju an island of world peace. All this against the seething opposition of the villagers of Gangjeong,

95 per cent of whom voted in a local referendum against the location of the base, a referendum the South Korean government refused to recognise, the views of the villagers brusquely brushed aside.

But not without a struggle. A struggle that has led to disruption, injury, hospitalisation, imprisonment and even a hunger strike, all wrapped in deep emotion, hurt, betrayal and anger. "We lost the battle," Ko Gwon-il (Gangjeong's Vice-Mayor in 2014) told me as, for my benefit, he relived scenes on his laptop of the direct-action protests. Hundreds of activists chained to vehicles to block contractors from entering the construction site. Helmeted armed police with flak jackets held the yellow t-shirted protestors at bay, crushing and corralling people away from huge machines as workers installed a six-meter-high perimeter fence.

"I'm so regretful," he tells me, tears welling in his eyes. "It was September 2011, about 1,000 mainland policemen were promptly dispatched to Jeju Island to stop us." Gwon managed to climb on to a twenty-metre scaffolding from which he directed the protestors below. It all came to naught. "It's the day of great sorrow. We were outnumbered," his voice breaking with emotion. "I am so regretful. We should have prepared better. From then on, we couldn't stop the construction. We lost the battle."

Emotion too from Yang Yoon-mo, former Professor of Film Studies at the Seoul Institute of the Arts. "The sound of them breaking the rock tears my heart apart," he tells me. Gureombi rock, the most sacred rock, "an uninterrupted kilometre-long rock formed by lava flowing into the sea and rocks rising from the seabed," according to the *Korea Times*. Despite pleas from the Governor of Jeju for a stay on its destruction, hundreds of kilograms of explosives blasted it into oblivion. Without deference to local custom, a Defence Ministry spokesperson casually and callously declared: "There is no such thing as a special Gureombi Rock. Such rocks can be found everywhere on Jeju."

Yang Yoon-mo was imprisoned for his defence of Gureombi rock. He immediately went on hunger strike for 76 days. He showed me a picture of himself at that stage. This hardy daily swimmer reduced to stick-like frail proportions. The following year he went on hunger strike for 34 days. And then in 2013 for 56 days.

"I have dedicated myself to this movement against the base for seven years. I have done so because of a continuous longing for justice. Can you understand that?" he asks me. I think the question was rhetorical. Our conversation was overshadowed by the clack-clack-clack sound of mechanised digger burrowing its way into rock.

From tangerine farmer Jung Young Hee came further emotion. "It hurts me very much. I've been living here in Gangjeong village for twenty-four years," she tells me. "The majority of people here are tangerine farmers. All of a sudden, in one day, this naval base project was first mooted in 2007. The navy did not hold public hearings or seek the views of the villagers. It is aching for Jeju Island."

The base is now a done deed. Completed in February 2016, the US navy's guided-missile destroyer *USS Stethem* (DDG 63) was the first to visit the base that spans nearly 500,000 square metres with docks running some five kilometres. In October 2018, Jeju hosted what the South Korean navy called "an International Fleet Review to promote world peace through the sea, while sharing ideas on harmony and co-existence". Some 10,000 troops from twelve countries and naval representatives from 46 countries attended. Celebrating the event, the *Korean Herald* wrote:

> The 103,600-ton Nimitz-class aircraft carrier of the US
> 7th Fleet based in Yokosuka, Japan, was among the 15

warships from 10 foreign countries that joined the naval event designed to promote trust and cooperation among world navies. The carrier, nicknamed a floating military base, can carry dozens of aircraft and around 5,700 crewmembers. The US deployed a total of three warships, including two cruisers, Chancellorsville and Antietam. Australia its 4,270-ton frigate Melbourne, Brunei its 1,600-ton patrol ship Darut Taqwa, Canada its 4,800-ton frigate Calgary and India its 5,500-ton destroyer Rana. Among the Korean warships were the 7,600-ton Aegis destroyer Yulgok YiYi, the 4,400-ton destroyer Dae Jo Yeong, the 10,000-ton logistical support shi1p Soyang and the 3,200-ton destroyer Gwanggaeto the Great.

Concluding the event, Admiral Sim Seung-seob, chief of South Korea's naval operations, stated:

> We want to give special thanks to the residents of Jeju Island and those who live in the town of Gangjeong for successful hosting of the first international fleet review at the Jeju Civilian-Military Complex Port. The South Korean navy will keep communicating with local residents and will keep working on finding ways for peace and harmony.

Truth and war. The presence of war and the absence of truth.

Now that the deed is done what worries Kristin Douglas is what will become of Gangjeong. "It will change the face of this village," she tells me. "Dramatically. There's not one bar in this village, that will change. You don't see prostitutes here. That will change." I suggest to her that the military would emphatically deny that there is any linkage between military bases and prostitution. "Look around you," she simply said. "Prostitution follows military around, whether it is US military or any other military."

For Kristin Douglas's assertion, there is ample evidence. "Wherever military go they spread their influence beyond their bases, they devour the landscape and they transform the local social scene. Militarised presences seep into towns and villages, disrupting and disturbing as they go." It is all one-way traffic. Civilian access to military bases is tightly controlled, strictly out of bounds. All that barbed wire. All those steel barriers. All those concrete slabs. None of which can disguise the reality of what lies behind.

I took Kristin Douglas at her word. I looked around me.

David Vine again. "Throughout history, women's sex work has been used to help make male troops happy – or at least happy enough to keep working for the military." But women's sex work comes with a price, chiefly for the women involved. But for men too. Sexually transmitted disease. And that cost hampers war's efforts, stymieing the ambitions of those who declare war, despite their enabling of the spread of the disease. Not just in Korea. Not just in Japan. Not just involving Japanese soldiers. Not just involving US soldiers. All wars. Present wars and past wars. And wars closer to home.

Sex work and prostitution are profoundly layered, contentious and much discussed concepts by feminist theorists and others. Central to the concept of sex work is that it is work undertaken as part of a livelihood, sometimes out of choice and sometimes not. Like all work. But sex work is also associated with recreation. Choice. Arguably part of sexual expression and freedom. Prostitution has an altogether different association. Criminality. Violence. Coercion. Pimps. Focusing on sexually transmitted disease, regarded as one-dimensional and reductionist by many, reflects a public health preoccupation of those who declare war, as evidenced by available detailed records, with maintaining a healthy if wholly exploited male military force. Irrespective of the cost to the women. And to the men.

175

Dating back to the Crimean war (1853-1856), venereal disease was identified as a significant threat to the British army. Frightened by the prospect of an epidemic which would further reduce the fighting ability of its armed forces, in 1864 the government introduced the first of three Contagious Diseases Acts. These Acts, according to Maria Luddy in *History Ireland's* "Women and the Contagious Diseases Acts 1864-1886", permitted the compulsory inspection of women in England and Ireland suspected of prostitution, and the forcible confinement for up to nine months of those found to be suffering from syphilis or gonorrhoea. Men were not subjected to similar inspections. The "subjected districts" of the Contagious Diseases Acts in Ireland were Cork, Queenstown (Cóbh) and The Curragh, all significant bases for either the British navy or army.

Venereal disease continued to be a matter of concern to the military effort during the First World War. According to a CNN report, as many as 18,000 men per day were invalided due to venereal disease during that war. Almost half a million (416,891) British and Dominion troops were hospitalised having contracted venereal disease during the war. The 1916 Defence of the Realm Act criminalised women who approached men in uniform. It had little impact on the soldiers' behaviour. And the Second World War was no different.

According to the US Army Medical Department, 1,324,748 military personnel contracted a venereal disease between 1942 and 1945. Venereal diseases were listed as the number one diagnosis in the army's monthly morbidity reports during the Vietnam War, according to medical historian Krzysztof Korzeniewski. Throughout the Korean War the incidence of venereal diseases was estimated at 184 per 1,000 soldiers, and gonorrhea accounted for three-quarters of all sexually transmitted disease diagnoses. In some units within the US army, the incidence rate reached up to 500 cases per 1,000 persons. That's every second soldier.

From Fort Bragg in North Carolina to Baumholder in Germany and the notorious Subic Bay in The Philippines, where Irish human rights activist Shay Cullen uncovered a child prostitution ring selling children to US army personnel, David Vine writes, "commercial sex zones have developed around US bases worldwide ... filled with liquor stores, fast-food outlets, tattoo parlours, bars and clubs, and prostitution in one form or another". One year (2015) prior to the opening of the military base in Gangjeong, presaging the potentially inevitable, flyers appeared in Seogwipo, the second-largest city on Jeju Island, advertising a new night club called the Aircraft Carrier. In large, bright yellow and red lettering set against an image of an aircraft carrier, the flyers advertised a fifty per cent offer on "cheap ladies".

Like its earlier British counterpart, the spread of venereal and communicable diseases exercised the US army headquarters as well. A VD Control Section was instituted with regular inspections and treatment for "entertaining girls". This category included licensed prostitutes, dancers, "bar girls" and waitresses. Between May 1947 and July 1948, medical personnel examined almost 15,000 women in Korea.

Korea has a longstanding and troubling history with prostitution where, according to David Vine, "camptowns" (read rape camps) around US bases have become deeply entrenched in the country's economy, politics and culture. Women were bought and sold by US GIs, sometimes for the price of a cigarette, and were "at the centre of an exploitative and profoundly disturbing sex industry, one that both displays and reinforces the military's attitudes about men, women, power and dominance". These were poor women, humiliated, bruised, battered, their exploitation driven by economic necessity. Girls as young as twelve, thirteen, fourteen, willingly sold by their families into prostitution according to political scientist and camptown expert Katharine H. S. Moon, professor at Wellesley College in Massachusetts.

Equally disturbing was the militarised enslavement of an estimated 200,000 "comfort women", or *ianfu* in Japanese, the euphemism used for women forced into rape camps by the Japanese Imperial Army before and after the Second World War, although Katharine H. S. Moon puts the figure closer to 400,000 as she argues that the number of Chinese women trafficked into these camps will never be fully known. Women were bought and sold and presented to soldiers as "royal gifts" from the Emperor Hirohito. Intended to ease the pressure on front-line soldiers and to reduce the level of "raping sprees" that alienated local communities, these "comfort stations" were first established in the 1930s.

Here too the spread of venereal diseases was a critical preoccupation. In an effort to address that concern the Japanese army created its own "comfort divisions", effectively state-controlled rape camps. According to the Center on Research for Globalisation, the government initially recruited women from Japanese brothels as a way of offering them the opportunity to repay their debts more quickly while serving the nation. As demand quickly exceeded supply, the government licensed contractors to procure more women. As well as Japanese and Korean women these contractors trawled far and wide to supply the Japanese soldiers. Women from China, Taiwan, the Philippines, Indonesia and other parts of Asia were recruited. Many were just children.

Born in the Philippines, Maria Rosa L. Henson, one of the "comfort women", was the first Filipino woman to speak about her experiences. "Sometimes twelve soldiers would force me to have sex with them and then they would allow me to rest for a while, then about twelve soldiers would have sex with me again."

Ninety-three-year-old Kim Bok-Dong was born in the city of Yangsan in South Korea. Told by her Japanese captors that she was destined for a factory making soldiers' uniforms, she arrived by ship at fourteen years of age in Taiwan, ending up in China where she, along with about thirty other young women, were met by a high-ranking Japanese official and prostituted. The soldiers talked among themselves, saying, "Isn't she too young?" Clearly, they did not think so. Ms. Bok-Dong recounted her war-time experience in an interview with YouTube channel Asian Boss in October 2018.

> I got dragged into a room, got beaten up so I had to comply. When the man was finished with me, the bed sheets were covered in blood. Later, I saw two girls crying because they just had the same thing done to them. We tried to figure out how to commit suicide.

They failed in their attempt. Ten days later, after having recovered consciousness, Kim Bok-Dong determined she would stay alive so the world would hear her story. But first she had to comply.

> On Saturdays I'd start at noon and finish at five. The soldiers stood in line, waiting. One after another. Sometimes banging on the door shouting to the soldier with me to hurry up. By five o'clock, I couldn't get up. On Sundays I had to have sex from 8.00 am to 5.00 pm. That was Sunday. Up to fifty men. That was how it went.

Ms. Bok-Dong was trafficked from Taiwan to Hong Kong, Malaysia, Indonesia and Singapore.

> As a woman, I had things done to me that are unfathomable.

When the war ended, she managed to return to her family. Her eight-year-long ordeal was over. But she could not tell anybody of her experience. As far as her family was concerned, she had been working in a factory. "I was angry and bitter whenever I thought about it and I thought things would get resolved if I told the truth. But it still hasn't been resolved to this day." She never married or had children. She simply could not.

Initially, Japan refused to acknowledge its complicity in the enslavement of women claiming that the women were voluntary paid prostitutes. But in August 1993, the Japanese government relented and issued the Kono Statement acknowledging state responsibility for the coercive recruitment of "comfort women" on the Korean peninsula.

Fourteen minutes into the eighteen-minute interview, Kim Bok-dong's tone abruptly changed. The narrative up to this point was controlled if heartfelt, even her sense of anger and bitterness told in a dispassionate, almost matter-of-fact way. Then anger with the deal concocted by the South Korean and Japanese governments, reached without any consultation with the still-living "comfort women", spills out.

"What kind of bastards would reach such a one-sided deal?" asks Kim Bok-Dong.

> I started cursing when I heard that. That kind of deal is not what we've been fighting for. What I want from Japan is an apology for having dragged us away and making us suffer. I want a formal apology. They should say, 'What we did was completely wrong, and we'll correct our history books'. And say to us, 'we sincerely apologise'. If they wrote that kind of formal apology, then we can forgive them.

And then towards the end of the interview Kim Bok-Dong's voice breaks. "I am heart-broken beyond belief."

Along with fellow survivor Gil Won-Ok, Kim Bok-Dong established the Butterfly Fund to help victims of sexual violence in armed conflicts around the world.

In January 2019, at the age of ninety-two, Kim Bok-Dong died. Prior to her death she requested that her coffin pass by Japan's Embassy in Seoul. Her request was honoured. The coffin passed the Embassy, accompanied on its final journey by mourners waving banners and holding yellow butterflies, the BBC reported. Cries of "Japan must apologise" rang out above the crowd, while others quietly sobbed.

However, the apology from the Japanese government she so desperately yearned for never materialised. An apology for a stolen and brutalised life.

"I was born a woman," she said, "but I never lived as a woman."

Other "comfort women" too sought apologies. Almost 90 years old, and 70 years after her ordeal, Yi Ok-seon in a CNN interview was unequivocal in her demand for an apology from the Emperor. "I want the Emperor of Japan to come to us and get down on his knees in front of us and reflect on what they have done and explain what actually happened. They are waiting for us old grannies to die," she says wiping the tears from her eyes.

As of January 2019, only 23 Korean registered "comfort women" survivors were still alive.

Reluctantly, and under pressure from the US House of Representatives and the European Parliament, the Japanese government issued an apology in 2015 and paid about $8.8 million (€7.9 million) reparation to a fund for the 46 surviving women. The deal was done with the government of Park Geun-hye, South Korea's first woman president (2013-2017), who was later impeached and sentenced to 24 years in prison and ordered to pay 18 billion won (€14.4 million) in fines for bribery, extortion, abuse of power and other criminal charges. A further year was added to Park's sentence by the appeals court in Seoul and her fine increased to 20 billion won, indicting her for receiving bribes from Samsung, the country's biggest conglomerate and one of the world's top technology firms. The court held that collusion between Park and Samsung was more expansive than the lower court had ruled. Daughter of former dictator Park Chung-hee, a second lieutenant in the Japanese army during World War II, Park Geun-hye adopted a very conciliatory approach towards Japan and was anxious to rush through the 2015 agreement which was to "finally and irreversibly" settle the "comfort women" issue.

Flawed as the deal clearly was, and unacceptable to the women and their representatives who were frozen out of the negotiation process, since 2015 there has been much back-sliding on the acknowledgement grudgingly made.

Japanese Prime Minister Shinzo Abe had long resisted any state apology. Citing lack of evidence in July 2006, he denied that there had been any coercion by the Japanese government or army.

Japan's Emperor Akihito has not apologised to the women. In August 2012, former South Korean President Lee Myung Bak demanded the emperor apologise for Japan's colonial rule of the peninsula if he wanted to visit the nation, leading to criticism from the Japanese public. No Japanese emperor has ever visited South Korea despite repeated invitations, including an invitation to the emperor from South Korea to attend the opening of the 2002 FIFA World Cup in Seoul.

There have been some muted acknowledgements. In a similar vein to what Queen Elizabeth of England said in Dublin Castle in 2011 – "the record over the centuries has not been entirely benign" – in 1984 during a banquet with South Korean President Chun Doo Hwan in Tokyo, Emperor Hirohito, in whose name the war was fought, stated: "It is indeed regrettable that there was an unfortunate past between us."

However, when the South Korean Speaker of the House Moon Hee-sang requested an apology from Akihito in 2019, Shinzo Abe described the request as "deplorable". Japanese sensitivity had been pricked in January 2019 when a "Comfort Woman" statue was unveiled in a Filipino shelter for homeless and elderly people in the city of San Pedro, in the province of Laguna. Two days later it was removed following an intervention from the Japanese Embassy in Manila. "We believe that the establishment of a 'comfort woman' statue in other countries, including this case, is extremely disappointing, not compatible with the Japanese government," the embassy said, according to a UPI report by Elizabeth Shim.

I asked a spokesperson from the Japanese Embassy in Dublin if it were the case that the Emperor had refused to apologise. The official confirmed that the Emperor had not apologised, informing me that the Emperor does not engage in day-to-day politics but represents the unity of the country.

No apology either from the South Korean government to the people of Gangjeong for steamrolling their opposition to the naval base. For disregarding their views. For disrespecting their culture and traditions. For the desecration of their sacred Gureombi rock. For the desecration of their "Island of World Peace". For adding another layer of militarisation on an already highly militarised area. For the escalation of tensions with the Chinese.

Meanwhile, the anti-naval base protests continue, albeit at a much-reduced level. The base may be up and running, but for the committed, the struggle against the pursuit of increased militarisation at the naval base at Gangjeong continues. And now a new struggle presents itself. The government plans to construct a second airport (an air force base?) in Seongsan on the east coast of the island, again despite the seething opposition of the local people. This is déjà vu all over again. Habitat loss. Environmental disaster. Cultural vandalism. Protests. No consultation. Hunger strikes.

"We may not be strong enough compared to the power of the government. We are like eggs thrown on hard rocks. However, we will become the unbreakable eggs and continue our fight," Kang Dong-kyun, Mayor of Gangjeong from 2007 until 2013, said to me. "We want peace. Some might say that peace can be protected by might, but peace achieved by might cannot last long."

There remains the forlorn hope that on this island of three Ws, the wind might come and blow the whole base down. Shortly before my arrival on the island, a typhoon lashed the Jeju coastline and smashed through a huge concrete structure at the mouth of the base. Those who oppose the base cling to the possibility that one more might blow the whole base down.

As a typhoon blew, I visited the gates of the base for the last time. "I hope this typhoon can blow all of it away," one man tells me. "This military base is built where my field used to be. Whenever I see the base my heart aches. It pains me to the core."

The struggle continues.

# 10

# A Stillbirth

## South Sudan

He told us on arrival at the airport that he would be our worst nightmare. Our fixer, that is. It was a joke of course. Nobody would introduce themselves as such if that were the case. A gentle ribbing gag – just to test us. Or so we thought.

Once we hit the ground, the fixer is the most important person on the crew. Everything that transpires happens through him or her. The name says it all. After that, the translator and then the driver come next in terms of importamce. The local crew. This fixer came highly recommended. I had been in contact with him for weeks in advance. His English was impeccable but there were indications of what was to come that I did not recognise. Fear was being hyped. Movement around the capital city of Juba was very restricted, he told me, and movement outside the capital impossible. But, of course, the fixer said we should still travel.

At passport control it was a free-for-all. There was just chaos. People leaving to catch the flight to Addis Ababa were trying to access the plane as we were trying to disembark. Two passport officers were trying to impose some order on a disorderly crowd. Without much success. We were swept along in a queue until our fixer appeared, took control of the situation, and we sailed through. His intervention was impressive.

And we felt lucky to have made it. Securing visas was incredibly problematic and it looked for a time as if we would not succeed. Then our fixer told us that putting an advance plan together was virtually impossible as the situation was so volatile that nothing could be planned more than a day or so in advance. So we arrived in Juba on 18 September 2014 somewhat fearful, not so much for our own security but about not being in a position to make the documentary.

For the first few days we were mired in prohibitions – it's not possible to go there, it's not safe – and being first-time travelers in South Sudan, a country teetering on the edge of existence, it was difficult to establish if that were the case or not. And then it gradually dawned on us that our fixer had a clear vested interest in heightening our sense of fear. There is an economic dividend to be gained from such fear-mongering. And the expenses were mounting up. Visas and film permits were four to five times the original price. Government officials would take cash only. Spot checks occurred in the most unusual of places – how could they know where we were? The only time we left the hotel during the first day-and-a-half was to visit more officials and each time it cost. We were being taken for a ride and not one in our best interests.

Eventually we decided to take control of the situation. We parted company acrimoniously amidst threats of not being allowed to leave the country, being picked up by army personnel late at night or just some unexpected happening that he would be helpless to prevent. Connections to people in high places were invoked. It was a tense time for all of us – Mick Cassidy, Mick O'Rourke and Bob O'Brien included. The stakes were high but on a hunch we felt he was bluffing. We were lucky: he was, but we couldn't really be sure of that until we had left the country. We began to make our own way.

And we did what we very often do – had conversations with local people, NGO people and journalists. Suddenly things began to fall into place. We met an amazing Irish woman who doesn't want her name known, and her help proved invaluable. Ayom Wol, a South Sudanese woman who lived the bulk of her life in London and who returned to help build the newly independent state, was also an enormous help. Aneta Brzostek, a Polish woman working for a Czech NGO, equally so, as was a young London woman, Shantal Persaud, who worked for UNMISS, the United Nations Mission in South Sudan.

In a sense our experience is a microcosm of what is happening in the country. Those orchestrating the conflict have no interest in resolving it. Five years of peace talks in plush hotels in Addis Ababa, far away from the reality of the conflict, were viewed with deep cynicism in South Sudan, and when yet another peace deal was signed in September 2018 the cynicism deepened. That cynicism was jolted when in April 2019 Pope Francis, along with the Archbishop of Canterbury, Justin Welby, the spiritual leader of the worldwide Anglican community, invited the warring sides to the Vatican for a two-day retreat at the end of which Francis knelt and kissed the feet of President Salva Kiir Mayardit, his nemesis Riek Machar (Vice President-designate) and Rebecca Nyandeng de Mabior, also Vice President designate. These pictures grabbed the attention of the world's news media in a way the conflict that has cost in excess of 400,000 lives failed to do. A celebrity photo does what hundreds of deaths, countless injuries and almost six million destitute people – more than 50 per cent of the population – cannot.

Previous pleas to agree a settlement have fallen on deaf ears. Previous peace deals held for only a matter of months before fighting resumed. The participants have more to gain from the conflict, it is widely believed, than in seeking a settlement. And the corruption is endemic – $4 billion allegedly siphoned off by 75 families. Just prior to the declaration of independence in July 2011, President Salva Kiir wrote to politicians and government officials, as well as corrupt individuals, whom he claimed stole this money, asking for it to be returned; not surprisingly, nothing came of it. South Sudan is not alone in having families-in-the-know bankrupt their country. Ninety-nine families in the equally oil-rich Angola, all connected with former President Eduardo dos Santos who ruled the country from 1979 to 2017, did likewise. It, too, experienced a bitter civil war that upended the country, from which it still has not recovered. His daughter Isabel is Africa's richest woman. Africa's first woman billionaire – a billion minutes in time is equivalent to 1,902 years, taking us back approximately to the time of Jesus. Her wealth is estimated at $2 billion, the equivalent in time back to when Africans were thought to have crossed the Strait of Gibraltar into Spain for the first time.

It is easy to be aghast at such self-serving fraudulent behavior and, given the level of poverty in each of these countries, not without reason. That is until we consider the complicity of western financial institutions and governments in that corruption. It is something that former Kenya National Human Rights Commission chairman Maina Kiai rails against. "Undeniably there is corruption," he told me some years earlier, "but the deals are done in London, done in Dublin, done in Paris."

On the recommendation of the Irish woman we met, we flew from Juba to Boro, located on the banks of the White Nile close to the Ugandan border, a distance of only 150 kilometres but where the roads were either non-existent or just too dangerous to drive. The conflict that has so traumatised the populace did not originate here, but in a simmering political power struggle between Kiir Mayardit and Riek Machar, former allies in the independence struggle against Sudan and both former members of the SPLM, the Sudan People's Liberation Movement. The tipping point was a barrack-room fracas in

Juba amongst rival supporters within the presidential guard at 9.30 on the night of Sunday 15 December 2013 that eventually spilled out onto the streets. Borrowing that Yeatsian line, the centre could not hold, things fell apart. The killing had started.

At 9.30 it was pitch dark. Street lighting in Juba, South Sudan's capital city, is practically non-existent. The only lights that cast shadows on the city streetscape are from charcoal fires as the women of the city hunker down to cook what is often the only meal of the day. These and the flickering lights from food stalls and other street sellers that act as a lighted cloister on the main thoroughfares of the city. But that night was like no other night. Fear and rumour gripped the city. Violence spread quickly. Allegations of mass killing. Social media went into overdrive. And people fled for their lives. By the Wednesday close to 20,000 people were seeking refuge in the nearest UN compound. And as the week went on, the numbers rose higher and higher.

Journalist Ayom Wol told me:

> Since the very early hours of the fighting there were extremely divisive and inaccurate reports on Twitter and Facebook reporting that certain things were happening, certain ethic groups were being affected in particular ways which actually weren't true, which spread very quickly and were used to stir up purely ethnically-based hatred and escalate the tension.

Born to an Irish-American mother and a South Sudanese father, Ayam Wol is a writer and journalist raised in South London who returned to South Sudan to help in the reconstruction of the nation following independence on 9 July 2011, still the world's newest country. A lifelong follower of Arsenal FC, she met us one evening by accident in a bar in the hotel where we were staying. It was, if ever there was one, a propitious meeting. And I have looked favourably on the trials and tribulations of Arsène Wenger ever since. She had been chronicling the way in which social media has inflamed and distorted the conflict, and in her distinctly south London accent she explained it to me.

> The morning after the conflict erupted images were in circulation, and not just in South Sudan but internationally, of thousands of bodies piled high on the street. They weren't true and they could not be true, because the conflict started in darkness.

It later transpired, she told me, that these images came from Boko Haram-prompted killings in Nigeria. But by the time that was established it was too late. People believed that an ethnic killing spree was underway and they either fled to the nearest UN compound in Juba or sought vengeance themselves. The harm was done.

If social media fanned the flames, mainstream media took up the torch. In Juba, *The Nation Mirror*, which styles itself as "Your First Authoritative Daily", headlined "Rebels Hoist Sudanese Flag in Areas Captured from SPLA", the governing party. South Sudan fought a 22-year civil war with Sudan, a war that cost something in the region of two million lives and displaced millions of others. The Sudanese flag is to the South Sudanese as the Confederate Flag is to African Americans – a symbol of years of oppression – and in Ireland we too know the incendiary power of flags. Notwithstanding the certainty of *The Nation Mirror's* headline, it went on to say in the body of the article that the rebels *were said* to have hoisted the Sudanese flag. In a country where just over a quarter of the population is literate the likelihood of misunderstanding was enormous. And in the context of a fragile state and a fearful people, misunderstanding was the harbinger of the violence and death that was to follow.

It was never meant to be like this. On 9 July 2011, South Sudan was born on a wave of hope and optimism. Watched by African leaders and foreign dignitaries, and with the help of Chinese engineers, the continent's biggest country was cleaved in two as the flag of the oppressor, Sudan, was lowered and that of hopeful, liberated South Sudan raised. The liberation of South Sudan from years of oppression and genocide was greeted by throngs of cheering, dancing, singing people as cars tooted horns, church bells rang, fireworks lit up the night sky and a new clock tower announced, "Free at last". The world's newest country had just been birthed.

Then death came to South Sudan with a vengeance. Hundreds of thousands of deaths. A Report by the London School of Hygiene & Tropical Medicine put the death toll as of September 2018 at 383,000, perhaps even in excess of 400,000. In addition, there are those who are traumatised and destitute. Over two million have fled their homes, another two million have fled the country and over six million are in dire need of humanitarian assistance. Numbers. But as Dr. Daniel Bul, Chair of the Committee for National Healing, Peace and Reconciliation pointed out to me, the crime is not the number of people killed. It is important that a human being is not to be killed.

Such was the speed that ignited the conflict that by the evening of the following day, 16 December, rebel forces allegedly loyal to Vice President Riek Machar attacked Bor, the capital city of Jongeli state with a population of approximately 20,000 people. The fighting lasted about four hours. Tall and thoughtful Alier Arem walked me through the town. In that time about 2,000 civilians lost their lives, he told me. Such was the level of fear among the people of Bor that huge numbers fled to the river in an effort to escape the rebels. Alier was among those who fled. Those who couldn't make it to the river were mercilessly killed, including all the patients in the hospital. All.

"We felt," Alier said, "that the rebels would have mercy on those in the hospital but unfortunately that did not happen. They were killed in their beds." Equally the church did not provide protection. Twenty-two people were killed in the church, their bodies buried in an unmarked grave opposite the plain, low-lying building with a simple cross on top. Two men and twenty women. The town itself was torched.

"There were bodies everywhere piled up on either side of the street," he told me as we walked through the newly built market area. Along the main thoroughfare, Alier pointed out various buildings; five people were killed there, two there, six here and on and on. Having emptied the town, the rebels daubed their names on buildings, which were now theirs. The spoils of war.

People fled in their thousands. I have tried to reconstruct the scene. I have no idea how many rebels there were or what they were armed with. Certainly, many had guns. People were shot dead. Perhaps machetes too. It is not unusual that people are hacked to death in these circumstances. But their arrival turned the day on its head. People in markets, children in schools, old men sitting under trees deep in conversation were suddenly under attack. At what point they decided to head for the water I do not know. Equally it is hard to comprehend thousands of people fleeing to the river. Women and men gathering their children in their arms. People perhaps stopping to grab some possession or other. A cooking pot. A bag of rice. A pair of flip-flops. The noise and the chaos. And then the chase, the shooting and the killing. The fall into water. The attempt to reach a boat. The clinging on. Parents struggling, children crying. Stretching for one, the other is let go. The uncomprehending shriek of the child as he or she is swept away. The last frenzied glimpse. The shriek heard long afterwards.

The possibility of boats. For those fleeing there were boats certainly. We could see that. These too were grabbed, pushed out, people clambering on board, people grabbing on to the sides and then fingers slipping, the inevitable struggle, submergence, the dead body drifts away. The river Nile was their only route to safety, but waters too can be treacherous and for countless numbers the waters offered no refuge. The fleeing townsfolk were followed by the rebels who continued shooting people in the water. The young, the elderly and those who could not swim were sucked into the river. Lost lives. Alier was one of those who survived.

> They were mercilessly shooting at us. So we had to run to the water and we swim. Many who could not swim were drowned. Parents watched their children drown, being carried away by the current. If they tried to rescue one child, they too would lose their lives. They had to try and save those they could. The dead bodies could not be saved either. You had to leave the dead body to the current. It is very strange watching people die.

All of this happened in a four-hour period.

We sat in a boat on the river as Alier recounted what happened. In the end his voice just trailed off and he looked away.

When it was all over the rebels disappeared back into the forest. What they thought of their four-hour work is impossible to second-guess. Perhaps they too were traumatised. They too are human after all. They too were manipulated, pawns in other people's war games. Perhaps they have compartmentalised those four hours. Consigned those events to the deep recesses of their minds and souls. Silenced the voices they heard that day. And now they go about their day, doing what they did before. Or perhaps they too live with the memory. Wracked by guilt. Tormented. Flashbacks. By night and by day. For the most part soldiers do not talk. And we did not get to talk to them.

A week later people began to drift back, Alier among them. There were bodies everywhere, most bloated beyond recognition from the African sun. All had rotted, many eaten by birds and other wildlife.

What we heard in Boro was truly shocking. I remember contacting a radio station back home to report on the atrocity. "That sounds like an interesting three minutes," I was told. "Perhaps on Friday." It didn't happen. Apparently Friday was a busy day in Ireland. And, we are told, black lives matter.

What happened in Boro left us yet again searching for answers as to our capacity for carnage and our inability to empathise with other human beings. We put these questions to Anglican Primate Daniel Deng Bul, chairman of the Committee for National Healing, Peace and Reconciliation. He had no answers. And the truth is there are no answers to such questions.

"They are all to blame," Archbishop Daniel Bul tells me as he reviews the carnage and disintegration of his beloved South Sudan. This is a plain-speaking man whose patience has been stretched to breaking point by recalcitrant politicians, former comrades of the ruling Sudan People's Liberation Army who fought a 22-year independence struggle only to engage in a bitter civil war that has beggared the country and traumatised its people.

Daniel Bul is as impressive a figure as his full title would suggest, "The Most Rev. Canon Dr. Daniel Deng Bul, Primate of Sudan and South Sudan". Despite his Dinka ethnic origins, he is regarded as an honest broker in this splintered society. His imposing frame easily fills his desk chair as he sits jacket-less behind his solid dark brown hardwood desk in his windowless office in Juba, South Sudan's capital city. Given his task he needs a big frame, sturdy shoulders and a thick skin. And all the support he can get.

His task was to try to bring some peace and reconciliation to the people of war-ravaged South Sudan. His is a towering presence and despite his Dinka ethnic origins, he is regarded as an honest broker in a highly splintered society where ethnic identity has been exploited and twisted by those who seek not just military and political gain, but also access the country's very significant oil revenue.

The Christian churches in South Sudan are engaged in the age-old practice of community-to-community peace-building. It is slow, tedious work but given the stalemate and procrastination that has characterised the political process it is the only hope for the future. And while Archbishop Bul has been given the equivalent role of his South African counterpart Archbishop Desmond Tutu, it comes without the global acclaim or worldwide support.

For the most part the South Sudanese conflict has passed the world by. It is perceived by outsiders as an ethnic conflict, the off-the-peg explanation for all of Africa's ills. And one that suits outsiders' view of Africa. It is much more convenient to explain away Africa's conflicts as backward black-on-black tribalism rather than confront any western complicity in that violence. Archbishop Bul gives a more nuanced, but nonetheless hard-hitting analysis.

> What has caused the crisis is the mismanagement of resources, corruption and nepotism. We did not manage our resources well. We did not re-distribute our resources well. That angered and triggered the fight amongst the people. These are the things to blame.

It is a view shared by Ayom Wol:

> There has been a use and abuse of ethnic tension particularly amongst the two largest ethnic groups, the Dinka and Neur, by people seeking to mobilise support for one side or another.

South Sudan is the most oil-dependent country in the world. It has one of Africa's biggest oil reserves and up to 2013, when drilling stopped, it accounted for almost all of its exports. Oil is the only wealth the country possesses but, as Carlos Figuereido said years previously in Angola, oil is a curse. And it seems the same is true for South Sudan. Corruption and nepotism. The country has an estimated 3.5 billion barrels of oil and 3 trillion cubic feet of natural gas in proven reserves – if trillions were seconds it would equate to 31,709.8 years or 31 millennia – and is seen by companies as one of the last frontiers for energy exploration in sub-Saharan Africa. But these riches are short-lived. South Sudan's oil is expected to be reduced to negligibility by 2035.

Beyond Bor, the killing was equally merciless. Aluel Kuol, a mother of five boys who all looked so close in age it was difficult to distinguish one from another, lived about a two-hour walk outside Bor on a road that only a motorbike could travel. "Before the war, we were self-sufficient," she told me. "We were able to cultivate our fields and we had enough sorghum, the staple here. There was no need for free food." Like many of her countrypeople, the crisis took them completely off-guard. Without warning men appeared shooting at them. "They came from all directions. They were shooting at us as we ran. I kept running with my children. I was really frightened. We saw so many dead bodies lying on the ground."

Aluel and her children managed to survive and for weeks afterwards lived in the forest, fearful of returning. When she returned her house had disappeared, everything burned to ash. Unlike other places of war, there was little material evidence of war's impact here. In rural areas, people's homes are generally made of flimsy material – mud walls, conical roofs made of sticks and covered with reeds which are easily torched. She showed us where her house once stood. There was nothing but scorched earth. She had returned to nothing.

Those that weren't burned to the ground were looted by the rebels, Aluel's neighbor Ateny Wel Alier told us. She too had fled to the forest, surviving on green grass. "We cooked it and added a small groundnut paste to make it taste good." Some evidence of the rebels' handiwork remained. Abandoned houses barely standing, some collapsed in on themselves, the occasional curtain blowing in the doorway. Inside one, an old spoon illuminated by a shaft of light that streamed in through a porous roof. In others discarded flip-flops, a plastic cup, a spoon, a crushed cooking pot. Pieces of clothing too. Once life's precious possessions, now war's debris.

Ateny has not yet been able to repair her house. She sits outside preparing groundnuts to add to the sorghum she, like her neighbours, has received from the World Food Programme provided by USAID. Her hard-worked hands work as she talks. Many of the people in this village have fled across the river too, many are still in hiding in the forest. Fearful of the power of the river, Ateny thinks many will never return. Now aged fifty, balding with her front teeth missing, Ateny was determined to return. "I was born here," she says. "I grew up here. I married here. This is my home."

Ayen Makuol Panyang also returned. She too lived in the forest following the rebel attack on Bor. She too was forced to cross the river. Almost matter-of-factly she described being shot at while running. She too saw children drowning. In this war "many innocent people have died and those who died do not even know the cause of their death".

Back in Juba, and despite the efforts of UNMISS's Shantal Persaud, it was not possible to film in their refugee camps. Permission had to be sought from community leaders who agreed, but younger, more radical people objected. While initially disappointed, it was good to see that within the camps people had agency, their voices were heard and that foreigners with cameras cannot just roll up and presume people will acquiesce to whatever is expected if not demanded. Thanks to Aneta Brzostek we did, however, get access to an informal displacement camp on the grounds of a mosque in the city. It was difficult to estimate how many people lived in this cramped space, no bigger than a football field – perhaps a thousand. It was difficult to judge given the close proximity of each new home to the other, but small in comparison with the UNMISS camp.

Along with her husband and three children aged four, five and six, Priscilla Madibo walked the 150 kilometers from Bor to Juba. Apart from the distance, it must have been a scary journey. The country was in turmoil from marauding well-armed groups of men. Fear of being killed, of rape, of kidnapping. Walking at night, they eventually made it to Juba. They now live in a one-room, one-bed shelter. Mats and cooking utensils hang from the roof and it is as neat as a pin, as is the whole place. Women with hand brushes sweep the narrow passageways between each of the huts.

"Life in war is very difficult as opposed to life when there is peace." Priscilla asserts this is no ethnic conflict. She is from the Murle tribe and lives here peacefully with the Neur and Dinka, the two biggest tribes in the country, each aligned with the two main protagonists in the war, President Salva Kiir Mayardit and Riek Machar. Even the children play here together, perhaps a chink of light in an otherwise dark world. "We will not return until the politicians agree peace," she tells me. "We are too afraid. But I want my children to go home, to go to school, so they can have a good future."

Whether the Pope's intervention or the September 2018 agreement can guarantee that future, nobody knows for sure. If past performance is anything to go by, the future is uncertain if not bleak. But all wars eventually end. What is often forgotten is the extent of the legacy of war on those who suffer most from it, which continues long after the inevitable compromises of the conference table.

The legacy of war is the legacy of trauma from war. "Many many people are traumatised from the war," Alier says. The people of South Sudan are traumatised. "Me too," he calmly tells me, yet stunned by the cruelty and barbarity of the world around him. "There is no way for me except to endure the trauma I have experienced. When I am sleeping at night and even in daytime the same scenario is recycled in my mind. All of what has happened."

Life's burden. Meanwhile we were always going to be able to leave. White western privilege counts. Black African lives caught in the maelstrom of war? Not even for three minutes on an Irish radio station on a Friday evening.

As for the fixer? Who knows? There are chancers and charlatans everywhere. Not everyone behaves honourably, particularly in war.

# 11

# HORROR IN ALEPPO

## *Syria*

Beirut's clogged streets inched us forward in the direction of Damascus. A sudden clearance appeared and the driver took off at a speed that had us digging our feet into the floor of the car. As if this would protect us, should his whisker-fine judgment fail him by, well, a whisker. Then unexpectedly around a bend, it clogged again. And so, we made our way until we realised the road had emptied out. Scarcely a car in sight as the night drew in.

As we got closer to the Syrian border we had the road to ourselves. At the border a somewhat idiosyncratic, three-foot-high Lego-like sign, brightly lit in rainbow colours, greeted us. Its individual lettering simply stated: Syria. Soldiers, cigarettes in hand, waved us to the side at ramshackle grey buildings. Behind them a somewhat diffident, if not doleful, image of President Bashar Hafez al-Assad looked down on us.

Inside the building, the image is the same. Equally glum are the passport control officials. Cigarette drooping from his mouth and with very little engagement, one stamps our passports and we take our leave. But not before he said, "Welcome to Syria". Given his demeanour, his welcome was surprising and appreciated. An unexpected portent, perhaps, of what's to come, I hoped. Welcome to Syria. It was good to hear those words.

It was a Saturday night. The main street into the city of Damascus was deserted. At the border we had changed cars and drivers. Our driver, who had impeccable English, took us to our hotel and then insisted that we see the old town. Like all good guides, he knew the best bars in the old city, now pock-marked with bullets but very much still standing. A UNESCO World Heritage site, the city dates back to between 8,000 and 10,000 BC and is considered to be one of the longest continually inhabited cities in the world.

The night was dark and damp and there were few people on the streets. We took refuge in Abu George Bar, the oldest in the city, where people leave messages on the walls – just like La Bodeguita del Medio, one of Hemingway's favourite watering holes in Havana. Here, the elderly hosts greet us with words of welcome. Clearly they are pleased to see us, not just because we are customers in an otherwise deserted bar, though that too, but the sight of foreigners in town is a reminder of what life was once like in this great city.

From there we stroll through the narrow streets ending up in a bourgeois bar all decked out for Christmas. Suddenly it seems as if we are in a different place. The in-house band, more redolent of Eurovision than traditional Syrian music, is in full voice. The young beautiful people are doing what young beautiful people do on such occasions – look beautiful. And so, we drift home as couples drift by. Life on a Saturday night in a capital city. And at that age, and after what they have been through, what would you expect? C'est la vie.

The following morning we went to the Ministry for Information to secure our permits. There is an inevitability about bureaucracy that drags at the soul, even when it is served with tea, black with a choice of lemon or basil. Or both. But not with the three spoonfuls of sugar that everyone here seems to take with even the smallest glass. The ever-tedious task of securing permits. The country – or at least those in government, and clearly the two are not the same – has had a fraught relationship with Western media. But our press passes are issued without too much ceremony. Now we are free to move between Damascus and Aleppo, our eventual destination.

Back to the old town, that narrow network of meandering streets and alleyways with needle-to-an-anchor shops and stalls. The covered cathedral-like Al-Hamidiyeh souk, with its three-storey arched black ceiling and its highly ornate windows, is busy. As in any Middle Eastern city, throngs of people weave their way through these alleyways.

Again, words of welcome are called out. One man selling fried *kubba* passes out a taste of his produce free of charge and without expectation. The camera is essentially ignored and, given how foreign countries have used this country in a proxy war, it's surprising that nobody shouts or jeers at us. There is not a hint of aggression or violence. And there is no fear or threat. Quite the contrary.

The following day we drove the seven-hour journey to Aleppo through the sun-scorched desert, marred only by the occasional burned-out tank. I remembered a previous occasion driving through such deserted beauty. Fadimata Walett Oumar, otherwise known as Disco and one of Mali's best known musicians, described the desert as Mali's ocean. "I love the desert," she told us. On this journey I could see why. This was, however, a different journey. Ken O'Mahony and I travelled in separate cars in uneasy anticipation. Signposts signalled what had now become familiar names. Homs, which we would skirt. Iraq's Mosul. Idlib's province. And then, as we approached Aleppo, the barrenness of the desert gave way to occasional abandoned, half-destroyed buildings.

The occasional buildings became clusters and then whole villages. All in ruins. In the distance we noticed a clothes line on one of the rooftops; two children scrabbling around in the dirt. In the distance too, two boys and a flock of sheep and goats – as if, out of the silence and the destruction, life was creeping back. And then the first sound of gunfire. It, too, from a sufficiently safe distance that it did not deter the driver. That was our cue. If the people around us were not bothered by the sound of gunfire or explosions, then we would not be either. It is, however, easier said than done. But these were the sounds that people had lived with and grown accustomed to over eight long years of warfare. And in the short time we were here, so did we.

After all, we had come to witness and report on that war.

How the war started is deeply contested. The prevailing Western narrative states that in February 2011 in Daraa, a tenth-grade student, fourteen-year-old Mouawiya Syasneu, along with about fourteen other youngsters, scrawled طقسي راشب ١٤٥ — literally meaning *falling is Bachar Al-A...* – on a school wall. Allegedly, they were arrested and tortured by the police. Reading from right to left in Arabic, it is clear that the graffiti is incomplete. As it stands it reads *Bachar Al-A is falling* or could be interpreted as *Bachar Al-A to fall.*

An innocuous enough piece of graffiti at one level, but in the feverish Arab Spring atmosphere of 2010/2011, enough to send cold shivers down the spine of the Assad government. Clearly the intended target was Bashar al-Assad who inherited his presidency from his father eleven years previously. The week prior to the appearance of that graffiti, both Egyptian President Hosni Mubarak and Tunisian strongman Ben Ali had been forced out of office by massive public protests. NATO had just recently intervened on behalf of rebels seeking to depose Libyan leader Muammar Qadhafi. From the perspective of Assad, the graffiti had only one meaning. He was next.

All parties are agreed on the significance of the moment. On what happened next, however, there is much disagreement.

Those who opposed the Assad regime claim that all fifteen children and young people were arrested, tortured, held for two weeks and then released. Newspapers and television stations in the West and in other parts of the Middle East are replete with descriptions of the torture they allegedly endured. One claimed that the young people were forced to sleep naked on freezing wet mattresses, strung up on a wall, left in stress positions for hours and tortured with electrically-charged prods.

Not all witnesses were present at the time of arrest, or of the events that flowed from the arrests. A CNN broadcast on what was happening inside Syria was based on the word of a novelist, activist and professor who was at the time living in Arkansas. The report stated that "police dragged protesters by the hair and beat them". It wasn't exactly a first-hand account. Neither did the broadcasters clarify the use of the word "activist".

Given the highly charged atmosphere that existed, given what was at stake and given that Assad was determined – as was his father – to secure his power base at whatever cost to othes, it is highly unlikely that, as one source said to me, the youngsters were given a clip on the ear and sent home. What is clear is that Western media, drunk on the possibilities they felt the Arab Spring represented, were anxious to maximise the potential of any anti-Assad protests. Israel too. And so were Saudi Arabia and Qatar. As to what actually happened, I have no idea. I wasn't there. To what extent the youngsters were self-consciously deeply political and heroic harbingers of an anti-Assad revolution or just young pranksters egging each other on, I also have no idea.

Now it is a matter of conjecture. Perhaps at this stage it doesn't really matter except to those directly involved. In all wars there is a moment of reckoning. The match sets fire to the embers that are already well prepared, often accidentally, frequently mundane, mostly unintentional. But time and again the wellspring of momentous global events has the most un-likely origins. In 1914, for example, the cavalcade of Austrian Emperor Franz Joseph took a wrong turn and drove metres in front of his nineteen-year-old Bosnian-Serb assassin Gavrilo Princip, who didn't miss and catapulted first Europe and then the world into a cataclysmic war. In March 1998, a tea-room fracas between three young students and a group of older mil-itary loyalists galvanised Burma's students onto the streets in open defiance of the dictatorial government, in what became known as the revolution of 08/08/88 that ultimately led to the accession to power of the 1991 Nobel Peace Prize winner (but now wholly discredited) Aung San Suu Kyi. And in Tunisia on 17 December 2010, when twenty-six-year-old Mohamed Bouazizi self-immolated following the confiscation of his un-licensed vegetable cart and its goods, having being slapped in the face, spat on and his father insulted, all of North Africa was set ablaze.

Such are the world's tipping points.

What matters in Syria is that whatever happened here quickly morphed into an international proxy war that not just subsequently traumatised Syria, but the whole Middle East region and the Western world as well. Darra, the city where it all began, with its mostly Sunni well-to-do families and close military and financial links to the state and the As-sad family in particular, was the spark that lit the fuse of one of the many conflagrations that have characterized the start of the twenty-first century.

As we drove into Aleppo on 11 December 2017, I recorded to camera a script I had prepared prior to coming to Syria. It was intended to set the scene, to give Irish viewers a sense of the complexity of the war and the geo-political jockeying for control that had so upended this country: an introduction to the film we were about to make.

The Arab Spring that became the Syrian Winter. Since March 2011, half a million people have been killed, almost two million injured and five million have fled the country. Six-and-a-half million people, including almost three million children, are displaced within the country itself, the biggest internally displaced population in the world. Central to the conflict, President Bashar Al Assad who, along with his father, has ruled this country for almost five decades. Central too are regional and international powers: Iran, Russia and Lebanon's Hezbollah on Assad's side. Opposed are Saudi Arabia, Turkey, Qatar, the United States, Britain and France. Involved too are China, the United Arab Emirates, Iraq, Israel and Egypt. Internally hundreds of militias, along with ISIS and Al Qaeda, fight for the soul of Syria. So too fighters from as many as sixty countries are involved in this proxy war that is also a civil war with regional and sectarian undertones. On this, the first anniversary of what the people of Aleppo call Liberation Day, we have come here to meet with those who stayed and those who survived.

We entered the city from the east, the devastated part that was reclaimed by government forces one year prior to arrival. As we drove into Aleppo we wondered at the destruction, which had a particular if grotesque aesthetic. Twisted metal, half-destroyed silhouetted buildings, suspended mortar clinging on as if for dear life. Carefully (in all probability rushed) constructed sandbag barricades with just enough space for a Kalashnikov rifle. Street after street. Shadowed by the early morning sun, silhouetted by the late evening sunset.

Creeping along with not a soul in sight in the eerily darkened empty night-time streets. Silence begetting silence. It had the feeling of Armageddon, a place like no other. And at that time and in that space it was just impossible to comprehend what had happened. Ken and I were outsiders and we had not experienced what had taken place. It took other people to fill that space. It is the case that you have to live through a war to know what war is.

Recalling a scene from *Apocalypse Now*, 24-year-old Antoine Makdis, a native of Aleppo who has been photographing the city since its destruction, recalled the words of Marlon Brando, "the horror, the horror", words taken from Joseph Conrad's *Heart of Darkness* to describe the destruction of the city. "It's really a horror to live in a war," Antoine told me. And over the next ten days we were witnesses to that horror. "The war has aged me not just psychologically but in the way of thinking. It aged me in my body. I have pain when I walk. I have pain when I'm sleeping. It has aged me a lot. I'm not wiser but I'm older."

He is not alone.

Reem Aslo is a 22-year-old pharmacy student at Aleppo University. Her life and that of her parents and older brother with whom she lives have been marked by war. "People don't realise what it's like to live in a war zone," she told me when we met the morning following our arrival. "I can't describe the feeling. You have to live it to understand it. When you hear stories, you can be touched by them but living them is completely different. Checking first thing every morning that everyone is alive." All aspirations towards living what passes for a normal life ebb away.

Reem was 16 years old when the war started. Perhaps not surprisingly, she idolises pre-war Aleppo. This bright, highly personable, sports-obsessed young woman comes from a wealthy middle-class family. Life held all kinds of possibilities. It was a life she took for granted, as any young person in her situation would have. And then came the deprivations. The coldness of winter nights. No electricity. No water and little food. A life haunted by fear. Leaving the house without a guarantee of return.

Living with the sound of the swoosh of overhead airplanes, shrapnel indiscriminately flying through the air. The sound of mortars falling. The crash of buildings. The sustained and repeated bombardment. The lone sniper's fire. The screams of the wounded and dying. The buried alive. The crying at graves. The night-time terrors. The living and the partly living.

I met with Professor Ibrahim Al-Hadid, Director of Aleppo University Hospital, against the sound of mortars, sounds that do not perturb him. He has been shot at several times: the car he was driving bullet-ridden; the hospital he previously worked in razed to the ground, completely destroyed. He invited me to visit the wards.

Here was evidence of war's egregious legacy.

A young teenage boy lay on a stretcher, his face bloodied, peppered by shrapnel. His lips were charred, eyes bloodshot and partially closed. His hair was matted with his own blood.

A body in a body bag left to one side. Three burqa-clad women sit passively at his side. I am presuming it is a "he". I have no idea.

A 56-year-old man, shot in the chest and abdomen. A sniper's fire. He lies completely still, mouth wide open.

A father stands stoically between two beds. His two sons, aged nine and ten, were injured beyond belief by a landmine. Both suffered head injuries, and other organs of their bodies suffered too. The father explains that another of his sons was killed in the explosion. One boy looks out at us from under a heavily bandaged forehead, his left hand in plaster. The other coughs intermittently, his eyes closed as he reaches under his blood-spattered t-shirt to a spot on his body to which a tube is attached.

Another eight-year-old boy, paralysed. On his own he cannot breathe. The doctor thinks he will not survive.

A 17-year-old boy hit by a mortar, mouth tightly shut from which various tubes protrude. His chest heaves. Should he survive, he will be crippled, Professor Ibrahim tells me. His name is Suliman Farage.

The people working here are confronted with such situations day in, day out. And they, too, are traumatised by what they see. An anaesthetist tells me he hasn't had a day off in three years. What it must be like coming to work each day knowing that you will be confronted by such trauma is hard to imagine. "Sometimes I cry when I see patients," he tells me. "We are all human." Something that is lost in the fog of war.

These are but seven stories. War's casualties. In 2015 in this hospital alone there were 18,000 in total. In 2016, there were more than 28,000. War's statistics.

As I left, I thought of what life might have been like moments before they were maimed. The young boy on the stretcher worried about homework on his way to school. The brothers possibly arguing whose turn it was to tend to the goats. Their father returning from work as a day labourer. The older man looking forward to a game of backgammon that evening. The 17-year-old boy standing in front of the mirror, worried that his fashionably oiled and coiffed hair would hold on a first date.

There are other casualties. Reem's father, Basher Aslo, a goldsmith, had built up an international business in which he had worked beside his father from the age of five. To the sound of underfoot broken glass we inch and half-crawl, careful at times not to bang our heads, to where his shop once stood. Surprisingly amidst all the destruction, his is still standing. A now shrunken figure in a jacket that is at least one size too big for him, Basher stands and stares. "It is heart-breaking," he simply says. "It is heart-breaking. A life's work."

On the ground, his business cards are strewn about, as are small envelopes that would have held the valuable jewellery he would have made. The detritus of a life's work. Inside the shop, everything had been ransacked, the safe blown apart.

The scales were twisted and broken, anything of value taken. Being here clearly hurts. Bashar moves about slowly as he surveys the destruction with just an imperceptible shake of his head. He seems to shrink further inside his jacket, his shoulders rounded and hunched. As he leaves he manages to close the door, the key he brought with him secures the lock. Why or from whom, he does not say. As he leaves he tells us it is for the last time. He will never return.

The loss of his shop was not just Bashar's sole source of grief. His daughter Nour was shot dead by a sniper. For him to recount what happened is beyond painful. His remaining daughter Reem described her sister's killing but is keen to emphasise that every family has a story.

> I saw my sister in the morning. We had breakfast. Then she went to watch Al-Jalaa men's basketball match at the Al-Asad court close to Sadallah Square. At the time, this area was known to be dangerous. We used to go together to watch basketball games. On that day, I did not go with my sister to watch the basketball game. She went by herself. After a while, we received a phone call. We were told that my sister was injured at Sadallah Square and she was transferred to the hospital. A bullet went through her heart.

A single bullet. One that passed from one human being through another. I have thought about that moment on Sunday, 8 February 2015. A young woman walks across Sadallah Square. A sniper high up on some building spies her. In all likelihood he does not know her. Does not know that she has represented her country in international basketball. Does not know her parents, her sister, her brother. Does not know anything about this 26-year-old woman except that she is a target. So he trains his telescopic lens on her. I have no idea if he has trained his lens on others prior to her arrival onto the square. He may have. But on Nour, he does. And then he moves the lens towards her chest, his finger on the trigger. I have no idea

*Aleppo, Syria, 2017.*

*Children of Aleppo, Syria.*

*Dr Ibrahim al-Hadid, Aleppo, Syria.*

*Youssef Ahmed Shawa and his family in Aleppo, Syria.*

*The Aslo family with photograph of their deceased daughter Nour, Aleppo, Syria.*

*Photographer Antoine Makdis with friend, Aleppo, Syria.*

*José Alberto "Pepe" Mujica, Montevideo, Uruguay.*

*Nicolas Rosa, Montevideo, Uruguay.*

*Uruguay's alternative to the "war on drugs".*

*Luis Parodi, Director, Rieles Prison, Montevideo, Uruguay.*

*Laayoune, capital city of occupied Western Sahara.*

*Mustafa Mohamed Ali, Chief of Defence Supplies,*
*Polisario Front, Sahrawi Refugee Camp, Algeria.*

*Mohamed Salem HallaHamma with his granddaughter in the liberated zone of Western Sahara.*

*Sahrawi Refugee Camp, Algeria.*

*Dide Bjtech with crew in Sahrawi Refugee Camp, Algeria.*

*Peadar King inside Western Sahara.*

if, at that very instant, he had a moment of doubt. Who knows? He pulls the trigger and kills her. Despite his accuracy, she does not die immediately. But her life soon ends.

Another needless death. Another statistic of war. Another family plunged into interminable grief. I have been watching the Netflix series *The Vietnam War* by Ken Burns and Lynn Novick. All the war combatants say the first person you kill is the most difficult, and that killing stays with you. Liking it to crack cocaine, one soldier also confided that there is an exhilaration in killing, that adrenalin pounds through the body, but also that it tears at and wrecks the body and the soul. War's secrets. I have no idea if the guy – and I'm presuming it was a guy – who killed her, if it was the first person he killed, if he experienced that exhilaration, that pounding of the body, if sweat rolled down his cheeks, if he had to wipe his eye to ensure he didn't miss, if he later regretted his actions or if it was just another target in this interminable war. Perhaps he has forgotten that moment, just one in a whole series, and he now cannot distinguish one killing from the next. Perhaps it haunts him to this day because he too is human, and he too is caught up in the maelstrom of other people's wars.

What I do know is the awful grief into which it plunged Nour's family, a grief they will carry with them for the rest of their lives. Burying people at the time was high risk. Cemeteries were targets. Throughout the city any green area became a temporary cemetery. Nour was temporarily interred in one such burial ground. Following what the people of Aleppo call Liberation Day in November 2016, when those opposed to the Assad regime were driven out of the city, Nour was finally laid to rest in the family cemetery. I went there with the family. They stood and prayed at her grave, lit candles and incense. Ken filmed them at the grave and then we moved back. Shortly afterwards they did too. But Nour remained behind, her life over. As we leave, they give me her mortuary card. I keep it with me. One side in English, the other in Arabic. The image that adorns her grave is also carried on her card. A young, smiling, bespectacled woman looking off to her left as if into the future. A future denied. An image frozen in time.

Throughout our time here I asked what life was like before the war. And the one common response was how integrated this city was, devoid of any sectarian bitterness or tension. The basketball team that Nour once played on, and the one that Reem continues to play on, included Christians and Muslims. While in Aleppo we ate at Youssef Ahmad Shawa's restaurant close to the Citadel that those opposed to the Assad government failed to take. Around the corner stood the shattered remains of the house in which he once lived with his wife and two adult children. Later we walk with them to the now-destroyed site. He and his wife stand hand-in-hand. Without apparent bitterness or rancour, he points to the precise location. There is mention of an ice-cream seller. He has a sprinkling of English. Then, as if we are not there, their conversation trails off into Arabic. They point to different ruins in what might have been a four-storey building but it is hard to tell, and reminisce about the people who once lived there.

Days later we sit in his restaurant and talk and eat. The absence of bitterness towards two foreigners is very real. A devout Muslim, he counted Christians among his friends and was determined that the war would not change that. It was after Friday prayers. He even found time for humour. "Friday is a holiday for all Muslims," he tells us, "but not for me. I wonder why?"

Earlier I asked Basher whom he held responsible for the destruction and grief that had befallen him. On that question he was very clear. "I don't blame the people who came and destroyed my shop. The people who make the bombs are the ones I hold responsible and the ones who provided the finance," he tells me.

Much has been made in the West about the alleged use of chemical warfare by Assad's government in this country. Indeed, chemical weapons have been fetishised as if all the other weaponry of war is harmless. Barack Obama's 2012 infamous "red line" is a case in point. Threatening invasion if chemical weapons were deployed by the Assad government, he elevated the threat posed by chemical warfare above conventional weapons. As if all weapons of war are not created with the intention to kill. Scientists, engineers, IT specialists, designers, tacticians, some of the best brains in the world, spend their time refining how best to kill other human beings. And while some weapons of war and some ways of killing attract more opprobrium than others, all are designed to kill.

Chemical weapons, abhorrent as they are, are no different than cluster bombs, barrel bombs, grenades, rockets, mortars, sniper fire and other explosives. Ultimately, all are designed to kill and maim. Basher Aslo is a witness to that truth. And these weapons have been made, supplied and profited from by a whole host of European and US-based companies who will never feel their insidious impact. Made in countries we deal with across the EU table at the WHO, OECD, the UN and a multitude of other international organisations. Countries we play against at the FIFA World Cup, at the Rugby World Cup, the Ryder Cup, the Tour de France. Behind the heavily merchandised image that these countries portray lies a much darker and sinister reality. Countries complicit with eyes shut, all implicated in the arms trade, all complicit in the killing machine. Ireland, with what is effectively a military base at Shannon Airport, is not out-of-step in that complicity.

What we say about war – the weapons of war and those who supply and profit from war, as well as those who suffer in these settings – matters. And despite our much-heralded neutrality, Ireland is both a supplier and facilitator of war. The EU plans to spend €19.5 billion on defence from 2021-2027.

Months prior to the grandiose gathering of world leaders in Paris in 2018, President Macron called for the establishment of a "true European army to protect the continent with respect to China, Russia and even the United States of America". Donald Trump announced in 2019 that he is seeking $750 billion for his defence budget. Shannon Airport is a facilitator of that spend.

But without serious pledges to stop wars, or without challenging those who have been centrally involved in fomenting past wars, to what extent do we dishonour all war's victims – the living, the partly living and the dead – irrespective of how we stand on ceremony?

It is difficult to leave Aleppo, that once most beautiful city, without a sense of the senseless and searing sadness of it all. Those young men and boys lying in Aleppo hospital. The father standing by his maimed sons. The doctor who has not had a holiday in three years and who, on occasion, is overcome by everything he sees. The restaurant owner re-visiting a shattered building that was once his home. The Aslo family standing at the grave of their dead sister.

When confronted with these realities, the big question I am often asked is, "what can be done?" And to that I say, the first thing is to know the reality of war. To know the stunning cruelty and barbarism we are all capable of. To know so that we cannot say, as in previous wars, we never knew. As to the why and how? We need to think about what we are being asked to think about. About the rationales for wars, for outside interventions, about the justifications and the self-justifications. And how easily we can find ourselves parroting these. And then the question: is there ever a justification for war? Is there ever a justification for killing another human being?

Leaving Aleppo, and a final piece of script for the documentary. A look-back at Aleppo:

Before the war this was a city of three million people. Nobody knows for sure how many people live here now. On the war itself, Antoine was right, "the horror, the horror". A constant refrain I have heard here is the way in which foreigners have destroyed this city. But this foreigner has received nothing but the warmest of welcomes. Gifted wherever I went with tea and cigarettes. And an invitation to come back. To come back and see and enjoy what's left of this most ancient, beautiful and elegant of cities.

# 12

# Pepe Talk

## *Uruguay*

He walked slowly with his head down. The slow gait of a country man who has known hard labour and now feels it in his bones. When we shook hands, his hard-worked hands with blackened nails firmly gripped mine. José Alberto Mujica Cordano, to give him his full title, now in his eighties is a former president of Uruguay, South America's second smallest country, and affectionately known as Pepe in his country and throughout Latin America. Famously dishevelled, he has always foresworn the conventional suit and tie – "maybe it is male coquetry, but I don't understand that rag that men wear around their necks" – in favour of working man's clothes of baggy trousers, open-necked t-shirt and unzipped fleece. While president, he once almost caused a diplomatic incident because of his refusal to wear a tie. "Once in Europe I was to meet with a king. When I arrived, they were waiting for me with a tie. So, I said 'we are leaving, we are not going to see the king'." An incident was averted. He was allowed meet the king without a tie.

The man and the face have become synonymous with a different world view, one that not only believes there is a different way to live, but lives that different way.

"I have always been a country man," he tells me. "Even when I was president." Before we sit down to talk, he shows me around his farm, curiously, from an Irish perspective, located on a dusty road past a lemon grove on O'Higgins Road. "This is the time of the year to prepare the summer nursery: tomatoes, peppers, pumpkins and some flowers too." Along with his wife Lucia Topolansky, once the country's vice-president, he sells their produce at the local market.

I ask whether he still has his car, the symbol of his austere lifestyle? Famously, he drove every day from 2010 to 2015 in his 1987 Volkswagen Beetle from his farmhouse to his presidential office. Not for him the opulent Suárez y Reyes presidential mansion, with its staff of forty-two. Such was the car's fame that an Arab Sheik offered him one million dollars for it on leaving office. He declined. But he offered me a drive in it. Flattered, I gladly accepted. Driving down that dusty road, windows open, a neighbouring farmer looked up and waved and Pepe responded, each with the ease and familiarity of two country men.

In Latin America and in left-wing politics elsewhere, the mostly revered Pepe's back story is well known. As a young man he had a political epiphany when he met Che Guevara in post-revolutionary Cuba. A bust of Che Guevara peers down from a bookshelf in his dilapidated farmhouse. Pepe tells me he has something special to show me. Che Guevara's last diary, given to him by Bolivian President Evo Morales. It's not the original but there are only ten copies in the world and this was one. Written in blue ink, the handwriting is neat, compact, as if nothing ought to be wasted. "Hadn't he good writing for a doctor?" Pepe muses.

I tell Pepe of the link between Ché and my home town of Kilkee, and the iconic poster of Ché by Jim Fitzpatrick based on a photograph taken by Alberto Korda. The image he knew, its origins, not surprisingly, he did not. Fitzpatrick, as a sixteen-year-old, met Che in the Royal Marine bar in Kilkee in the summer of 1961. At the time, Che's flight from Shannon to Moscow was delayed so he travelled to the seaside town of Kilkee for some rest and relaxation. Kilkee now hosts an annual festival in his honour and his image adorns the walls of the town. A keen observer of Cuban politics, Fitzpatrick recognised him immediately.

Like so many other Latin American revolutionaries of his era, 'Pepe' Mujica sought to emulate the Cuban revolutionary model. The old order was beyond reform. It had to be destroyed. "Che Guevara was unforgettable, a mould-breaker, the true spirit of universalist Latin American values. He marked our entire youth."

On his final revolutionary expedition to Bolivia, Che Guevara passed through Uruguay securing a fake Uruguayan ID that allowed his onward journey. "I saw him two months before he died," Pepe tells me. "Yes of course I went to his funeral." Che's body was repatriated from Bolivia to Cuba for a pomp-filled state burial in 1997.

But Pepe is also a realist. He knows that the methods employed by Che and Fidel Castro were of their time.

"Che Guevara was part of a moment in time. He represents that insurrectionist world. It seemed at the time that social change was around the corner. We were really mistaken. I think it is more complex. The reality is much more complex."

The former revolutionary, who at the age of seventy-five became the country's fortieth president in 2010, left office with an approval rating of almost 70 per cent. During his presidency, he parted with 90 per cent of his salary, which earned him the moniker "the world's poorest president". On his inauguration, his annual personal wealth declaration – mandatory in Uruguay – was $1,800, the value of his Volkswagen Beetle.

Mujica joined the MLN-Tupamaros in 1966, an armed revolutionary group dedicated to the overthrow of what they regarded as the kleptocratic Colorado and Nationalist parties that had ruled Uruguay for 160 years, and sought to replace them with a Cuban-style Marxist government. Three years later Pepe, at thirty-five years of age, along with nine comrades, all MLN guerrillas, attacked the quiet industrial town of Pando with a population of 12,000. They robbed the bank and attempted to take control of the local government offices. In what has been described as a chaotic shoot-out in broad daylight, a police officer and a civilian were killed. It was an event that marked his life and caused him later to renounce violence.

In 1970, Mujica was shot six times by police. Expected to die in the hospital, he made a miraculous recovery. In 1971, he escaped from prison. Quickly re-arrested, he managed to escape again the following year. In August he was again arrested and spent the next thirteen years in prison, three of them in solitary confinement in a drained swimming pool covered with sheet metal. At one point he was held in a watering trough.

The poet, novelist and playwright Mauricio Rosencof spent eleven years in a tiny cell next to Uruguay's future president. The prisoners could only communicate by tapping morse code on their cell walls. Allowed to use the toilet just once a day, they urinated into their water bottles, allowing the sediment to settle and drinking the rest because water was also scarce. It was even worse for Mujica, whose six bullet wounds had seriously damaged his stomach and his health. The self-educated guerrilla turned politician who quotes at will from the Greek and Roman classics – Seneca is a particular favourite – recalls those years.

> I spent a very hard decade in complete isolation; they moved me every six or eight months from one military unit to the other. I couldn't read for seven years. Man is a harsh animal.

This was a cruel deprivation on top of the others inflicted on him. But these weren't wasted years.

> Until I was nineteen years old I was a passionate reader,
> with a discipline of six or seven hours of severe reading.
> I was poor but I went to a public library. Then my life
> changed and in the years I spent in prison I searched
> in my memory for knowledge that I didn't even know
> I had.

It is that knowledge that now draws people to him. On the
day I visited him at his farm, a young Italian man had travelled especially to Uruguay in the hope of meeting him. A US
film crew were scheduled to meet him afterwards. All wanting
to see and hear how this most unorthodox politician lives, and
hear from the former president whose life is like no other's.

Released in 1985 when Uruguay returned to democracy,
Mujica and other former guerrillas joined together to create the
Movement of Popular Participation, a left-wing political party.
He became a senator in 1999. Six years later he was Minister
for Agriculture, conjoining his passion for politics and farm-
ing. In 2010, he was elected president of Uruguay. "My goal is
to achieve a little less injustice in Uruguay. To help the most
vulnerable and to leave behind a political way of thinking,"
he said at the time. Both a modest and an audacious ambition.

"We live in the most unjust continent in the world, probably the richest, but with the worst distribution of wealth," he
has stated on numerous occasions. Challenging the model of
development based on untrammelled growth, he singles out
hyper-consumption as doing irreparable damage to the planet.

During Mujica's time as president poverty was reduced, as
was income inequality, although for him poverty cannot sole-
ly be measured in financial terms. Quoting again from Seneca
he tells me:

> Poor is the one that needs a lot. My definition is old.
> I am a neo-stoic. In the market society nothing is
> enough, I am not poor, I am austere in the way I live,
> I try to go with little luggage.

He supported the nation's ground-breaking legalisation of marijuana. Uruguay became the first country in the world to regulate the legal production, sale and consumption of marijuana. His intention was to take the market away from the ruthless drug traffickers and treat drug addiction as a public health issue.

This was my reason for coming to Uruguay. In Peru, Colombia, Mexico and the United States, I had witnessed first-hand the social upheaval caused by strict prohibitionist drug policies. The emphasis was always on cutting supply, Latin America being the fall-guy for US consumption. What was happening in Uruguay was an altogether different story and I was anxious to get a first-hand account. But all stories need context and this is Uruguay's, a context it shares with every other country in the world.

For years the international drug trade has been characterised as a supply problem and not a demand problem, a disproportionate focus on first stage production rather than on the consumers. Its problematisation in itself a problem. While precise figures are hard to come by given the nature of illicit drug conumers, according to the UN World Drug Report 2018 an estimated 5.6 per cent of the global population aged 15–64 years, or approximately one in every eighteen people, had consumed illicit drugs at least once in the previous year. The actual number of people who use drugs increased by twenty million people from 2015 to 2016. Nearly half the population of the United States say they have tried marijuana at least once in their lifetime. Cannabis was the most commonly used drug globally in 2016 with 192 million people consuming it at least once. In 2017, Global Financial Integrity (GFI) published a report that estimated the value of the global market in drug trafficking at between $426 billion and $652 billion, the second most lucrative illicit market in the world, behind counterfeiting and ahead of illegal logging.

Dating back to antiquity, the vast majority of cultures have sought ways and means of ingesting substances in the expectation that these would at best produce a feel-good response, or at worst go some way towards assuaging pain and distress. Such experimentation would appear to have been openly tolerated and considered a normal part of the human condition since time immemorial.

Since the beginning of the twentieth century, particular kinds of drugs have been problematised and criminalised, cannabis being a case in point, while other kinds of drugs, promoted and produced by for-profit pharmaceutical companies, have been sanctioned in what would appear to have been a very arbitrary process. The sanctioning of some drugs has resulted in enormous profits for some, while the criminalisation of others has also generated enormous profits for many people but has also resulted in terrible social upheaval and loss. Much of this loss and destruction has accrued from the "war on drugs".

In a seamless continuity of policy, each president of the United States since the World War II has identified a particular war that characterises his presidency. In some cases, the war baton is passed from one president to the next. The "war on drugs" is one such war. Nixon's war on drugs became Reagan's war on drugs, then Bush senior's war on drugs, then Clinton's war on drugs, then the younger Bush's war on drugs, and these wars then morphed into the war on terrorism.

Richard Nixon was the first president to declare a "war on drugs", a war that has not only had a calamitous influence on drug policy but has destabilised the USA's neighbouring southern nations and deepened US military involvement across Latin America. This was, he claimed, "America's public enemy number one." Not poverty. Not white supremacy. Not gun violence.

Seven months after taking office in 1969, Nixon announced a global campaign against drugs and their traffickers. Nixon "saw evil Mexican traffickers exporting marijuana into the

United States," a phrase echoed by the current churlish incumbent in the White House. Nixon attempted to seal off the 2,500 mile-long border between the United States and Mexico, a policy that disrupted social and economic activity. Mexican farmers and traders held up at the border for hours on end as traffic was stopped and searched were particularly hard hit. Their perishable goods just rotted in the hot sun.

Echoing Nixon's declaration of war on drugs, Ronald Reagan allocated over $1 billion to his first war on drugs in 1982. In 1986, Ronald Reagan signed the National Security Decision Directive 221 declaring drug trafficking a threat to national security. George Bush senior followed with a similar declaration and in addition mobilised the US army for the war. Bush senior briefly reactivated Richard Nixon's 1969 short-lived Operation Intercept. He too attempted to seal off the border with Mexico and block the supply of narcotics coming into the country. Federal spending on combating the movement of illicit drugs from outside its borders increased from $1.65 billion in 1982 to $17.7 billion in 1999.

In the year 2000 Clinton launched Plan Colombia, initially at a cost of $1.3 billion, to combat drug trafficking and guerrilla violence. In 2012, long after he left office and long after he could effect change, Clinton acknowledged that his administration's attempt to limit drug trafficking from Colombia "hasn't worked" and that the global war on drugs "is a failure".

At the time of writing in 2019, the present incumbent of the White House has followed the same line of thinking, claiming that 90 per cent of the drugs coming into the United States come through Mexico and the southern border, a claim the US Department of Justice's Drug Enforcement Administration cannot verify. The claim aims to bolster his demand to fund an $18 billion border wall with Mexico and a $50 million anti-drug media campaign. Such campaigns, previously tried, like Nancy Reagan's alarmist and ultimately futile "Just Say

No" that continued for a decade, and which Congress elimi-
nated in 2012 after studies showed that their hysterical nature
may actually have led to an increase in drug consumption.

The stubbornness, tenacity and ferocity with which the war
on drugs has been fought by each successive US president has
increased over time and has been replicated across the world.
Since its inception in 1972, the US government has spent over
a trillion dollars or an average of $51 billion annually on its
war on drugs. Every facet of US life has been affected. The
incarceration rate has sky-rocketed. At a cost of $9.2 million
every day, one-fifth of the current incarcerated population in
the USA is serving time for a drug charge, while another 1.5
million are on probation or parole. People of colour account
for seventy per cent of all defendants convicted of charges
with a mandatory minimum sentence – African Americans are
four times more likely to be arrested for marijuana possession.
Hundreds of thousands of people (230,000) have died from
drug-related causes, 72,000 deaths by overdose in the USA
during 2017 alone.

Others have taken their cue from the United States. Filipino President Rodrigo Duterte embarked on a mercilessly sav-
age attack in an effort to eliminate drug traffickers and users,
resulting in the extrajudicial execution of more than 27,000
people since June 2016. Between 1 July 2016 and 30 September
2018 4,948 suspected drug users and dealers died during police operations.

The "war on drugs" formally declared by Nixon in 1972
was essentially a war on blacks, a war on hippies and a war
on anti-war protestors, something his former domestic policy
advisor John Ehrlichman subsequently acknowledged. "You
want to know what this was really all about?" Ehrlichman said
in a later interview.

> The Nixon campaign in 1968, and the Nixon White
> House after that, had two enemies: the anti-war leftists

and black people. We knew we couldn't make it illegal to be either against the war or black, but by getting the public to associate the hippies with marijuana and blacks with heroin, and then criminalising both heavily, we could disrupt those communities. We could arrest their leaders, raid their homes, break up their meetings, and vilify them night after night.

The war on drugs, Nixon's Trojan horse.

It is against this background that Uruguay's ground-breaking legislation on marijuana needs to be understood.

In stark contrast, Mujica recognised that the drug trade could not be defeated militarily. A military solution had been tried and failed spectacularly. "Narco-trafficking is defeating us in the whole world. It corrupts every institution and the current prohibitionist policy is [mired] in violence. Repressive politics do not give us answers," the former president told me.

The profit is so high that there will always be people ready to risk their freedom for that kind of profit. Reality is reality, you can't change reality because it is ugly. We must learn to accept it and manage it in the best way possible.

Recognising he could not defeat them, he sought to undermine them.

While Mujica was the first president in the world to legalise cannabis he was not out of step with recent thinking within Latin America. In April 2012, thirty-three heads of state and government of the Organisation of American States commissioned a report on the drug problem in the Americas with the following guidelines:

The report should be frank, thorough, and shed light on actions taken so far to confront the drug problem, without shying away from sensitive issues and without fear of breaking taboos in order to pave the way for new approaches to the drug phenomenon.

225

One year later, in May 2013, the report's conclusions testified to the pressing need for governments to revisit the policies that had predominated in the hemisphere and yet had failed to achieve expected outcomes. The *New York Times* wrote that the report "effectively breaks the taboo on considering alternatives to the current prohibitionist approach". The starting point was that there is not just one drug-related problem but rather a host of problems.

In its conclusions, the report asserted that sooner or later decisions will need to be taken that lean toward the decriminalisation or legalisation of the production, sale and use of marijuana. This new debate shifted from one principally concerned with economics, morality and law to a focus on public health. Ricardo Soberon, a Peruvian global drug policy expert whom I met in Lima, summed it up as follows: "The drug problem in essence is a health problem and not a security problem." That realisation has changed perspectives not only within Latin America but also with those affected, and people working with those affected, by chaotic drug use.

The steps that Mujica, who has never smoked cannabis in his life – "I am old-fashioned and marijuana does not suit me" – and the Uruguayan government took to legalise the production, sale and consumption of marijuana were cautious and considered. Some believe the agreed system is too restrictive and too paternalistic as the government determines the price, quality and volume of production and sets limits to consumption. Unlike cigarettes, smoking cannabis in public places is proscribed. In addition, driving under the influence of cannabis is prohibited. A core element of the legislation was a public campaign promoting responsible use of marijuana. These measures, one user told me, are there to benefit the user and to ensure that people have a good and safe trip.

The legislation, which was enacted on 20 December 2013, was no free-for-all. The law applies only to those over eighteen years of age:

> The state will take control of regulating the activities of import, export, planting, cultivation, harvesting, production, acquisition in any capacity, storage, marketing and distribution of cannabis and its derivatives, or hemp when appropriate, through the institutions to which it grants legal mandate ... the growing or cultivation of plants must be authorised beforehand by the Cannabis Regulation and Control Institute (IRCCA) ...

While the law decriminalised cannabis for personal use, those who exceeded the prescribed level of cannabis production would be severely punished.

> Anyone who, without legal authorisation, produces – in any manner – raw materials or substances capable of producing psychological or physical dependency, as the case may be ... shall be punished by a prison sentence ranging from 20 months to 10 years.

The law allows for residents to grow up to six "certified and unadulterated" plants at home. Cannabis can also be bought from a local pharmacy or people can create their own cannabis clubs. Members of the club, with a maximum membership of forty-five, can withdraw forty grams per month from the club's cannabis crop. Each club can grow a maximum of ninety-nine plants. The Ministry for Health can prescribe cannabis for health reasons. It is estimated that 160,000 cannabis users have officially registered since December 2013.

Over seven days in 2016 I met with several people, mostly young, who are availing of the new dispensation. "Being stoned is a pleasure, it's nice" was how one young teacher described why he smokes cannabis. It's a self-evident but barely-heard perspective. "It's a feeling of peace and quiet." Acknowledging that some people think marijuana is the devil, he went on to say, "I don't bother anyone and I don't do much harm to myself. I think I am a responsible user." This teacher is quite open with his students about his consumption. "The legislation and the social consensus around it make that possible. No shame. No fear."

The caveat of "I don't do much harm to myself" is what those opposed to the new law emphasise. But on the day I visited a grow-farm club, there was very little talk of that harm. Up to a dozen people in their twenties and thirties, some with young children, were involved in various stages of production. It was low-intensity yet organised and efficient work. On this farm, nobody was breaking a sweat. Open ground was being broken by hand-held tools. Plants were being propagated in a germination room. People were drinking tea, talking and, of course, smoking. Children were playing, potting their own plants. All with an air of normality. It could be any community garden anywhere in the world.

The cannabis club was established in 2014, I was told. The land rented from a farmer, far from the public road. People are still coy about the location of such farms. Those opposed to the legalisation of cannabis destroy any crops they come across. Potential thieves willing to take advantage of other people's work pose another threat. "In the club we are workers, students, mothers, fathers, young people and not so young," I was told. The forty-five members of the club are no longer buying weed on the black market. "With our own plants we know what we are smoking, we no longer need to go to the 'bocas' to buy it."

Fear of the "bocas" was keenly felt by those who sought outlets from which to purchase marijuana prior to legalisation, particularly for young middle-class Uruguayans. Much of the illegal trade was located in the barrios and poorer areas of Montevideo, Uruguay's capital city of 1.4 million people. Part of Mujica's motivation in legalising marijuana was to ease the pressure on the barrios and provide some protection for the city's poor. "To buy marijuana, I used to go to the 'bocas'. There was a house with some kids who sold marijuana and it was quite complicated. My legs were shaking every time I went there."

For those living in the "bocas" the sale of marijuana added another layer of challenges to their lives. Now "there are fewer *casitas* (little houses) where they sell weed", one woman who lives in one of the "bocas" told me. "And that's been possible thanks to marijuana legislation."

That fear has now dissipated. Marcel Renaud, a precocious and engaging IT specialist, personified that new-found confidence. Working along with five or six colleagues, his office has the now *de rigueur* paraphernalia of IT offices. A table football sits in the middle of the office. A guitar leans against a wall. People are sitting intently in front of screens. Most ignore me. "We are from the software area and we are developers."

In his distinctively American-accented English, Marcel tells me with some swagger:

> We are part of Silicon Valley. Not everyone smokes in the office. Most people don't actually in the office hours. But some of us do. Some relax time or some lunch time. I like it. I like our liberties and our freedoms.

We go up on the roof of the building. It is oppressively hot. The midday sun. Not the most auspicious time, I would have thought, for smoking. "When I have most of my work done, I take some free time and enjoy a joint." He offers me some; smoking is a communal activity. The joint is passed around to whoever wishes to partake. I accept. It's potent. And I find it difficult to imagine how one could so easily integrate smoking cannabis into a work routine. But Marcel has no such difficulty.

For those highly critical of the legalisation, one of the young people on the grow-farm pointed to the failure of years of prohibition.

Abstinence is not real. People have lived with drugs from the beginning. If we are talking about health, it will be always worse to get whatever you consume from the black market than from here on this land. The war against drugs has failed. And it continues to fail. It has been very expensive in terms of human lives lost and money, the corruption it generates and the effect it has had on many democracies. It is time we stop something that does not work.

It's a view shared by two unlikely people: HIV and addiction specialist Dr Julia Galzerano, and Luis Parodi, Director of Rieles Prison in Montevideo. Both are supporters of the current legislation. Consumption of cannabis is less addictive than cigarettes and less addictive than alcohol, Dr Galzerano tells me. She lists all the illnesses that cannabis can treat. Included are:

> ... neurological conditions: refractory [drug-resistant] epilepsy, multiple sclerosis, Parkinson's disease. Then there is chronic pain of various etiologies. Chronic pain related to cancer, either caused by the cancer itself, or chronic pain related to the treatment of cancer with chemotherapy. Chronic neuropathic pain, pain related to the pathophysiology of the spine [back pain], migraine. We also use it with anxiety. We use it with depression. We have some colleagues who have treated post-traumatic stress disorder. And we have many children and young people with general developmental disorders and autism. This is a new use and brings about neuro-cognitive improvements.

I ask about side-effects and these are acknowledged, but with a caveat.

> It does have some side-effects. In some people we see a higher incidence of testicular cancer. Yes. But I'm talking about chronic use. A higher rate of infertility. Chronic use, but not the significant adverse side-effects other medications have.

Dr Galzerano is also clear that cannabis is not a gateway drug to cocaine or coca paste or alcohol. And then she adds: "And another thing to note is that it does not have a lethal effect. Cannabis is a substance that has not caused a single recorded death anywhere in the world." This is a view almost universally shared. Nearly all medicines have toxic, potentially lethal, effects. Marijuana is not such a substance. For marijuana to kill, a person would have to ingest about one-third of their body weight or 680 kilograms in one dose. An unlikely scenario. In contrast, according to the World Health Organisation, three million people die each year from alcohol-related illnesses (5.3 per cent of all deaths) while tobacco kills up to half its users – 7 million each year plus 1.2 million passive smokers.

While marijuana is widely available, state prisons are still a no-go area, a situation Luis Parodi would like to change. "The fact that drugs are prohibited within the prisons gives immense power to the narcos inside the prison," Luis tells me.

> Legalising will always be better than not legalising. Drugs must be legalised. They're here. People have them. So, the best thing we can do is legalise them, talk about them, make them visible.

Like his former president, Luis is only too conscious of the destruction wrought by drug traffickers across Latin America. We have a situation where electoral campaigns are financed by traffickers.

> If the traffickers occupy the place of the state, we really will have a problem. It's alarming: they pay for your campaign and then you're their prisoner. At one point in Colombia, the traffickers proposed to the government that they would pay the national debt, for example. They'd pay it, and then: Bye Bye!

In coming to Uruguay, it wasn't my intention to hear from the nay-sayers. There is enough of that. It's well established

231

that the legalising of marijuana does not meet with universal approval. One woman selling lottery cards on the streets of Montevideo, whom I briefly stopped to talk to, was determined to have her say. "Marijuana is no good for young people, they lose all sense of responsibility. They don't want to work, they are deluded." It was clear as well she was no fan of Pepe.

> His government was shameless, I can say it as a Uruguayan woman, born in this land. It was a disaster because he helped those who do not work and give nothing to the country. He gave them houses and all kind of benefits, and he never gave anything to Uruguayan workers, to those who have worked all their lives.

I came to Uruguay to hear about the country's unique experience of legalising marijuana and to meet its former president, José Pepe Mujica. With Pepe I discovered you get more than an insight into his innovative drugs policy. Now that he is out of office, it is his philosophical rather than just day-to-day political reflections that people come to hear.

An avowed agnostic he may be, but Mujica inhabits that crossroads between secularism and spirituality from which he calls forth a more generous world, in stark contrast to the dystopian vision that the current (2019) president north of the Rio Grande embodies. In a world weary of hectoring and discordant rhetoric that divides and manipulates, his quiet-spoken gentleness and firm convictions that there is another way, that there is an alternative, are reassuring for many.

Mujica is opposed to war and militarism. "The world spends $2 billion a minute on military spending," he exclaimed once in horror to students at an American University. "I used to think there were just, noble wars, but I don't think that anymore," said the former armed guerrilla. "Now I think the only solution is through negotiations. The worst negotiation is better than the best war, and the only way to ensure peace is to cultivate tolerance."

The excessive concentration of wealth and the global increase in inequality is another theme that Mujica returns to again and again.

> Along with the environmental problem and the nuclear danger, the excessive concentration of wealth is one of the main threats to freedom in the world. The concentration of wealth is concentration of political power, is anti-democratic.

He is also concerned with the extent to which we now dedicate so much of our time to the pursuit of wealth. The pursuit of wealth over the pursuit of happiness.

> When I buy something, I don't buy it with money but with the time I had to spend to earn that money. But what I can't buy is time. To be clear: if I work all day to pay the bills, I don't have time left to live. That's the thing. Life, it is not only about economic progress, we have to fight for happiness. And happiness means having time for our beloved ones and for the good little things in life, which don't give us money, but create feelings. And that's one of the keys of the contemporary pain.

He is reluctant to discuss his own legacy. With Pepe there is no sense of triumphalism. He is far too sure of himself for that. And he has known life in all its triumphs and failures.

> I dreamed of achieving more than I did. To end poverty and indigence. It went down, but we still have a 9 per cent of poverty and 0.5 per cent of indigency. But in a very unfair continent, Uruguay was always the one that distributed the most. But still, we have many social debts.

I was coming to the end of my visit with this seemingly out-of-step former president in his out-of-step attire who thinks politics is as much about personal and collective happiness, care for the earth, encountering alternatives to the shallow seduction of consumerism, and the joy of conviviality as it is about the cold logic of GDP, GNP or the Gini co-efficient.

233

Not that he isn't concerned with income inequality or wealth distribution. His record says otherwise. Mujica is as far from a neoliberal apologist as one can get, but neither does this former Marxist guerrilla fighter wish to give credence to what he regards as the polarised binary ideologies of right-wing/left-wing politics. Pictures of Che Guevara might adorn his sitting room walls but he believes his politics, while necessary for his time, now belong to another era.

On meeting Pepe, there were some stand-out moments. On his own life he had this to say.

> It's been an interesting life, an intense life and full of obstacles, like the life of everyone who tries to change the world, with better or worse luck. I have been very lucky because I am still alive, that is almost a gift, but I spent some years in prison, have some injuries, a lot of clandestine years. But I am no hero.

And then as I left, a reminder…

> Being alive is a miracle, and sometimes people, in the middle of the noise around us, do not realise that. But being alive is miraculous. So we have to be happy in this life. Because we have only one life, and it is always going away.

As I take my leave the young Italian man continues to hover. "This is the way it is," one of Mujica's security guards tells us, although the term itself is a misnomer. The security guard just controls the flow of traffic as Pepe takes his leave of us and slowly and patiently awaits another foreign journalist.

# 13

# A DESERTED PEOPLE

## *Western Sahara*

Words are whispered in Laayoune, the capital city of occupied Western Sahara, particularly certain words. Whispered words and furtive eyes. And the eyes are everywhere. People anxiously watching, particularly the Sahrawi people. People feeling that they are constantly being watched. And the words hidden behind hands, whispered at the lowest possible decibel level. This is a fearful place.

Laayoune is an occupied city, and has been for over 40 years now. While the winds of change have liberated more than 80 countries, an estimated one billion people across the world, following the establishment of the United Nations in 1945, Western Sahara has remained an occupied country. And notwithstanding the numerous resolutions the United Nations has passed dating back to 1963 that assert Western Sahara's right to self-determination, that illegal annexation continues.

In 2014, on the 39th anniversary of the annexation of Western Sahara, King Mohammed VI declared: "Morocco will remain in its Sahara, and the Sahara will remain in its Morocco until the end of time," further adding that, "Moroccan sovereignty in the whole of its territory is unalterable, inalienable and non-negotiable."

The Sahrawi people see it all so differently.

"We are suffering from invaders who polluted our home-land," one old wind-lined and sun-lined woman told me as she sat in her tent in that sliver of desert Morocco has no strategic interest in annexing. Rather than live in her original home close to the sea, she chose the nomadic life of the desert. "They took our homeland from us. They have oppressed us. We want to be free from the filth of the invaders." I asked her if she were to meet with the King of Morocco what would she say to him. Her vehemence shook me. Her vitriol was not what I was expecting.

> I don't want to meet the King of Morocco. I don't want to see him ever. Seeing him is a disgust. He oppressed me and why would I see him? We don't like him. I'm going to spit on his face and tell him to get out of my homeland, you oppressor and invader, get out of my home. They murdered my brothers, my sons, my cous-ins and many Sahrawis so I don't want to see his face.

Given the scale of the Moroccan presence, Mauritania eventu-ally withdrew from Western Sahara leaving the spoils of vic-tory to the Moroccans. And the spoils are indeed rich. Fishing and lots of it, and phosphates, used in agricultural fertilizer. It is the second largest producer (30 million metric tons in 2018) of phosphates in the world, most of it illegally mined at the Bou Craa mine, exported to the rest of the world for the ben-efit of the Moroccan government and to the detriment of the Sahrawi people of Western Sahara. The extraction, sale and purchase of which is unethical and constitutes a violation of the human rights of the Sahrawi people. And now, in an age when the world has become increasingly aware of the fossil fuel risks to the survival of the planet, oil and gas are also among the spoils.

Filming in Western Sahara is strictly forbidden. Morocco does not tolerate western journalists in its annexed territory and any foreign journalist who manages to inveigle their way into the territory, if caught, is summarily expelled. Among the expelled was *The New Yorker* journalist Nicolas Niarchos and his brother. Before they could disembark from their plane in Laayoune in December 2018, they were met with "a swarm of plainclothes policemen … [who] began filming us and yelling … for half an hour the official shouted at us … reminding us of Morocco's support for the post-revolutionary United States". They were deported on the next flight.

High-profile human rights activist Kerry Kennedy, daughter of Senator Robert Kennedy and president of the Washington-based RFK Centre for Human Rights and a long-time supporter of the Sahrawi people, along with her then seventeen-year-old daughter Mariah Kennedy Cuomo, did manage to get to Laayoune in 2012. Kennedy claimed she and her daughter were roughed-up by the police.

These fates I was anxious to avoid.

Expulsion would have been, at worst, an inconvenience. Reporters without Borders ranked Morocco 135th out of 180 countries (2019) for safety for journalists, describing its media climate as "very difficult" citing "judicial harassment" as a regular feature of journalists' working lives. The organisation reported that, in addition to legal proceedings against professional and citizen journalists, Moroccan "authorities deliberately obstructed national and foreign media…". In 2012, Morocco expelled nineteen journalists from Western Sahara, of whom fifteen were Spanish and four Norwegian. Between May and August 2017, Morocco arrested eight journalists. From within Morocco comes criticism too. Freedom Now, a coalition of human rights defenders, claimed that press freedom in Morocco in 2019 is the worst since the 1990s.

Morocco's Ministry of Culture and Communication rejected these findings, claiming that the country enjoys "an atmosphere of freedom and independence, without any direct and indirect censorship".

That was not my experience.

Following protracted communication with key informants within Western Sahara, representatives of the Sahrawi Arab Democratic Republic (SADR) government in exile, representatives of that government in London as well as in the refugee camps in Algeria, a colleague and I surreptitiously entered Western Sahara in October 2015. My colleague was celebrating his half-century birthday. For him, entering Wetsern Sahara was a lifelong dream. The call of the Sahara, the world's most iconic desert, Africa's internal ocean. The largest hot desert in the world. That was our story, if asked. Perhaps we looked like a hapless pair. After a cursory questioning, we were allowed through.

Our detailed pre-arranged plan worked. We spent three days in Western Sahara, facilitated at enormous personal risk by two Sahrawis living in Laayoune. On the city's footpath at a designated meeting place, a man on a mobile phone, without making eye contact, walked by us and said, "follow me". We did, at a distance, through a warren of streets. At one point two men emerged from one of the side streets and took our rucksacks. We didn't object. A white jeep was parked ahead of us. The door opened and we were hurriedly ushered in. Minutes later, we stopped and were steered into two separate cars. We were driven separately for about half an hour before arriving at a nondescript apartment building. Told to wait until the apartment door was open, we exited kerb-side and hurried up two flights of stairs. It never crossed our minds that we may have been intercepted, that these may have been interlopers. Heading down a warren of side streets in a city where we didn't have the language, in a city we didn't have permission to be in, in the company of strange men. Perhaps we *were* a hapless pair. But as it transpired, we were in the safest of hands.

We had arrived. Life in Western Sahara.

Western Sahara, that sprawling swathe of African desert wedged between the Atlantic coast to its west and the largely inhospitable, barren Hamada region to the east. The last un-resolved colonial conflict in Africa bar the Chagos Islands.[1] In 1974, the United Nations Special Committee on Decolonisation declared Western Sahara a "non-self-governing territory", and pressure mounted on Spain to decolonise. Dating from 1884, the Spanish colony imploded in 1975, along with the General Franco-led dictatorship.

In expectation of the decolonisation process, Morocco and Mauritania claimed sovereignty over the territory, ties that they believed pre-dated the Spanish colonisation of Western Sahara. In October 1975, the International Court of Justice (ICJ) formally rejected both Morocco's and Mauritania's claims, concluding that the evidence presented "does not establish any tie of territorial sovereignty between the territory of West-ern Sahara and the Kingdom of Morocco or the Mauritanian entity". The ICJ found that the right to self-determination for the Sahrawis was "paramount".

Shortly after the ICJ declared that Western Sahara had the right to self-determination, Spain relinquished its administra-tive control over the territory. Without the authorisation of the UN Special Committee on Decolonisation and without the consent of the people of Western Sahara, Spain bequeathed two-thirds of the territory to the Kingdom of Morocco and one-third to Mauritania. One month after the ICJ determination, Morocco sent 350,000 settlers and soldiers to colonise West-ern Sahara, an incursion that became known as the "Green March", a momentous event in recent Moroccan history that is still celebrated every year.

On 28 February 1976, the Moroccan national flag was hoist-ed in Laayoune.

---

1 See *What in the World? Political Travels in Africa, Asia and the Americas.*

Marking the forty-third anniversary of the Green March, Moroccan journalist Tarek Bazza wrote:

> The march succeeded in recovering the southern prov-
> inces peacefully and civilly, recalling the words of the
> then Moroccan King Hassan II: "We have to do one
> thing, dear people, and that is to undertake a peaceful
> march from the north, the east, the west to the south. It
> behoves us to act as one man in order to join the Sahara."

Bazza's journalistic colleague El Houssaine Naaim described the march as "the largest, longest, and most peaceful
march anywhere in the world".

It is not how the Sahrawi people saw it at the time, or see
it now.

The Moroccans were met with resistance from the Frente
Para la Liberación de Saguia Al Hamra y Rio de Oro (Polisario), Western Sahara's national liberation movement backed
by Algeria. In 1975, the Polisario Front began a sixteen-year-
long guerrilla war against Moroccan forces' occupation of
what they regarded as their country, which ended with a 1991
UN-brokered cease-fire. Sporadic violence has occurred since.
Nobody knows for sure what the precise death toll from the
war is but estimates range from 14,000 to 21,000 over 43 years
of conflict.

In 1976, Polisario proclaimed the Sahrawi Arab Democratic Republic (SADR)[2] and three years later, Mauritania withdrew from the territory and admitted the wrongfulness of its
1975 occupation of Western Sahara. As Mauritania withdrew,
Morocco extended its control over 80 per cent of the territory,
which it still controls today. The remaining 20 per cent is a

---

[2] Ireland's longstanding position on SADR was reiterated by Tánaiste
and Minister for Foreign Affairs Simon Coveney in the Dáil (Q.68) on 6
December 2018 as follows: While Ireland does not recognise the Saharawi
Arab Democratic Republic, the state declared by the Polisario Front, it does
recognise the Polisario Front as a party to the dispute, and my officials meet
regularly with its representatives to seek their views on the current situation.

narrow desert strip of no strategic or commercial value, home to a few nomadic families and their herds of camels and goats.

Following the Green March, the Kingdom of Morocco incentivised Moroccan settlers with higher public servant wages and offers of houses once owned by the Sahrawis to move to the Western Saharan territory. This was analogous to the seventeenth century Plantation of Ulster and the sixteenth century Plantation of Munster in Ireland, a deliberate and calculated attempt to erase any vestiges of Sahrawi life and physically mark the landscape with the ubiquitous Moroccan flag which, at the time I was there, was flying from every possible vantage point, not just in the city but on all major roads leading to it. The Moroccan occupation was complete. While no census has been conducted, it is believed that Moroccans in the Western Sahara currently outnumber the Sahrawis.

Meanwhile, tens of thousands of Sahrawis fled the violence and the Moroccan army's advances for the baking hot "desert within a desert" in southwestern Algeria. By October 1976, 50,000 Sahrawis were living in the Tindouf refugee camps in Algeria. The memory of that flight lives on among the older generation.

"I left Western Sahara in 1975, when the Moroccans invaded the area, I was among the people who witnessed the Moroccan invasion," Dide Bjtech – dressed for the desert in her beautifully textured aquatic blue darra robe that leaves only her face exposed to the blistering sun – told me over tea. There is always tea in Tindouf refugee camp. Tea and welcome. "Indeed, you are welcome here, welcome as guests regardless where you came from, any time you come."

> We are living on borrowed land. Our home is in Western Sahara but for now we live here. I fled with my family. I was with my father, my mother and my brothers. My father died in the battle. We arrived at a place called Gelta, but they followed us and attacked us there, then we fled to a place called Mahbes and it was already

crowded with people. And we kept moving, stopping only in places where we could be safe from the attacks until we reached the Algerian borders and found safety. We slept between plants and under trees, we did not carry our tents with us because we were in a rush just to get out for safety. Sometimes we slept under the shadow of some trucks or a tree or whatever we could find. Some trucks were fully packed with people, mostly old people running for safety. Some old people were carried by their sons. I have seen some young people carrying old ladies on their shoulders.

Ours was a less eventful journey – another privileged western dividend that allows us to travel pretty much where we wish across this planet.

Prior to travelling to Western Sahara, in October 2015, along with my crew colleagues, I visited Tindouf, a town with a population of under 60,000 people located close to the Mauritanian, Western Saharan and Moroccan borders. To get to the Sahrawi refugee camps, we flew to Algeria's capital Algiers, from there to Tindouf and then under an armed Algerian guard for the fifty-kilometre journey to the outskirts of the refugee camps. Polisario Front soldiers in desert-battered cars took us to Smara Camp, one of five (El Aaiun, Boujdour, Awserd, Smara, and Dakhla, all called after towns in Moroccan-occupied Western Sahara) scattered throughout the desolate desert, now home to an estimated 173,600 people according to 2017 UN data. These refugees remain "the longest warehoused refugee groups in the world" according to the US Committee for Refugees and Immigrants.

It was dark on arrival. Mustafa Mohamed Ali, Chief of Defence Supplies with the Polisario Front, was our host. His is a large extended family and it is difficult initially to establish precise family relationships. Given the circumstances in which they live, their generosity was remarkable. His home is in

Smara Camp, the largest of the Sahrawi camps with perhaps as many as 50,000 refugees.

The morning sunlight greeted my early rise. Stepping outside Mustafa's home, everything, bar the sky, is brown with the exception of the colour-dotted clothes lines. Brown and silent as far as the eye can see across this flat, barren, yet beautiful wasteland. Desert brown mud-built flat-roofed homes were scattered randomly across the brown landscape. Constructed initially, Dide Bjtech tells me, from bricks "made from our own bare hands". Even the rocks that break through the desert were covered in a thin layer of sand that gives them a veneer of brownness.

These early-morning moments are the ones to savour in the desert. Later, I was told, temperatures would rise to over 40°C. In summer they reach over 50°C. So hot the camps have earned the sobriquet "The Devil's Garden". As I stood at Mustafa's front door, I watched a woman wash the exterior walls of her home with water. Unless homes are regularly watered, Mustafa tells me over breakfast, they will crumble from the searing sun. The uniform landscape is both beautiful and grim. And it's not just the sun. The wind, when whipped up, is biting. Women, men and children move, where possible, in the shadow of the houses, cowering against the wind's piercing impact.

In fluent English, a downbeat and disheartened Sahrawi Students' Union leader Jalihenna Mohamed, born in the refugee camp 27 years previously, described the harsh reality of life in the camps.

> I have experienced the hardness of the living in the camps, as have all of the Sahrawis. In the summer we live here in more than 50°C. And of course, in the winter we face a lot of problems with the very very cold. To live under more than 50°C in the summer, that means that you cannot go out from 10 o'clock in the morning till nightfall. You are waiting all the day for the night

to fall to go out in the fresh air. And the night can be hot as the day. The Moroccans not only occupied our country but they keep prolonging our sufferings. Here in the camps, the conditions, we feel like we are living in a prison. And that's all because of the Moroccan occupation of our land.

Morocco's stance is not recognised by the fifty-four-member-strong African Union (AU), not recognised by the United Nations, not recognised by the European Court of Justice, not recognised by the United States of America.

In 1991, a United Nations Mission for the Referendum in Western Sahara (MINURSO) was created to oversee a ceasefire that ended the sixteen-year civil war between the Moroccan army and the Polisario Front, and to pave the way for a referendum on the status of Western Sahara. No referendum has ever taken place and currently there are no plans to hold one. In 2011, the UN Security Council recommended establishing a human rights monitoring mandate within Western Sahara, but due to pressure from Morocco, this has also not happened. Furthermore, Morocco as late as 2018 has threatened to break with the 1991 ceasefire, claiming that the Polisario has repeatedly broken the terms of the agreement. The United Nations has found no evidence of such breaches.

In 2017, Morocco re-joined the AU more than three decades after it left in 1984 when the membership voted to recognise the independence of Western Sahara. Among the most stalwart supporters of Western Sahara are the Southern African countries, Swaziland excepted.

In Tindouf I met with Dennis Thokozani Diomo, South Africa's ambassador to Western Sahara. "For many years the people of South Africa," he tells me, "have struggled against internal colonialism and apartheid and our people have been in receipt of international solidarity and support. We believe it is only natural to support those still in bondage." And with some confidence he then predicts: "What we will see in our lifetime is the freedom of the people of Western Sahara." In his address to the South African parliament, President Cyril Ramaphosa reiterated the support of his country for what he called "the legitimate struggle of Sahrawi people for freedom and self-determination".

Western Sahara in bondage. An apt description from the Western Sahara perspective.

A more unlikely support for the people of Western Sahara has come from the Trump administration in Washington, while allowing for the erratic nature of any pronouncement from the same administration. John Bolton, Trump's normally bellicose former National Security Adviser, better known for his hawkish views, particularly his desire to see regime change in Iran ("the outcome of the president's policy review should be to declare that the Ayatollah Khomeini's 1979 revolution will not last until its 40th birthday") is surprisingly emollient on Western Sahara. And on Western Sahara Bolton has form, having worked alongside James Baker, former Secretary of State and White House Chief of Staff to US President George Bush Sr. and UN Secretary General Kofi Annan's personal envoy in Western Sahara. Bolton was a strong advocate of Baker's peace plan, a plan supported by the UN General Assembly, the ICJ, and the AU, to hold a referendum on self-determination for the disputed area. The problem was that the representatives of the Sahrawi Arab Democratic Republic (SADR) and the Moroccan government could not agree on the eligibility criteria for voting. The referendum proposal died a slow death.

Bolton has repeatedly accused Morocco of engaging in delaying tactics to thwart negotiations. He wrote, in 2007, "Morocco is in possession of almost all of the Western Sahara, happy to keep it that way, and expecting that *de facto* control will morph into *de jure* control over time." A spokesperson for the Moroccan government has cried foul claiming that

245

Bolton unfairly sided with the Polisario separatists. "[He] distinguished himself by taking positions that are openly close to those of the separatists," claimed journalist Tarik Qattab, reflecting the views of the government. In a barely disguised effort to mollify Bolton, Morocco cut off diplomatic ties with Iran in May 2018, ostensibly because it claimed Iran was arming the Polisario but essentially to curry favour with Bolton in what has become known as "the Bolton effect".

Whatever it takes, it appears that there are no limits to which the Moroccan government will go to copper-fasten its colonisation of Western Sahara. Ending diplomatic ties with Iran did not have the desired effect. In an interview with *The New Yorker's* Nicolas Niarchos, Bolton said: "You have to think of the people of the Western Sahara, think of the Sahrawis, many of whom are still in refugee camps near Tindouf, in the Sahara desert, and we need to allow these people and their children to get back and have normal lives."

The European Union has a more ambivalent position. While the European Parliament's non-legislative resolution of 16 January 2019 stated that:

> the EU and its Member States do not recognise the sovereignty of Morocco over the territory of Western Sahara ... recalls that Morocco is a privileged EU partner that covers political, economic and social aspects as well as security and migration highlights that Morocco has been granted advanced status within the European Neighbourhood policy.

At no stage in the forty-two articles does the European Parliament demand Morocco withdraw from its illegal occupation of Western Sahara.

However, under pressure from Spain and France, the EU Fisheries Policy buckled under the demands of its fishermen and approved a deal with Morocco. In the Dáil debate on 8 February 2007, then Labour Party Foreign Affairs spokesperson

Michael D. Higgins described the deal as "a flagrant breach of international law and one that prejudiced a solution in the dispute between Morocco and the Sahrawi Arab Democratic Republic". That agreement ended in 2011.

Notwithstanding the concerns expressed by Higgins, party colleague Pat Rabbitte and others, on 15 July 2014 the EU announced a new EU-Morocco Fisheries Partnership Agreement.

European Commissioner for Maritime Affairs and Fisheries, Maria Damanaki, stated:

> The European Commission welcomes Morocco's ratification of a Fisheries Protocol which is set to open the door for European vessels to go back fishing in Moroccan waters after a pause of more than two years.
>
> I am glad that this protocol can finally enter into force: our fishermen have been waiting for this day for more than two  years. Now we need to make sure that our fleet can resume its  activities as soon as possible. This new protocol is an example of responsible international fisheries governance.

Up to 120 vessels from eleven EU countries (Spain, Portugal, Italy, France, Germany, Lithuania, Latvia, Netherlands, Ireland, Poland and the United Kingdom) will benefit from this partnership. That benefit increased by a third compared to the previous protocol and will now total 80,000 tonnes for small pelagic species, with further fishing opportunities available for demersal, tuna and artisanal fisheries. In total, six fishing categories *exploited* (the EU term) by both industrial and small-scale fleet segments are covered by the protocol. The cost to the EU of this access amounts to €30 million a year, of which €16 million compensates Morocco for access to the resource and €14 million is directed towards supporting the fisheries sector in the country. In addition, the ship owners' contribution is estimated at €10 million, giving a total financial envelope for Morocco of an estimated €40 million.

There is no guarantee that the €16 million compensation will not leak into the repression of the Sahrawi people.

As President, Michael D. Higgins became the first European Head of State to meet with Polisario Front leader Mohammed Abdelaziz, prompting the Moroccan government to temporarily withdraw its ambassador from Ireland. Following Mr. Abdelaziz's death in 2016, President Higgins sent his condolences to the people of Western Sahara, further straining Irish-Moroccan relations.[3] President Higgins said:

> I met the late Secretary General (Mr. Abdelaziz) both in Africa and in Ireland. Ireland has been among those countries which have provided personnel to the United Nations peace-keeping forces in Western Sahara. On behalf of the people of Ireland, I offer my condolences to Mr. Abdelaziz's family, to the Polisario Front and the people of Western Sahara, as they mourn his untimely loss. I remain supportive of all those who are seeking to achieve peace in the region.

Former German president Horst Koehler is the latest in a long series of high-profile international figures to try to mediate a resolution to the conflict. Appointed by UN Secretary General António Guterres, he managed to get Morocco, the Polisario Front, Algeria and Mauritania around the same table in December 2018. They may be willing to talk but there is no indication of substantial change. Home rule versus independence. That binary world all too familiar to students of Irish history.

On the Moroccan side, its UN Ambassador has set out their stall: wide-ranging autonomy. "That's the top. That's the bottom. That's everything, and within the sovereignty of Morocco," he said. "On this basis, we are ready to negotiate. Outside autonomy, nothing. We are not ready to negotiate anything."

---

[3] Ireland is one of the few EU countries not to have a full diplomatic mission in Morocco but in 2019, Foreign Affairs Minister Coveney announced that Ireland is to appoint its first ambassador to Morocco in 2020.

For Polisario, its UN representative Sidi Omar said a referendum with independence as an option was a red line for the people of Western Sahara. "Our position is very clear," he said. "The only way for the Sahrawi people to exercise self-determination is through a referendum."

Red lines. And stalemate.

The most potent symbol of that stalemate is the 2,720 kilometre-long wall or berm (literally meaning a mound or wall of earth) constructed by the Moroccans between 1980 and 1987. This is the longest contiguous wall on earth stretching from southern Morocco to the southwestern tip of Western Sahara. Not quite as long as the Great Wall of China but that wall, unlike the Moroccan wall, is not contiguous. My host Mustafa Mohamed Ali offered to take me there and we travelled under the protection of the Polisario army. The berm is a couple of hours' drive across the flat dusty desert, and I was anxious to see it. It was a hot, uncomfortable journey. At times spectacular, the desert begets its own monotony, broken betimes by the mysterious emergence of a caravan of camels and their lone driver.

In the distance the berm emerged, the Moroccan fortifications the only break in the seemingly endless wall that ended only at the cloudlessly blue skyline. The idea of the wall is to pen in the Sahrawi people who did not or could not flee from the Moroccan army and keep at bay members of the Sahrawi living in the refugee camps.

We got within perhaps a half a kilometre of the wall. The whole area is heavily landmined, about seven million in total. This is the most heavily concentrated area of landmines on the planet. According to the *Landmine & Cluster Munition Monitor*, during the three-year period between 1976 and 1978, Morocco imported a total of $6.5 million worth of VS-50 antipersonnel and VS-1.6 antitank mines from the Italian company Valsella. Morocco is also known to have mines of Spanish, Russian, French and US origin. Morocco refused to sign the Convention on Cluster Munitions adopted in Dublin on 30 May 2008 and signed the following December in Oslo.

Mustafa stopped for prayers. Watching him kneeling in the sand facing Mecca, I wondered what it was like for him to pray on this side of the wall, cut off from the land of his birth. Seeing the wall plunges him from being what was heretofore an open, hospitable, warm man into retrospection and despondency.

> I have brothers and sisters on the other side of the wall. Some of them were born in my absence, grew up and had children, and their children now are as old as I was when I left there in 1975. It is very sad because beyond this wall we have families, memories and a homeland.

Mustafa is deeply moved by this visit and I am moved by his emotion. I had not expected it. This was a big man, a military man, who knew war, having fought in the sixteen-year war with the Moroccans. "I have shots in different parts of my body, my left arm, my thighs, three in one, four in the other, two shots in my right lung. Now, I have only twenty per cent of my lung left."

I ask him what it would feel like if the wall could be magicked away.

"I would cry," he simply said.

If we ever got to Western Sahara, I told him I would touch the ground for him. I did.

That was after we were ushered up the stairs in Laayoune some weeks later. House rules were strict, even as the hospitability was generous. We could not leave. Could not be seen near any window. Could not go out on the stairwell. For a cigarette? I asked. A blowhole for my exhalation was found.

Before the camera could roll, everything in the apartment had to be covered in white sheets. My hosts told me that the Moroccan police would subject the film to detailed analysis, when they eventually located it as my hosts believed they would. Frame by frame. Nothing left to chance.

People willing to talk to us would come and go, arriving at all hours of the day and night. We had just a basic camera and an iPhone for sound. Over the next couple of days, we met with three human rights activists, one woman and two men. Brave people, all three. They were prepared to talk directly to the camera. All alleged torture by the Moroccan state police.

I asked the woman activist why she was willing to take this risk. "I am happy for my face to be shown in front of an international camera so the world may know about the suffering of the Sahrawi people who just want their freedom and independence." She was arrested for her membership of the Polisario Front, detained in December 1980 and released in June 1991. Just over ten years. She detailed the various forms of torture to which she was subjected.

> They tied me on a long table with ropes. Then they flipped the table and stuffed dirty cloths in my mouth. After that they put electricity through my toes and my ears. On other occasions, they would hang us from the ceiling by our feet. They would beat us with electric cables. Sometimes they would put us facing the males and hang us from the ceiling naked or they would put males in front of females.

She told the story almost matter-of-factly. Her pure strength. Her sheer resilience. Her utter determination. For her and all those who survive the experience of torture, perhaps the telling is a way of giving meaning to their suffering, suffering on a scale I cannot imagine enduring. Perhaps the telling offers some catharsis, some way of disowning the suffering, externalising it. I watch her face and her hands in the telling, which is in Arabic and I have to wait for the translation. There is no sense of her body tensing as I have witnessed with other victims of torture. The intake of breath before a crucial telling.

The drying of the mouth. The wetting of the lips. The sacrificial body.

And I think of that other sacrificial body. The Lamb of God. This is my body. This is my blood. "Who his own self bare our sins in his own body on the tree, that we, being dead to sins, should live unto righteousness: by whose stripes ye were healed." [1 Peter 2:24, King James Bible]. Her table, her tree. The wood that entered her soul.

Self-identified political activist, thirty-eight-year-old Ali Saaduni was not only prepared to talk to us on camera but also to have his name published. He was twenty-one years of age when he was first detained. Attempted sexual humiliation was also a key tool of his torturers.

> We were stripped naked and beaten. They blind-folded us. During the interrogation, someone would kick you from behind, randomly and unexpectedly. Two interrogations every day. Two hours each time. They even attempted to sexually abuse me with sticks. They would insert the stick deep into you and if you didn't talk, they would push it deeper into you. It was the most brutal thing I have ever witnessed, truly inhumane.

Ali Saaduni had been recording what the Moroccan authorities regard as illegal public demonstrations against its presence in Western Sahara. He shows me the evidence on his laptop from one such demonstration in 2013. A non-uniformed armed man beats a woman, throws her against a car and she falls to the ground. Unbowed she takes off her shoe and throws it at him. These men, he claims, are plain-clothes policemen working for the Moroccan government.

None of the three people I spoke to is protected by the UN mission in Western Sahara. MINURSO is the only UN peacekeeping mission in the world that lacks the ability and authority to monitor human rights.

Back in the refugee camps in Algeria, talk turns to war. "I don't want a war," Students' Union leader Jalihenna Mohamed told me.

> I don't want to be the person to start the war but if it starts, I will be very convinced to participate. Not because I am violent or Sahrawi people are violent. But because the international community, the United Nations, we have given them more than twenty-five years to make it peacefully but they didn't. So, this is a good argument for the young people who are pushing for to go back to war. And this is also very convincing when you see us living in these hard conditions for more than forty years.

With her young daughter at her feet, recently married Nanaha Bachri, granddaughter of Dide Bjtech, one of the first to arrive at the Tindouf refugee camp, told me that she would fully support her husband if he decided to go to war. "I would go myself, to fight, to die to take it back."

"When I leave this camp," Mohamed tells me, "I will go to my old town Smara in Western Sahara, my old town, and I will live in the same house as my family, taken and occupied by Moroccan settlers. That will mark the end of the occupation when I go back to the same house where my family lived."

Exile. Loss. And that sense of abandonment are now central narratives in the Sahrawi story. Feelings that infuse their lives and their poetry.

> Resist your wounds,
> The desert is treeless.
> A place of dissatisfaction.
> Peace and rest can never dwell
> Here our pain is ceaseless,
> Remains while we wear the chains of conquest.

(Extract from "Resist" by Mohammed Hadri from *Settled Wanderers: The Poetry of Western Sahara* by Sam Berkson and Mohammed Sulaiman.)

# CONCLUSION

## *And a World Turns Away*

"**W**hen you look at the earth with your own eyes, changing very fast, at a speed of eight kilometres per second, what you see is beautiful. You have tears in your eyes so even if you are a tough person you can't avoid becoming a child again". Jean-François Clervoy flew twice on the Space Shuttle *Atlantis* and once on *Discovery*, spending a total of 675 hours in space.

It is something most know. Not everyone. We live on a beautiful but fragile planet. And Irish people are particularly lucky in that we live on a most beautiful island on that planet. Most of us don't need to go into space to know or appreciate that. As of 19 September 2019, only 565 people have had that privilege. And those who have invariably struggle for words to describe the feeling. For veteran astronaut and aquanaut Nicole Stott, "awe" is one of those words. Kathy Sullivan, who in 1984 became the first American woman to perform a space walk, has said that while in space you never tire of looking at the world.

Up close the world is an altogether different place for many people, perhaps the bulk of the earth's population, something a succession of astronauts acknowledge.

NASA astronaut Ron Garan is one of those:

As I approached the top of this arc, it was as if time stood still, and I was flooded with both emotion and awareness. But as I looked down at the Earth - this stunning, fragile oasis, this island that has been given to us, and that has protected all life from the harshness of space - a sadness came over me, and I was hit in the gut with an undeniable, sobering contradiction.

In spite of the overwhelming beauty of this scene, serious inequity exists on the apparent paradise we have been given. I couldn't help thinking of the nearly one billion people who don't have clean water to drink, the countless number who go to bed hungry every night, the social injustice, conflicts, and poverty that remain pervasive across the planet.

Human suffering in Paradise. War in Paradise.

We may not like to admit it, but war and conflict largely define the way human beings have lived on this planet. Cave art from Europe dating from the Late Mesolithic and Early Neolithic periods, approximately 10,000 years ago, are testimony to the human proclivity to conflict. Similar scenes from the same period are found in Africa and Australia. More recently, the Crusades, the Mongol conquests, Inca wars, the Thirty Years War, the Hundred Years War, and the list goes on and on. And it's not just these historical wars that mark human experience on this planet.

According to research conducted by the Australian-based Institute for Economics and Peace (IEP) (Global Peace Index, 2019), the world remains considerably less peaceful now than a decade ago, with the average level of peacefulness deteriorating by 3.78 per cent since 2008. Peace was improving more or less continually every decade since the Second World War, but those gains have now been reversed.

The IEP ranks 163 independent states and territories, covering 99.7 per cent of the world's population, and estimates that the economic impact of violence on the global economy

255

in 2017 was $14.76 trillion in purchasing power parity (PPP) terms. This figure is equivalent to 12.4 per cent of the world's economic activity (gross world product) or $1,988 for every person. The economic impact of violence increased by two per cent during 2017 due to a rise in internal security spending, with the largest increases being in China, Russia and South Africa. Since 2012, the economic impact of violence has increased by sixteen per cent, corresponding with the start of the Syrian war and rising violence in the aftermath of the Arab Spring.

In *The Genocide Contagion*, Israel Charny, a New Yorker who emigrated to Israel, confronts us human beings about our violent predilections. And in doing so he does not spare us, does not spare our pretensions about ourselves as a caring, peace-loving people, does not spare the self-serving rhetoric with which we cloak our most violent actions. Charny does not spare us at all. His book, Robert Fisk has written, "makes for uncomfortable reading".

> What I see is another replay of a truth that we haven't faced fully enough. And this is that the human species – with all of its beauty – is a horrible, uncaring, destructive species that has delighted and excelled in the taking of human life for centuries. And there is no real addressing of this issue in our evolution that I know of.

This is Ron Garan's "undeniable, sobering contradiction". The gift we have been given, and what we have done and continue to do with that gift. It is an uncomfortable view. A dystopian view. Armageddon.

And it's hard to escape the truth of his assertion. In the fifteen years in which I have travelled across Africa, Asia and the Americas, I have encountered stories of the most egregious violence. Stories of horrific abuse. Stories of the most fundamental violations of human rights. The chapters in this book are testimony to that.

Reem Aslo's desolation at the killing of her sister by a lone sniper in Syria.

Brazil's Zilda Maria de Paula's distress at the killing of her son by state police.

Amjad Saffar in Mosul who carries images of the charred remains of his extended family on his phone.

Libya's Mohammed Busidra, whose still bruised body carries the scars from years of torture and abuse.

A Mexican cartel member who graphically recalled the first time he killed someone. He was at the time a mere fourteen-year-old kid.

Serafimove Kazakova's recollection of the Nazi search for Jewish people in her home village of Mozhaisk.

The images of a bomb in Mogadishu that will continue to haunt Ahmedweli Hussain.

The violation Jung Young Hee feels about the desecration of her village by the South Korean and US military.

Alier Arem's description of people tumbling into the river Nile in an effort to escape marauding South Sudanese militias.

The seven brothers of Abdul Miamat, lost in Afghanistan's myriad wars.

The plaintiff cries of Mustafa Mohamed Ali longing to return to his native Western Sahara.

Plaintiff cries too from Rami Elhahan and Bassam Aramin, whose young daughters were killed in Palestine/Israel.

José Mujica's observation that "man is a harsh animal", on his decade-long incarceration in complete isolation.

In *Regarding the Pain of Others*, Susan Sontag chronicles the way images have sought to record war, the use and meaning of these images and how these images shape us or not. Engagement with such images evokes a binary response. Sontag asks, "are we changed after seeing them or do we simply become numb to their effect over time?" Do images simply reinforce longstanding oppositional politics or do they have transformative potential? Conveners of a shared humanity? Sontag thinks not.

> To an Israeli Jew, a photograph of a child torn apart in the attack on the Sbarro pizzeria in downtown Jerusalem is first of all a photograph of a Jewish child killed by a Palestinian suicide bomber. To a Palestinian, a photograph of a child torn apart by a tank round in Gaza is first of all a photograph of a Palestinian child killed by Israeli ordnance.

All photographs wait to be explained or falsified by their captors, as Sontag argues:

> During the fighting between Serbs and Croats at the beginning of the recent Balkan wars, the same photographs of children killed in the shelling of a village were passed around at both Serb and Croat propaganda briefings. Alter the caption, and the children's deaths could be used and abused.

And yet. For all that, Sontag believes in the power of the image. Why else did British Prime Minister Margaret Thatcher seek to limit the number of journalists covering the 1982 Falklands War to two? Only three batches of film ever reached London before the islands were recaptured. No direct television broadcast was permitted.

US President George H.W. Bush followed suit during the 1991 Gulf War. Top military and political figures were happy to see images of the techno-war above the dying transmitted. But when the broadcaster NBC acquired footage of the thousands of defenceless Iraqi conscripts who were carpet-bombed with explosives, napalm, depleted uranium and cluster bombs – as consistently described by Denis Halliday – on the road to Basra as they fled Kuwait in what one US officer famously described as a "turkey shoot". NBC, under military orders, refused to show the footage.

Likewise, in Afghanistan in 2001 journalists were excluded from most of the US missions. Sontag argues that the current political context is the friendliest to the military in decades. The same could be said for reporting. The embedded journalist: the term given to reporters who travel with the military. First encountered in the 2003 Iraq war as a sop to journalists who felt excluded from covering previous US military adventures, objective reporting in such circumstances is simply not possible.

Military censorship. Commercial censorship. Self-censorship. The latter is perhaps the more sinister. Commercial sponsors are not interested in what they regard as distant wars. An obsession with ratings and the insatiable preoccupation with celebrity trivia conspire against confronting the awful realisation with which Israel Charny confronts us.

Military-imposed censorship spilled over into media self-censorship. And long before the Gulf War. "The eighties were the worst of times," argues film director and political activist Ken Loach in an interview in *The Irish Times*. "There was a conscious effort on the part of those who controlled news and film to shift culture to the right. Channel 4 actually advertised for right-wind producers." Such is his incredulity he repeats himself. "They advertised for that." Channel 4 was a "cunningly concealed right-winger", Loach claims. And then comes his big claim. "As most broadcasters are."

Notwithstanding Rami Elhahan's assertion that we are not doomed, the generosity of spirit embodied by former Uruguayan president Pepe Mujica, the willingness of the people of Kabul to keep going despite it all, and the willingness of the peace activists on Jeju Island to do likewise, Charny's realisation is worth repeating: "that the human species – with all of its beauty – is a horrible, uncaring, destructive species that has delighted and excelled in the taking of human life for centuries".

"We don't get it," Sontag concludes.

> We truly can't imagine what it was like. We can't imagine how dreadful, how terrifying war is; and how normal it becomes. Can't understand, can't imagine. That's what every soldier, and every journalist and aid worker and independent observer who has put in time under fire, and had the luck to elude the death that struck down others nearby, stubbornly feels. And they are right.

From those horrors, for the most part, the world in all its beauty turns away. As W.B. Yeats reminds us in "The Stolen Child":

> While the world is full of troubles
> And anxious in its sleep.
> Come away, O human child!
> (...)
> For the world's more full of weeping than you can understand.

# INDEX

# Index

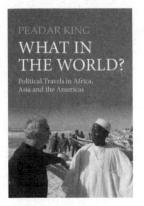

# What in the World?

*Political Travels in Africa,
Asia and the Americas*

### Peadar King

ISBN 978-1-908308-41-2;
paperback; 2013; 300 pages;
50+ colour photos.
€19.95 (Stg£18.95)

"This book brings to real people as opposed to the often jaded "experts", or worse politicians, what inequality, failed development aid, misplaced humanitarian "generosity" can do to those with very little. And those with very little constitute the majority of humankind. This is humankind that sees very little hope for improvement in their lives and for the lives of their children."
– *Denis Halliday, former Assistant Secretary General of the UN*

"We live in a global village and first hand accounts, such as that contained in Peadar King's description of his travels, are vitally important in helping us understand our neighbours – and our responsibility to them.... Peadar's passionate and convincing arguments on the stark divisions between the rich and poor, the powerful and the powerless, should prompt us all to act on our responsibilities to the excluded and disfavoured of the world."
– *Mary Robinson, former President of Ireland and former UN High Commissioner for Human Rights*

"This remarkable travelogue, inquiry, and illuminating analysis provides a sympathetic and searching look at a world we have helped create but do not see – a world of painful and needless suffering, courageous resistance, and even inspiration and hope. And it offers a compelling opportunity to look at ourselves as well, at what we have wrought and what we can do."
– *Noam Chomsky, Author and Political Activist*

*The Liffey Press, 'Clareville', 307 Clontarf Road, Dublin D03 PO46, Ireland
Tel: +353 (0)1-8337814. Email: theliffeypress@gmail.com. www.theliffeypress.com.*